# THE QUEST FOR VICTORY

John I. Alger

# THE QUEST FOR VICTORY

## THE HISTORY OF THE PRINCIPLES OF WAR

*Foreword by*
General Frederick J. Kroesen

Contributions in Military History, Number 30

GREENWOOD PRESS
Westport, Connecticut • London, England

**Copyright Acknowledgment**

"Mao's 10 Principles of War," by Kenmin Ho, in
the July 1967 issue of *Military Review,* is
reprinted by permission of *Military Review.*

**Library of Congress Cataloging in Publication Data**

Alger, John I.
    The quest for victory.

    (Contributions in military history, ISSN 0084-9251;
no. 30)
    Bibliography: p.
    Includes index.
    1. Military art and science—History.   2. War—His-
tory.   I. Title.   II. Series.
    U39.A43        355'.02            81-13319
    ISBN 0-313-23322-5 (lib. bdg.)        AACR2

Library of Congress Catalog Card Number: 81-13319
ISBN: 0-313-23322-5
ISSN: 0084-9251

First published in 1982

Greenwood Press
A division of Congressional Information Service, Inc.
88 Post Road West
Westport, Connecticut 06881

Printed in the United States of America

10 9 8 7 6 5 4 3 2 1

To our children and their generation.
May their hardships be lessened and their prosperity and joys increased by efforts to understand more fully the labors and follies of earlier generations who tried to do and to sustain what is worthy and just.

# CONTENTS

# FOREWORD

THE "PRINCIPLES OF WAR," INTRIGUING guides for military
leaders and theoreticians that I had never heard of until after I had
fought in my first two wars, are now staple in the Army officer
education system. And a good thing, too, because there is something
satisfying about a set of postulates that can be discussed, argued
about, and referred to by the members of our profession who take
seriously the intellectual challenge of war and combat operations.
John Alger and *The Quest for Victory* provide grist for such ses-
sions, an understanding of the centuries of development associated
with today's "principles."

I have long believed that there should be a tenth modern principle
which explains that war is an art, not a science. A rough, clumsy,
undisciplined, and some might say unprincipled art, but an art
nonetheless with characteristics of most art produced by a free-
thinking mankind. Recognition of this principle goes back at least
to Sun Tzu, whose treatise was entitled "The Art of War."

But no art exists without certain fundamental truths, which can
be derived from analysis, from logic, and from the successes and
failures of those who have plied the art. The derivation of these
truths is a demand placed on scholars, and this book provides
synthesis and summary of the what, when, and why of the truths
known as the "principles of war."

As with any doctrine, blind adherence cultivates seeds of disaster; therefore, one is tempted while extolling the virtues of a work, which contributes so valuably to our general knowledge, to express the caution that the knowledge of how and when to apply these principles becomes far more important than knowing the principles themselves. There are probably no two principles more respected and universally accepted than those of "the objective" and "the offensive." When I think of them I am always reminded of the first exhortations of the Mass, "This is the first and great commandment . . . (the objective), the second is like unto it . . . (the offensive)." Yet it was stubborn adherence to these two principles that brought the carnage of World War I. The offensive became an end in itself, a faulty objective, and the cost in human lives became a terrible monument to the reasonless attempts to mount offensive operations without the tools required to cope with the overwhelming advantages that technology had forged for the defense.

This caution is well expressed, and I commend John Alger's work to military men and women as a valuable addition to their collective intellect and intelligence. A knowledge of the evolution of today's version of the principles of war can only add breadth and depth to the understanding that tomorrow's military captains must have to employ military power successfully. I would like to know that today's practitioners of the art of politics have similar reference material available so that we might be spared a new test of the "principles of war."

General Frederick J. Kroesen
Commander-in-chief, United States Army, Europe

# PREFACE

AS A STUDENT AT the United States Military Academy in the early 1960s, I, like every other cadet presumably since the founding of the academy in 1802 (in the minds of most cadets, little, if anything, had changed since the academy's founding—and certainly not the principles of war), was required to learn nine principles of war. They were expressed as titles:

The Principle of the Objective
The Principle of the Offensive
The Principle of Mass
The Principle of Economy of Force
The Principle of Maneuver
The Principle of Unity of Command
The Principle of Security
The Principle of Surprise
The Principle of Simplicity

My classmates and I quickly learned that it was important for examination purposes to memorize this list, and the farsighted among us possibly realized that there was some connection between the memorization of the list and success in future military endeavors.

The practical purposes for the list prevailed, however, and the particularly astute, or perhaps the intellectually lazy, learned that it was easier to memorize a mnemonic acronym, made up of the first letter of each principle, than to memorize the nine principles. Some preferred "MOS-MOUSSE" and others "O-O-SUM-MESS," but both terms became part of the cadet lexicon and a key to victory in the quest for academic excellence.

After learning the principles, or at least learning to recall them with the help of an acronym, in tactics courses, we found that as first classmen in the very popular History of the Military Art course that the principles were used extensively to judge and evaluate military operations from the time of the early Greeks to the present. It was somehow presumed, at least by the students, that those nine principles had prevailed throughout history and therefore that they must have been at least as well known to Alexander the Great as they were to us. Imagine my surprise when I learned as a graduate student that the list of nine principles first appeared in the U.S. Army *Field Service Regulations* of 1949.

My interest was piqued, and with the encouragement of Professor Peter Paret, I began to seek the origins and antecedents of those nine principles. My search began in eighteenth- and nineteenth-century military theory in Professor Paret's seminar on the History of Military Thought, Institutions, and Policy at Stanford University in the spring of 1971. The scope of the search increased until it ranged from the significant concepts of principles of war found in ancient and medieval treatises on war, through the period of definitive codification by the British and U.S. Armies in the early 1920s, to the latest doctrine of the world's major military powers. *The Quest for Victory* is the culmination of that search.

In the course of such an undertaking, I encountered some notable difficulties. For example, the current manuals of some armies are restricted from public circulation and hence cannot be quoted directly. In other cases my lack of language abilities restricted access to original doctrinal sources, and I had to rely on translations or secondary sources—if they existed and could be found. Translations raised problems of semantic and conceptual interpretation, and even though some concepts cannot be perfectly equated from language to language and even from source to source, I have tried to follow the spirit as well as the letter of concepts that I have encountered in foreign sources. Semantic problems exist in English, too. The judgment and interpretation necessary to resolve such problems hopefully have not distorted the facts.

Throughout this book I have tried to distinguish between "principles of war" in the modern sense of a short, definitive list of titles and/or aphorisms and principles of war in the earlier established sense of the myriad fundamentals that relate to war by consistently using quotation marks with "principles of war" in the modern sense. Even though the convention is abandoned in direct quotations in order to maintain the accuracy of the original, and even though at times the distinctions are based on hindsight and interpretation, I hope that the convention will help to emphasize and clarify the important differences in the meaning of this key phrase.

# ACKNOWLEDGMENTS

THIS BOOK IS A DIRECT result of my study of military thought and doctrine, which began under the direction of Professor Peter Paret at Stanford University in 1970. His guidance and encouragement have been steadfast. For the opportunity to study history at Stanford, to pursue interests in doctrine and in writing, and to serve as an instructor and assistant professor in the Department of History at the United States Military Academy, I am indebted to Brigadier General (Retired) Thomas E. Griess. I thank Lieutenant General (Retired) John H. Cushman, who was the commandant of the United States Army Command and General Staff College during my tenure as a student there, for his sincere interest in promoting a balanced view of the principles of war. I thank Commander (Retired) Thomas B. Buell for his encouragement to publish. I thank General Donn A. Starry, former commanding general of the United States Army Training and Doctrine Command, for providing a copy of his address, "History, the Principles of War, and Military Doctrine," and for his insights into recent doctrinal debates concerning the "principles of war." To the staffs of countless libraries, among them the Library of Congress, the Stanford University Libraries, the United States Military Academy Library, the United States Army Military History Institute (formerly the United States

Army Military History Research Collection), the Bibliothèque nationale, the Command and General Staff College Library, the United States Army Infantry School Library, the Hoover Institution on War, Revolution and Peace, and the William R. Perkins Library at Duke University, I extend thanks for valuable assistance. I thank colleagues at Stanford, at the Command and General Staff College, and in the Department of History for their encouragement, comments, and criticism. I am indebted to Colonel A. T. P. Millen, Colonel Jean R. Bour, and Colonel Wolfgang Gerhardt, former chiefs of the British, French, and German liaison sections at the Command and General Staff College, respectively, for providing insights and documents relating to their respective services' concepts of principles of war. Above all, I thank my family of close friends and relatives for counsel, love, and care.

# INTRODUCTION

WAR, IN SPITE OF THE PAIN and destructiveness that accompany it, has been a fundamental and intrinsic part of human existence. And because of the serious consequences of war, especially in defeat, the quest to understand the essence of war has attracted some of the world's greatest thinkers. Many of these thinkers have directed their efforts toward identifying fundamental precepts that can be easily taught and that can serve as guides to success in war, but universal agreement concerning the form and content of such precepts has been lacking. Even the common title assigned to such precepts has been a matter of dispute, but increasingly in the nineteenth and twentieth centuries, the word *principle* has been applied to the most fundamental precepts that affect the conduct and outcome of war. The search for principles has been synonymous with the quest for victory.

Doctrine is intimately associated with principles. *Doctrine* means principles or tenets, especially those sanctioned through usage or by the authority of certain offices that by design, if not in fact, are the repositories and workshops of knowledge related to a given subject. Current military doctrine is written by soldiers assigned to such offices, and in the present century, many of these soldiers have endorsed and promoted the idea that military doctrine is based upon precepts that are few (generally less than twelve) in number, that are often expressed by a title or phrase, and that have become widely known as the "principles of war."

"Principles of war" serve many needs: they are guides for the effective conduct of war; and they are often used to facilitate the study of military history. Finally, they provide a simple—perhaps too simple—expression of many of the intricacies and complexities of war. The usefulness of principles in the study and understanding of complex disciplines is accepted by scholars, and the existence of such principles as those of falling bodies and of planetary motion is known to every student. But the principles of war differ markedly from those of other disciplines. They are expressed neither as algebraic formulas, such as $F = ma$, nor as philosophic truths, like the principles of Christian morality. Although the generally accepted form of the principles of war has differed from age to age and from army to army, they have been expressed, at least in English-speaking societies for the past half-century, as brief lists of apothegms that purport to represent ultimate truths concerning the conduct of war. For example, the 1920 British *Field Service Regulations* summarized the principles as maintenance of the objective, offensive action, surprise, concentration, economy of force, security, mobility and cooperation.

Since World War II, "principles of war," as defined in official service publications, have been used extensively in British and American courses intended to prepare military men and women for assignments in the profession of arms. To candidates for commissions, the principles have a special value: strict attention, too often through rote memorization, to the titles and definitions of the principles results in appropriate rewards at examination time. At the staff colleges, the intermediate level of officer education, many students and faculty members have questioned the officially accepted principles, but few have thought about the origins of their modern form and content. Officers attending the war colleges, the highest level of formal military education, have generally accepted the official list of principles but with modifications of their titles and revised explanations of their meaning. In spite of their present significance, however, no serious investigation of the history of the principles of war has been undertaken by the capable officers and civilian scholars who have written and thought about them. In fact, it rarely occurs to those who cite a "principle of war" that it often was not recognized as a "principle" until quite recently. Furthermore, many great leaders of the past who are judged according to the modern principles were ignorant of the importance that modern doctrine has assigned to the certain selected precepts now known as "principles of war."

Where did the principles come from? Whose principles are they? What, if any, is their value? Such questions have been rarely asked, and when they have been asked, the conclusions have been shallow, misleading, and in many cases incorrect. Perhaps the principles have been so convincingly presented in the primers of the military profession that they become intuitively accepted by all who deal with military theory.

An examination of military thought in the United States suggests that like so many other American institutions, its origins are found in Europe. Therefore, this study examines concepts of principles of war as they developed not only in the United States but also in the major European states. The Orient, too, has, on occasion, influenced the development of Western ideas on war, and hence, some Chinese and Japanese ideas are considered. In an examination of the development of ideas about martial principles in a variety of nations and services, different forces can be identified that contributed to the development of different theories of war. An examination of the concepts and content of the principles themselves will lead to a clearer understanding of the writings of such influential theorists as Sun Tzu, Antoine-Henri Jomini, Carl von Clausewitz, Alfred Thayer Mahan, J. F. C. Fuller, and Mao Tse-tung; better insights into the use and usefulness of the lists of "principles of war" can be achieved; the forces that influence doctrine can be better understood; and our understanding of the essence of war might be improved.

In examining the origins of the "principles of war," I frequently encountered a familiar dichotomy that exists in the military services of nearly every major military power. On the one hand, there are those who find the quest for victory to be a practical matter decided by brute strength and cunning upon the field of battle. At the other extreme are those who maintain that the outcome of battle is determined by the adherence to or violation of certain doctrinal precepts or "principles." The dichotomy is important because it helps to explain the conflicting schools of thought that recur throughout the development of military theory. The dichotomy can be illustrated by an analogy from Greek mythology.

The military traditions of the Greeks were founded in mythology, and their gods and goddesses were believed to possess and grant the qualities needed to guide humans in their mundane endeavors. Among these endeavors was war, associated with Zeus, the father of the gods, with his son, Ares, and with his daughter, Athena, also known as Pallas Athene. Ares was the Trojan war god; he delighted in blood, lust, and death. He represented the proud spirit of battle, but neither his fellow gods nor his parents were proud of him. He stood for the distasteful physical aspects of war: brutality, slaughter, and suffering. To survive war's destructiveness, he, like other ancient warriors, relied upon physical strength and protection afforded by a shield of dried and hardened goatskin. Impervious to the missile weapons of its day, the goatskin represented the physical side of battle, and the term *goatskins* is used to describe those who rely on brute physical strength to prevail in the face of battle. "Goatskins" can be readily identified with Ares.

Most modern professional soldiers, however, tend to identify with Athena. Her helmet adorns the crest of the United States Military Academy, and her statue is carved in stone above the main entrance of the academy's library. She was the giver of wisdom and beauty, and she argued for justice tempered with mercy and reason. Her solution to the scourge of war existed not in force and goatskins but in spiritual, moral, and intellectual qualities. Victory and success could be achieved by using the mind as well as the body. Those soldiers who identify with Athena almost without exception possess in their collection of wall hangings a diploma, a "sheepskin," from a recognized college or university. They prize and emulate the thinking soldier-leader and strive to establish a theory of war that lends clarity and reason to the complexity of war.

Goatskins and sheepskins are admittedly extreme examples, and few would readily characterize themselves as fitting comfortably into only one category. However, the models suggest the dichotomy that has plagued modern armies and profoundly affected military education and military doctrine. The sheepskins generally argue in favor of extensive, formal military education; the goatskins generally favor the commonsense approach to the practice of war. Most among those who have ever been involved with war are hybrids, but by defining the extremes, the entire spectrum of attitudes toward the doctrine of war can be better understood. And even though most are admittedly hybrids, most also tend toward one group or the other. For example, Robert E. Lee and George C. Marshall favored sheepskins; Ulysses S. Grant and George Patton tended toward goatskins. A study of the history of the principles of war should make the principles themselves and doctrine in general better understood, and the dichotomy between goatskins and sheepskins will be recognized as less extreme than it is often perceived to be.

Although a clearer understanding of doctrine and principles should result from such a study, at times, words and their meanings can be troublesome. For example, the words *strategy, tactics, doctrine,* and even *principle* are each extremely important to the proper understanding of concepts pertinent to the conduct of war, but each of these terms and many others suffer from imprecise, mercurial, and often misused definitions. Part of the semantic problem exists in the penchant among the army's policy makers (mostly sheepskins) to coin new words and acronyms. There is even a word in the U.S. Army vocabulary to describe the resulting, and often unclear to the uninitiated, language: Pentagonese.

When military concepts are examined over a long period of time, it becomes evident that Pentagonese existed long before the Pentagon was constructed in the early 1940s. This observation is instructive for two reasons. First, concepts can exist long before a word to describe the concept is coined, and second, new words often are used to describe concepts that were known by other names in other times. The sad result of these observations is that the historian's understanding and often the understanding of those affected by doctrinal language is obfuscated. For example, in the last half-century, while the concept of "principles of war" was steadfastly developing, the term "principles of war" has been repeatedly used and abandoned in U.S. Army handbooks and manuals. It first appeared in U.S. doctrine in the U.S. Army *Training Regulations* of the 1920s, but criticism of the form and to a lesser extent of the content of the *Training Regulations* list led to doctrine in the early 1930s that intentionally avoided the use of the term "principles of war." In 1931, however, the "principles of offensive combat," a list of ten aphorisms, appeared in an army manual, *Tactics and Techniques of Infantry in Offensive Combat.* In many cases the principles in this list were identical with "principles of war" that had appeared in *Training Regulations.* In 1936, the U.S. Army Command and General Staff College at Fort Leavenworth, Kansas, published a list of seven "principles of strategy," in substance identical to seven of the nine "principles of war" found in *Training Regulations.* In 1939, the staff college published a pamphlet, *The Offensive,* in which six "principles of war" appeared. Again the six repeated in form and content ideas that had been included in earlier U.S. Army doctrinal sources under different headings. In 1941, a similar list of seven aphorisms appeared but under a unique heading, "The Exercise of Command; Doctrines of Combat," and in 1949, the U.S. Army *Field Service Regulations,* at the time the most general doctrinal source in the U.S. Army, published a list of nine titles and explanantions—again under the heading "principles of war." The form and content of this list and the notion that its nine aphorisms are indeed the "principles of war" have been relatively steadfast for the past three decades, at least as far as the U.S. Army is concerned. In other services and other nations, other aphorisms have been ensconced as the fundamental "principles of war."

To follow the development of these martial concepts expressed as aphorisms, a clear understanding of their definition and realm is necessary. The title of this book implies that "the history of the principles of war" will be examined, but the term "principles of war" was not always applied to the concept as currently accepted in U.S. Army circles. At times a principal concept contributing to their development took a quite different title, such as "doctrines of combat."

Of central interest is the word *principle* itself. A principle is a fundamental truth that is professed as a guide to action. Synonyms occurring in the history of the "principles of war" have included *axiom, law, rule, guide, fundamental, essence, maxim, lesson, aphorism,* and *doctrine.* In other languages, a similar list of cognates and equivalents exists. Although the connotations of each term differ from those of the other terms, and these differences can be significant, every one of the terms has been involved with the history of the modern concept of "principles of war" and can be considered a principle according to the definition given above.

The realm in which the principles are operative also involves a variety of terms. Are the "principles" valid for all aspects of war, for strategy, for tactics, for combat, for operations, for campaigns, or for some other facet of war? Some writers, for example, J. F. C. Fuller, offered a list of principles for strategy and another list for tactics. Lists of principles have been published that deal with administration and with organization, and some lists purport to be operative in the realm of specific types of war, for example, in guerrilla war or in primitive war. The principal focus of this study, however, is on the principles that purport to guide commanders toward success when their unit is confronted by a comparably armed and relatively equal foe. When small units, such as squads, platoons, companies, and battalions, have been considered, the term *principles of tactics* has often been used to refer to what are otherwise "principles of war." Similar guides for commanders of large units, such as corps and armies, have sometimes been called *principles of strategy.* As with the synonyms for *principles,* however, the operative realm does not necessarily affect the contribution of a given concept to the development of modern lists of "principles of war." The appendixes, "The Essence of Victory— A Chronological Compendium," show the variety of thoughts, formats, and milieus associated with the history of the modern "principles of war." Scrutiny of the lists reveals some common themes, but consensus regarding content and form is notably lacking.

"Principles of war": Do they exist? Where did they come from? What are they? How have they been expressed? Are they a pedantic bane as the goatskins sometimes claim? Or are they an intellectual boon that sheepskins have distilled from centuries of military experience and from assiduous reflection upon that experience?

# THE QUEST FOR VICTORY

# 1

# MARTIAL PRINCIPLES
# BEFORE NAPOLEON

IT IS INCONCEIVABLE THAT any intelligent being would knowingly surrender any clear advantage to an opponent in war. Even though the date when humans first orgainized themselves for warlike purposes long precedes the beginning of extant recorded history, it can be safely assumed that the earliest of military organizations used intellectual power in combination with their physical power in their attempt to defeat their enemies. Neither technology nor military thought was sophisticated in prehistoric times, but as civilization advanced, man directed his efforts toward the study of war, study that focused on correct methods. In war correct methods are those that lead to victory.

Individuals who have contributed to the knowledge concerning war are variously called military thinkers, military theorists, or military philosophers, and their writings are often referred to as military theory or military philosophy. Although the distinctions between the terms are slight and are generally overlooked, they can serve useful purposes. A military thinker is one who questions the methods and practices associated with military activity. A military theorist has thought extensively about war or some aspect of it and has systematized his thoughts in a cohesive written form that others can readily examine. A military philosopher seeks to uncover fundamental truths concerning war. Such subjective measures as depth of thought and degree of revelation also distinguish the military thinker from the military theorist and the military philospher.

Because principles of war are fundamental truths pertinent to the practice of war, the earliest known writers who contributed to the understanding of such fundamentals are rightfully called military philosophers. In the millenniums of recorded history that preceded Napoleon, military philosophers identified fundamentals that to them conveyed essential information concerning the practice of war. They organized their thoughts in varying ways and generally called attention to some precepts that they considered to be of greater importance than many or most of the others that they addressed.

The terms for these important precepts varied. They were called principles, maxims, theories, axioms, rules, or judgments. Regardless of the generic term used or the number of precepts identified, concepts that today are accepted as "principles of war" frequently appeared in early writings on war. For example, the importance of security and surprise was included in nearly every treatise dealing with military operations. Many early military writers published extensive tomes on the practice of war, and their advice and observations on war were expressed in thousands of principles. On occasion, important concepts were included in brief lists, but no single list was advanced that purported to enumerate all or even the most important of the fundamental considerations in the conduct of war. An examination of some of the more important writings on war—by Sun Tzu, Vegetius, Machiavelli, the duke of Rohan, Jean Charles de Folard, the marquis de Feuquières, Frederick the Great, Maurice de Saxe, the marquis de Silva, and Henry Lloyd—conveys both the form and concept of martial principles before Napoleon.

The earliest known treatise on the conduct of war is Sun Tzu's *The Art of War*. Written in China in about 500 B.C., the work attracted attention in the Western world following its translation into French in the late eighteenth century.[1] Sun Tzu dealt with the fundamentals of the art of war as he understood it, and in part because of the nature of the Chinese language, Western-language translations have been aphoristic. In chapter 1, which deals with estimates or plans, Sun Tzu stated that war should be appraised in terms of five factors (moral influence, weather, terrain, command, and doctrine) and seven elements.[2] In the Lionel Giles translation, published in London in 1910, the seven "elements" were posed as questions, and the statement, "By means of these seven considerations, I can forecast victory or defeat," followed the enumeration of the elements[3] (see appendix 1).

Throughout Sun Tzu's treatise, pithy statements concerning such areas of concern as discipline, morale, and the importance of deception and other psychological measures abound. To conclude, however, that Sun Tzu provided a list of aphorisms that carry the same force or connotations as the lists of modern "principles of war" or that are antecedents to modern lists (except that all military theory can be generally construed as a basis for later theory) is erroneous. In fact, a statement by Sun Tzu suggests that he would argue against the often prevailing view that a few fundamental principles guide and determine the outcome of military operations. He wrote, "In the art of war, there are no fixed rules. These can only be worked out according to circumstances."[4] He thus was more the antecedent of those who maintain that the uniqueness of circumstances argues against the statement of immutable principles rather than the antecedent of those who accept principles as the enduring guides to the conduct of war.

The most influential treatise on war to survive from the era of Roman domination is Vegetius's *De Re Militari* (On military institutions). Written during the decline of the Western empire but extolling the virtues of early Rome, it was used little by the Romans. During the Renaissance, however, nearly a millennium later, *De Re Militari* was the most popular work, and possibly the only work widely used, on the practice of war. Vegetius, like every other serious writer on military topics, well understood the importance of victory in war and attempted to point out the fundamentals essential to it. Vegetius included neither enumerations nor terse lists, however, focusing instead on discipline, organization, training, and administration.

Vegetius was heavily relied upon by Egidio Colonna and Christine de Pisan, the principal military writers of the early Middle Ages, and by Niccolò Machiavelli, who published his *Arte della Guerra* (The art of war) in 1521.[5] Since Vegetius's treatise on war was nearly one thousand years old when Colonna, de Pisan, and Machiavelli were writing, the constancy of military institutions must have been apparent to them. In fact, from the Renaissance until Napoleon's consistent military success suggested to some theorists that a new generation of war had dawned, men who wrote and men who were educated studied the Greeks and Romans, their classical languages, and the history of these ancient civilizations in depth in their search for the truths of the ancients, especially in the humanities. In the study of war, writers like Machiavelli discovered that certain fundamentals had not changed in the millennium between the decline of the ancient civilizations and their own time. An enthusiasm for the study of Roman institutions resulted, and the attitude that what was good and true for the Romans was also true for Renaissance man prevailed. Constancy, reflected by the prevalence of the idea that certain fundamentals, which were often referred to as principles, existed, was evident in military writings throughout the period from the sixteenth through the eighteenth centuries. The treatises that appeared, however, suggested that there was no limit to the total number of such principles.

Machiavelli provided far more in his chief military work, *Arte della Guerra,* than a mere repetition of the platitudes known to the Romans. In his keen insights concerning the conduct of military operations, he recognized that circumstances influence the actions that a commander should take in war, but he also included a series of "general rules" in the dialogue of his *Arte della Guerra* (see appendix 2). When discussing the importance of the relative sizes of opposing forces, he stated, "You must make it a general rule to contract or extend your front according to the number of your own men and those of the enemy."[6] When discussing psychological dimensions of generalship, lacing the discussion with examples from Hannibal, Caesar, and other Roman and Carthaginian commanders, Machiavelli stated, "Let me recommend a general rule to you: *to frustrate any of your enemy's designs, it is best to do of your own volition what he endeavors to force you to do.*"[7] Machiavelli's writings marked the beginning of nearly three centuries of military thought that was strongly influenced by classical thought, that reflected an interest in the search for principles, fundamentals, general rules, or any of the variety of synonyms used to define such basic concepts, and that increasingly was influenced by technological growth and scientific inquiry.

Technological growth was significant in the centuries following the "rebirth of knowledge." Gunpowder became the principal force on the battlefield. Pikes and halberds gave way to bayonets and flintlocks, and artillery took its place as an important and essential combat arm. Military writers had to deal with the technological innovations in precise and clear language, and procedures for the carrying, care, and use of the new weapons were precisely enumerated and often illustrated by hundreds of meticulously drawn pictures. By the early nineteenth century, detailed drawings were also used to illustrate the "principles" of other military activities, such as deployments and maneuvers.[8]

Scientific inquiry, which called for and achieved precise and clear definition of natural phenomena like the precision and clarity associated with technological developments, also influenced military thinkers. It influenced the acceptance of the existence of principles in military thought as well as in other humanitarian fields of study, for

the word "law" came down trailing clouds of glory from Galileo and Newton. Students of society, consciously or unconciously asserting the scientific status of their studies, adopted the same language and believed themselves to be following the same procedure.[9]

Military theory increasingly used the language of science, and the word "principle" became a central part of the language of both science and war.

Science also indirectly influenced the development of modern concepts of "principles of war" through the schools of war established in the eighteenth and early nineteenth centuries to teach technical, scientific subjects, such as artillery and engineering skills. Some military schools had existed long before the eighteenth century, but the scientific age increased their number considerably and brought new purposes to the schools. The Royal Military Academy at Woolwich, for example, was established for instructing "the raw and inexperienced people belonging to the Military Branch of Ordnance in the several parts of Mathematics necessary to qualify them for the service of the Artillery, and the business of the Engineers."[10] In 1794, amid revolution in Paris, the Ecole polytechnique was established to provide a complete education for public service. It became a preparatory school for the training of both civilian and military engineers. Schools of application, such as the engineer and artillery school established at Metz in 1802, completed an officer's scientific education. In Great Britain, the Royal Military College was founded in 1799 to educate young officers and to provide staff officers for the army; mathematics was the chief subject taught. The United States Military Academy was founded in 1802 to form "the basis in regard to science, on which the establishment rests," and a military school for officers was founded in Berlin in 1810 to provide the means "for acquiring the knowledge requisite for higher ranks of the service, for the duties of officers of the staff, and for all other appointments which demand military and scientific studies of a higher and more general character than the common ones."[11]

The schools in Paris and Berlin had successful antecedents, but the recognition of the need for scientific education among the officer corps of an army in general was a primary factor in rekindling an awareness in the value of formal military education. In the late nineteenth and twentieth centuries, many of these schools altered their curriculums to include operational as well as technical subjects. The pattern of teaching principles—that is, specific fundamentals and rules rather than abstract generalities—was sufficiently imbued in the system of military education that had existed since the beginning of the age of science that an operational science of war was readily accepted by faculty and students in the schools. "Principles" were established as an accepted part of the educational system of the professional soldier.

An examination of some of the attitudes concerning principles of war that exist in the writings of significant military writers of the late Renaissance and the Enlightenment, the period when reason and rationality ruled the thoughts and discussions of learned men, gives further evidence concerning the form and content of martial principles before Napoleon.

Although immutable principles that purported to serve as guides to victory in war did not exist before the twentieth century, seventeenth- and eighteenth-century writers provided an occasional enumeration that gave advice to military commanders. Henry, the duke of Rohan, was such a writer. Born in Brittany in 1579, he served for a time in the royal French Army, and he later became the champion of the Huguenots in their fight for religious freedom. Rohan was a prolific writer, and among the many political and military volumes to his credit is *Le Parfait capitaine* (The perfect captain), which deals with the history and art of war. In this military memoir, Rohan presented a list of seven guides for the general who wishes to engage in war (see appendix 3). Much of his advice remains valid today, though none compares directly with any of the British or American "principles" enunciated as eternal in the twentieth century.

A decade after Rohan's death in 1638, Antoine Manassès de Pas, the marquis de Feuquières, was born in Paris. Like Rohan, he became an experienced soldier and writer, and his most famous publication, *Mémoires sur la guerre* (Memoirs on war), provides insights into his views concerning the form and content of martial principles. The work is full of criticisms of commanders who served Louis XIV from 1672 to 1710. The chapters of the first volume each address a given aspect of operations: chapter 5 is entitled "Of Military Discipline," chapter 8 is "Of the Disposition and Plans of War," chapter 9, "Of Secrecy," and chapter 11, "Of the Manner of Assembling an Army." The first volume of the English translation of 1736 contains thirty chapters, and the second volume continues with twenty additional chapters on other aspects of operations. Each chapter was short and contained advice on the proper conduct of military operations. According to de Feuquières, his volumes also contained all the maxims or rules that generals need to know. He wrote, "In a word,

I have collected all the general Rules which can be given, with Regard to this grand Operation of War."[12] The "general rules" were spread throughout the narrative. For example, in chapter 7, de Feuquières wrote, "But it would have been agreeable to the true Maxims of a Prince who prepares to engage in a War, to have raised a considerable Body of Foot, antecedent to the Publication of . . . the Declaration of War," and in the chapter on battles, he wrote, "[The general] always ought to give Battle in Consequence of his own voluntary Choice, and endeavor to prevent his Enemy from forcing him upon that important Action."[13] In fact, de Feuquières presented a critique of the wars in which he had participated, and he elevated the lessons that he learned in those campaigns to the level of maxims or general rules.

Another French writer and soldier, who participated in many of the same campaigns as de Feuquièrcs, was Jean Charles, the chevalier de Folard, whose interest in military theory was based in large measure on his study of Caesar's *Commentaries*. De Folard's life (1669-1752) spanned the period of military history in which linear formations dominated tactics. However, he was an adherent of the column, and in his *Traité de la colonne* (Treatise on the column), he proposed the maxim that "greater depth gives a stronger formation."[14] His comments on the column were occasionally supported by other observations that he referred to as "established [*ancien*] principles." In addition to citing maxims or principles, de Folard's writings pointed out the affinity of science, classical Roman history, and the importance of principles to learned men of the eighteenth century. The anonymous author of the preface to Folard's *Histoire de Polybe* (History of Polybius) observed, "Science has made progress only through the knowledge of its true principles. War is no different. The knowledge of its principles becomes the foundation on which its study is made."[15] By the mid-eighteenth century, the existence of principles within the realm of war was widely accepted. Their number, form, and substance, however, were not definitively addressed.

Thinking about principles was encouraged, perhaps unwittingly, by one of Europe's most colorful soldiers, Maurice de Saxe. Born in 1696, he was the eldest of 354 illegitimate children sired by

Augustus the Strong of Poland. De Saxe's worldly experiences in carnal and military matters began at an early age; he was thirteen when he first went to war and to debauching. At the age of thirty-six, after gaining fame as a soldier and a court intriguer, he wrote a treatise on war that was published posthumously in 1757. Entitled *Mes rêveries* (My musings), it was received as a farce by some and as an astute treatise on war by others. Even the role of principles held by de Saxe was variously interpreted, for in the preface to the volume he wrote, "War is a science covered with shadows in whose obscurity one cannot move without an assured step. . . . All sciences have principles and rules; war has none. The great captains who have written of it give us none."[16] Even though de Saxe stated that war has no principles, it seems more accurate that he meant that the principles of war were not presented clearly in extant studies, for he also wrote in his preface, "It is impossible to erect any edifice, or establish any system, without first knowing the principles that support it."[17] That he argued against the form in which principles were presented—as myriad ideas spread through multivolume treatises—rather than against the existence of principles is further supported by prefatory remarks that accompanied a collection of his military writings published in 1762:

> Most of the authors who have written on the art of war have confused and mixed together the sublime parts with the simplest details. An infinity of repetitious and quite useless explanations have made their works so lengthy that often to find the sense of a discussion, which could be presented in a dozen lines, one must read a hundred pages.[18]

De Saxe's *Rêveries* was short, very short in comparison with most works on military theory published in the eighteenth century, but the principles of war, however he understood them, remained part of the general narrative.

Other eighteenth-century authors held the view that principles were the key to the understanding of war. A 1766 treatise, *Elémens de l'art militaire* (Elements of the military art), stated, "Books alone will not make an officer, but they will allow him in three or four years of service to make more progress than he could gain in thirty if he worked without principles."[19] And in 1773, the marquis de Silva wrote: "When one has principles, when one knows how to apply them, and when one has a view of war, he can determine with some justice a general plan of operations."[20] Five years later, de Silva published *Pensées sur la tactique, et la stratégique ou, Vrais principes de la science militaire* (Thoughts on tactics and strategy or, true principles of military science), in which he presented a list of ten enumerated principles of maneuver (see appendix 4). His first principle, which stated in part, "All maneuvers must be simple, prompt, easy and sure," is similar to the modern "principle of simplicity." The ideas expressed in his second and third principles, in which he spoke of "direct movements," "single purpose," and "single objective," are suggestive of the modern "principle of the objective." His fourth principle, that all movements should be "covered," is suggestive of the modern "principle of security." In spite of the similarities between "principles" in current doctrine and de Silva's principles of maneuver, however, it is doubtful that de Silva had much influence on the modern expression of principles. Even though the substance of his principles may have been widely known, his list, his book, and his reputation as a military writer have been obscure.

The listing of principles that serve as guides for military commanders was not original with de Silva, but his work was published at the start of the period when such lists became relatively popular means of summarizing and emphasizing considerations for commanders. A few years after de Silva's publication of the principles of maneuver, Henry Lloyd, the Welsh officer who fought for the French and later the Prussians during the Frederician wars, provided numerous lists of principles for sundry activities within the realm of war. The idea that war, like other earthly phenomena, had principles was expressed by Lloyd in 1766: "This art, like all others, is founded on certain and fixed principles, which are by their nature invariable."[21] His ideas concerning the nature of these principles were expanded upon in his military memoirs, first published in 1781. In this work he intended to

> establish first a few general ideas on the principles of war; then to explain the plan of operations of several campaigns;

in the third place, to give a military description of the theatre of war and finally, a specific topographic description of the places where the most remarkable actions took place.[22]

The principles Lloyd discussed were not presented in a single list, and they also reflected the wide range of topics that concerned the eighteenth-century commander. For example, the "first of all the principles," according to Lloyd, was presented as a list of three terse imperatives:

1. The soldier must be dressed and armed according to the action anticipated.

2. He must be instructed in all the variety of circumstances that might occur before the enemy, but nothing more.

3. He must also be instructed in all the things he might do in the particular circumstance where he might find himself.[23]

These imperatives, however, do not immediately involve the conduct of operations, and they do not serve as guides for operational decisions. Other pithy statements Lloyd presented met these criteria, but they were scattered throughout the first part of his work. He stated as a fundamental axiom, "No maneuver . . . can be made . . . without cover and protection."[24] He wrote that one general principle is "the best maneuver is that which can be accomplished by a given number of men in the least amount of time and space."[25] He presented three rules concerning firepower (see appendix 5), two principles, called "geometry" and "genius," for determining the choice of camps, and three axioms on lines of operations (see appendix 6), but he did not distinguish the terms *axioms, principles,* and *rules.*

Because of his clear statements of principles, rules, and axioms, Lloyd has been identified as "apparently . . . the first to discern and define 'the principles of war.' "[26] But he left much doubt concerning the differences among principles, rules, maxims, and axioms, and he failed to state which of his lists, if any, represented the most important principles of war, and he did not try to specify the number of principles in existence.

In the course of military history before Napoleon, many learned men recognized the need to study systematically the conduct of war. Nearly all were soldiers of high rank and reputation, and nearly all spoke of the principles, axioms, maxims, or rules of the military art in such a way that it is apparent that they accepted that such principles, axioms, maxims, or rules exist. Some, like de Rohan, de Silva, and Lloyd, listed and enumerated guides for commanders, but no one presented all or even the most important principles of war in a single list or even said precisely or approximately how many principles exist. Also, there was little agreement even in the lists that were presented concerning the substance of the concepts. Those tasks awaited the military theorists and philosophers of the nineteenth and twentieth centuries.

## NOTES

1. See appendix III, "Sun Tzu in Western Languages," in Sun Tzu, *The Art of War,* trans. Samuel B. Griffith.
2. Ibid., p. 63.
3. The Giles translation is included in Thomas R. Phillips, ed., *Roots of Strategy: A Collection of Military Classics.* Quotation from p. 22.
4. Sun Tzu, *Art of War,* p. 93.
5. See Felix Gilbert, "Machiavelli," in Edward M. Earle, ed., *Makers of Modern Strategy: Military Thought from Machiavelli to Hitler,* pp. 7, 21.
6. Niccolò Machiavelli, *The Art of War* [trans. Ellis Farneworth], p. 111.
7. Ibid., p. 121.
8. See, for example, the two folio volumes by C. de Buzelet, *Cours de science militaire contenant les principes et les actions des grands généraux.* Examples for this study of "the principles and actions of great generals" are taken from the history of warfare from Alexander the Great to Napoleon.
9. Edward H. Carr, *What Is History?* p. 72.
10. Great Britain, *Report of the Commissioners Appointed to Consider the Best Mode of Re-organizing the System for Training Officers for the Scientific Corps Together with an Account of Foreign and Other Military Education,* p. xli.
11. Edward C. Boynton, *History of West Point,* p. 202; Henry Barnard, *Military Schools and Courses of Instruction in the Science and Art of War,* rev. ed., p. 395.

12. Marquis de Feuquières, *Memoirs Historical and Military: Containing a Distinct View of All the Considerable States of Europe,* trans. anonymous, II, p. 2.

13. Ibid., I, pp. 92-93, II, p. 1.

14. Jean Charles Folard, "Traité de la colonne," in *Abrégé des commentaires de M. de Folard sur l'histoire de Polybe,* I, p. ii, my translation.

15. Anonymous, Preface to Jean Charles Folard, "Histoire de Polybe," in ibid., p. ii.

16. Maurice de Saxe, "My Reveries upon the Art of War," trans. Thomas R. Phillips in Phillips, *Roots of Strategy,* p. 189.

17. Ibid., p. 192.

18. *Esprit des loix de la tactique et de differentes institutions militaires ou Notes de M. le maréchal de Saxe,* I, p. i, my translation.

19. M. Cugnot, *Eléments de l'art militaire, ancien et modern,* p. vi, my translation.

20. Marquis de Silva, *Considérations sur la guerre présente entre les russes et les turcs,* p. 2, my translation.

21. Henry Lloyd, *History of the Late War in Germany between the King of Prussia and the Empress of Germany and Her Allies,* I, p. 5, quoted in Michael Howard, "Jomini and the Classical Tradition in Military Thoughts," in Michael Howard, ed., *The Theory and Practice of War,* p. 5.

22. Henry Lloyd, *Mémoires militaires et politiques du général Lloyd,* p. xxxiii, my translation.

23. Ibid., p. xxxvi.

24. Ibid., p. xli.

25. Ibid., p. xlii.

26. John R. Elting, "Jomini: Disciple of Napoleon?" *Military Affairs* 27 (Spring 1964):18.

# 2

# Napoleon and the
# Birth of Modern
# Military Thought

NAPOLEON CAUSED A RADICAL change in military thought and institutions. His active mind was responsible for many changes, but his military success was more responsible because it caused others to search for the reasons behind the success. Ideas and attitudes that had existed for centuries and millenniums changed, largely as a result of this one man. Even the concept of principles of war changed. Rather than representing a commonly accepted philosophy concerning the myriad activities that collectively compose the operations of war, the term began to connote a brief list of aphorisms intended to guide commanders. The former definition has been used by military writers throughout the centuries and continues to be used today. The latter definition, which has become the standard in English-speaking nations, originated in the Napoleonic era, quite possibly with Napoleon himself. In a conversation reported by Marshal Saint-Cyr, the emperor

> utterly denied the difficulties of the art of war, which he said were far from being understood. He added that if he ever had the time he would write a book in which he would demonstrate the principles of the art, in so clear a manner, that they would be within the comprehension of every military man.[1]

His contribution to the origins of the modern concept of principles of war has often been traced to this statement made to Saint-Cyr, but Napoleon referred to principles on many occasions. For example, in 1804, he wrote:

> Remember always three things: unity of forces, urgency, and a firm resolution to perish with glory. These are the three great principles of the military art that have brought me success in all my operations.[2]

And from his maxims:

> Gustavus, Turenne and Frederick, as well as Alexander, Hannibal and Caesar, have acted on the same principles. To keep one's forces together, to bear speedily on any point, to be nowhere vulnerable, such are the principles that assure victory.[3]

Similar thoughts about principles of war dominated the theoretical and historical works of Antoine-Henri Jomini, who became the most influential interpreter of Napoleonic warfare in the nineteenth century. Jomini wrote in his *Précis de l'art de la guerre* (Summary of the art of war), first published in 1838:

> Twenty years of experience have strengthened in me the following convictions: "There are a small number of fundamental principles of war, which can not be deviated from without danger, and the application of them, on the contrary, has been nearly always crowned with success."[4]

This concept of the principles of war molded generations of military writers and teachers and has become the basis of modern military thought relative to the statement of martial principles.

Although Napoleon endorsed the concept of a few fundamental principles, he also expressed reservations about their applicability. In 1817, for example, he spoke well of Jomini's enunciation of principles but added, "Genius acts by inspiration. That which is good in one circumstance is bad in another, but it is necessary to consider the principles like the axes that give reference to the graph."[5] Napoleon's ultimate contribution to the development of the modern concept of principles of war, however, consists not of references that can be gleaned from his writings or conversations but in his example, which inspired the belief that success in war can be simply and consistently achieved. Many writers accepted the challenge concomitant with this belief—that is, to identify and present in a didactically and generally acceptable form the components of success in war.

The modern concept of principles of war originated in the Napoleonic era, but to identify unequivocally the ultimate source of this widely accepted and variously defined concept remains difficult.

> The most eminent thinkers sometimes do no more than codify and clarify conclusions which arise so naturally from the circumstances of the times that they occur simultaneously to . . . obscurer, but more influential figures. . . . And sometimes strategic doctrines may be widely held which cannot be attributed to any specific thinkers, but represent simply the consensus of opinion among a large number of professionals who have undergone a formative common experience.[6]

In spite of the truth of these caveats with regard to the development of the modern concept of "principles of war," Antoine-Henri Jomini is undoubtedly the individual whose thought and writings most profoundly contributed to the emergence and growing popularity of the idea that a small number of principles guide the commander in his quest for success on the battlefield.

But no intellectual origin is absolute, so the work of Jomini's predecessors cannot be ignored. Jomini clearly profited from and used paths that Henry Lloyd had charted earlier. In fact, Jomini's borrowing from Lloyd's history of the Seven Years War was very nearly plagiarism, even though he did credit Lloyd in the preface to the first volume of his earliest published work, the *Traité de grande tactique* (Treatise on grand tactics):

[Lloyd] presents several profound ideas on lines of operations, on strategical movements, and principally on systems of battles, but his ideas are poorly developed, poorly summarized and often contradictory. Lloyd, nevertheless, convinced me of a truth that had been unknown to me; he showed me that the operations of war can be reduced to simple and incontestable principles.[7]

Many authors have pointed to Jomini as the prime contributor to the development of the modern principles of war, but the claim that he provided the first list of principles of war cannot be supported. Like his eighteenth-century predecessors, he was not consistent in his methodology or in his definitions. Nevertheless his ability to translate experience into readable prose and his pragmatic approach to the conduct of war made his writings popular and extended his influence to professional military institutions throughout the Western world. In his *Précis*, he wrote of his own perception of his contribution to military thought:

It is extraordinary enough to accuse me of having said that the art of war did not exist before me. . . . What I said is, that there were no books that proclaimed the existence of general principles and made application of them through strategy to all the operational requirements in a theater of war.[8]

Even in this last major work, it is not clear what Jomini meant by "general principles," but a review of his writings indicates significant changes in his own concepts concerning the regulating principles of the conduct of war.

The full title of Jomini's first published volume was *Traité de grande tactique, ou relation de la guerre de sept ans, extraite de Tempelhof, commentée aux principales opérations de la dernière guerre; avec un recueil des maximes les plus importantes de l'art militaire, justifiées par ces differents événements* (Treatise on grand tactics, or a discussion of the Seven Years War, taken from Tempelhof, commented upon and compared to the principal operations of the latest war; with a collection of the most important maxims of the military art justified by these different events). The title indicated that the work was to be an essay on grand tactics, and hence, the "collection of maxims," which the title also announced, must have been considered useful to grand tactics rather than strategy or war in general as his later works maintained. The volume was composed of chapters translated and rewritten from Tempelhof's accounts of the Seven Years War (Lloyd continued the Tempelhof account where Tempelhof left off), and Jomini's observations on the operations reported upon provided the theoretical thrust of the work. These theoretical discussions dealt primarily with lines of operations, for Jomini believed that Frederick's campaigns demonstrated that the choice of operational lines was "without contradiction, the most important part of grand tactics; it forms the foundation of the science of war."⁹ Since Jomini believed that grand tactics, the branch of war that concerns the movements of large troop organizations, such as corps and armies, prior to and in battle, formed the foundation of the science of war, he also believed that principles determining success in war would be applicable to grand tactics. Furthermore, Jomini assumed that the successes achieved by Frederick with relatively small numbers of troops could be achieved by much larger armies, like those typical of Napoleon's day.

On occasion Jomini explicitly enumerated guides for commanders. The first volume of his *Traité* included an enumeration of five maxims on lines of operations (see appendix 7) and a didactic resume on lines of operations (see appendix 8). In the thirty-fifth chapter, "Observations of the Author on the Preceding Discussion of the Battle of Leuthen; Maxims on the Oblique Order and on the Combinations of War," Jomini wrote that the

last maxim of Lloyd comprised the general principle on which all the combinations of war must rest. This principle maintains that a greater number of men than the enemy must be put into action at the most important point on a line of operations or on a line of attack. . . . It appears incontestable that all the rules of the art, all the mistakes that can be committed in war are affiliated with this maxim.¹⁰

Jomini added that the reduction of the system of war to a single principle had "many advantages: it makes instruction easier, operational decisions more sound and hence, faults less frequent."[11] In the second volume of Jomini's *Traité de grande tactique,* which has the same full title, the same format, and was published in the same year as the first volume, a further list of six maxims on lines of operations appeared (see appendix 9). It is presumed that these lists and the "general principle" were part of the "Collection of the most important maxims of the military art" that the title promised. Jomini's first two volumes hardly differed from the earlier work of Lloyd as far as "principles" were concerned. Maxims and principles were identified but scattered. Some summaries were provided, and little attention was paid to semantic distinctions among the various branches of war and among the terms *principle, maxim,* and *rule.* Furthermore, little attention was given to clarity; frequent repetition of similar thoughts and redundancy confused the stated concept.

Napoleon supposedly read Jomini's first two volumes after the Battle of Austerlitz in December 1805 and apparently was little bothered by their semantic deficiencies or by their lack of originality. Napoleon recommended the *Traité* to Alexander Berthier, his chief of staff and principal aide and often Jomini's antagonist; Berthier criticized the volumes soundly for being inconclusive.[12] Jomini responded to this criticism by publishing a separate conclusion to his *Traité* in December 1807 in Glogau, Silesia. This chapter, "Resumé of the General Principles of the Art of War," brought the scattered maxims on the conduct of war together in a single listing, but Jomini did not claim that the resulting list was a complete exposition of all the principles of war. He merely stated, "I am going to try to point out all of them."[13] His semantic inconsistencies persisted in this chapter, too, but since he seemed to use the words *principle* and *maxim* interchangeably, the inconsistencies are of little consequence.

The format employed in this chapter was consistent with Jomini's earlier statements concerning maxims and principles, and he expanded on the statement he made in volume 1 of the *Traité* concerning the "general principle on which all the combinations of war must rest." In the 1807 version, he stated:

The fundamental principle, whose application is necessary to insure the success of strategical decisions and without which all strategical decisions are fatal, is to operate with the greatest mass of forces, in a combined effort, against the decisive point. . . . The means of applying this great maxim are not very numerous; it is enough to read of the operations of Napoleon and Frederick to gain an exact idea of them. I am going to try to point out all of them.

1.   The first means is to take the initiative of movement. The general who succeeds in gaining this advantage is the master of the employment of his forces at the place where he chooses to take them. On the other hand, the general who waits for the enemy can make no strategical decision since he has subordinated his movements to those of his adversary and since he does not have time to stop the troops that are already in motion. The general who takes the initiative knows what he is going to do; he conceals his movements, surprises and crushes an extremity or a weak point. The general who waits is beaten at one point before he learns of the attack.

2.   The second means is to direct movement against the most important weak point of the enemy's forces. The selection of this point depends upon the position of the enemy. The most important point will always be the point that offers the most favorable opportunities and the greatest results: for example, positions that may lead to the severing of the line of communications between the enemy force and his base of operations.

3.   The result of the preceding truths is that if preference is given to the attack of the extremities of a line, then care must be taken not to attack both of the extremities at the same time. . . .

4.   In order to be able to act in a combined effort on a single point, it is important to hold your forces in an area that is very nearly square so that they will be highly dispatchable. Large fronts are as contrary to good principles as broken lines, large detachments and divisions isolated beyond supporting distance.

5.   One of the most efficacious ways to apply the general principle is to make the enemy commit errors that are contrary to the principle. . . .

6.   It is very important when one takes the initiative to be well in-

formed of the positions of the enemy and of the movements that he is capable of undertaking. Espionage is a useful means. . . .

7.   It is not sufficient for success in war to skillfully bring masses to the most important points; it is necessary to know how to employ them there. If a force arrives at a decisive point and is inactive, the principle is forgotten; the enemy can counterattack. . . .

8.   If the art of war consists of bringing the superior effort of a mass against the weak points of the enemy, it is undeniably necessary to pursue actively a beaten army. . . .

9.   In order to make superior shock of a mass decisive, the general must give care to raise the morale of his army. . . .

10.   By this rapid review, it is seen that the science of war is composed of three general activities, which have only a few subdivisions and few opportunities of execution. . . . The first is to hold the most favorable lines of operations. . . . Second is the art of moving masses as rapidly as possible to the decisive point. . . . Third is the art of simultaneously bringing the greatest mass to the most important point on the field of battle.[14]

The concepts presented in these ten paragraphs were sometimes referred to as maxims and sometimes as principles, but the fact that they were presented as a list of general truths whose application contributes to success in war qualifies them as the prototype of the modern "principles of war." This list was reprinted with minor changes in chapter 35, "Conclusions of the Work, the Art of War Restored to Its True Principles," of the first half of the second edition of Jomini's *Traité* in 1811 and rewritten and again placed at the conclusion of the second edition when the final two volumes were published in 1816. The title of the 1816 conclusion was changed to read, "Exposé of the General Principles upon Which the Art of War Rests," and the maxims that support the general principle were increased from ten to twelve (see appendix 10). The conclusions of subsequent editions of the *Traité* closely followed the text of the 1816 chapter.

In the same period that Jomini was writing and revising his summary of the general principles of the art of war, Archduke Charles of Austria published two works that also sought to enunciate general principles upon which the conduct of war was founded. The first of these, *Grundsätze der höheren Kriegskunst* (Principles of the great art of war), was published in 1806, and in the first chapter, "A General Discussion of War," the archduke wrote that principles lay in "the nature of war" and that they "give proper definition to the art of war."[15] The chapter concluded:

> It consists in the art of war to use and to unite a superior number of troops at the decisive point. This principle must serve as a guide to every general in the largest operation and in the smallest battle, in offensive as well as defensive war and in every possible situation.[16]

The work continued with brief instructional chapters on the operational aspects of the conduct of war. As in Jomini's and most other theoretical works of this period, the principal focus was upon bases, lines of operation, and lines of communication, but unlike Jomini, the archduke made no attempt to summarize his principles, although he declared in the conclusion, "The principles of the science of war are few and unchanging."[17]

In 1813 the archduke published *Grundsätze der Strategie* (The principles of strategy), a work that Jomini declared to be "more complete than my own" but intended only "for accomplished military men."[18] The first volume of this three-volume study explained the principles, and the second and third volumes demonstrated the manner in which they had been applied in the campaign of 1796 in Germany. Spaced type was used frequently in the initial section, and if it is presumed that the most important dictums were emphasized in this way and hence indicated the "principles," then only fifteen or twenty principles would be discovered. For example, spaced type was used to emphasize the following:

> Every position and every movement must assure security for the zone to the rear, for the base of operations . . ., for the communications with the base and for the line of operations.[19]

The greatest advantage is achieved by forcing the enemy, by

sheer force or by maneuver, to deviate from the principles of strategy without abandoning them yourself.[20]

A point is considered strategic when its occupation gives a decisive advantage in an operation.[21]

The ideas were similar to those expressed by Jomini, but unlike Jomini, Charles offered no summarized list of principles. In spite of the translation of Charles's volumes into French, Italian, Turkish, and Hungarian, he never achieved the influence that Jomini's volumes exerted on the theory of war.

Throughout the Napoleonic period the lack of well-defined taxonomical distinctions within the realm of war created inconsistencies in the area of application of the principles. In his *Grundsätze der Strategie,* Archduke Charles wrote, "Strategy is the science of war. . . . It is the only science belonging exclusively to the highest commanders."[22] He believed that strategy was a science and hence that it must have concomitant "scientific principles." Jomini had declared in 1805 that the science of war and the concomitant principles lay in the realm of grand tactics, but in 1830 he wrote in the *Tableau analytique des principales combinaisons de la guerre* (Analytical tableau of the principal combinations of war):

The essential goal of this work is to point out that there exists a fundamental principle of war for all the operations of war, a principle that must be adhered to in all proper combinations.

It is:

1.   To carry the greatest part of the available forces of an army on the decisive point whether it is in the theater of war or on the field of battle.

2.   To operate in such a manner that this mass is not only present at the decisive point, but that once there, it is also skillfully put into action.[23]

And in 1838 in his *Précis,* Jomini again expanded the statement of the fundamental principle. He wrote,

It is embraced in the following:

1.  To throw by strategic movements the mass of forces of an army, successively, upon the decisive points of a theater of war, and as much as possible upon the communications of the enemy without compromising one's own.
2.  To maneuver to engage the mass of forces against fractions of the hostile enemy army.
3.  On the day of battle, to throw by tactical movements the mass of forces on the decisive point on the battlefield, or upon the most important part of the hostile line.
4.  To insure that these masses are not only present at the decisive point, but that they are vigorously and simultaneously engaged.[24]

In the *Tableau* the fundamental principle was to apply "to different combinations of strategy and tactics."[25] In the *Précis* the fundamental principle was included in the chapter on strategy, but it was introduced as "the one great principle underlying all the operations of war,—a principle that must be followed in every operational decision."[26]

Jomini's concept of the principles was complicated by additional lists of maxims that appeared in the *Tableau* and *Précis*. In the section of the *Tableau* that concerned lines of operations, he listed seven "principal maxims that are expanded upon in the course of this essay" (see appendix 13).[27] In the *Précis* he summarized the contents of the chapter on strategy by pointing out six "maxims that support the application of the fundamental principle of war" (see appendix 16).[28]

If Jomini's various lists of principles or maxims presented between 1807 and 1838 were collated, a brief list of imperatives would result. But Jomini did not use such a format in his final theoretical works, the compendia of more than thirty years of thought and experience relative to the conduct of war. He merely stated, "There exists a small number of fundamental principles of war."[29] When the second edition of the *Précis de l'art de la guerre* appeared in 1855, it included an appendix that sought to confirm the immutability of the fundamental principles of war in light of new weapons and inventions. The appendix closed with the following remark:

That war, far from being an exact science, is a terrible and impassioned drama, regulated, it is true, by three or four general principles . . . but also dependent for its results upon a number of moral and physical complications.[30]

Jomini never explicitly identified the general principles or even the "small number of fundamental principles of war," but he certainly insisted upon their existence and identified the one great fundamental principle.

One of the fundamental problems facing every military theorist is to reduce the numerous forces with which a theory of war must contend to a manageable level. Jomini based his theory of principles predominantly upon material forces. He recognized the role of "moral and physical complications," but in his theory he generally ignored the forces that make war "a great drama, in which a thousand physical or moral causes act more or less powerfully, and which cannot be reduced to mathematical calculations."[31] Although the consideration of this multiplicity of forces complicates the phenomena of war, it does not of itself negate the possibility of the existence of fundamental principles. It only shifts the milieu of the principles from the material world to the philosophical, to the psychological, or even to moral foundations. For example, a manuscript written by a general officer in 1815 on the art of war began by listing five principles of war:

I. Examine yourself and seek to know yourself. See what you are capable of so that you understand only what you can achieve. Neither over- nor under-estimate your forces. If you have a choice, do not accept a command nor a task beneath your ability, your courage or your means. . . .

II. Generals and soldiers must at all times and in all places, far and near, materially or philosophically, have a goal. When one knows well where he wants to go, it is rare that he does not arrive at his destination. . . .

III. There are some happy men whom fortune favors and who trust fortune for all success. Do not imagine yourself to be one of these men, but put every possible advantage for success on your side. Neglect nothing, not even the smallest detail. . . .

IV.   Responsibility alone leads to what is just, but responsibility must be united in a single person. . . .

V.   Subordinate yourself; never criticize the orders of your superiors. Respect a position full of difficulties.[32]

The philosophical overtones of these statements are obvious, and their contribution to success in war is surely no less significant than the operational dictums presented by Jomini and Archduke Charles. Some operational concepts, like those found in the modern "principle of the objective" and the "principle of unity of command," were clearly stated. This particular list, however, had no significant influence as far as subsequent theory is concerned.

Carl von Clausewitz, on the other hand, was an individual of considerable influence. His life and writings, like Jomini's and Archduke Charles's, were part of the Napoleonic experience. Clausewitz argued against the one-sidedness of Jomini's theory and others like it, and he sought to present a more complete theory "whose components and totality could stand the test of experience, historical interpretation and logical analysis."[33] But in spite of this high goal, which was only partially achieved in his posthumously published thoughts, *Vom Kriege* (On war), Clausewitz has been spuriously labeled a prime contributor to the modern concept of principles of war.

Although Clausewitz himself frequently spoke loosely of certain "principles" to be observed and followed, . . . he specifically rejected the notion that there could be any well-defined body of particular rules or principles that universally dictated one form of behavior rather than another.[34]

In the 1920s, however, he was referred to as the enumerator of certain principles of strategy that merely used different terms from those used in the British *Field Service Regulations* of that date.[35] And in a pamphlet, *Jomini, Clausewitz, and Schlieffen,* used at the United States Military Academy in the 1960s, "Clausewitz's principles" were said to have included the objective, mass, economy of force, surprise, mobility, and simplicity.[36] Clausewitz never used such titles, but he did tersely state a few "principles" in a brief memorandum. The memorandum was didactic in its intent and content and directed toward the instruction of a teenaged and militarily unaware prince. Even though the memorandum barely suggested the depth of thought and thoroughness that permeated the mature writings of Clausewitz, it was significant to the development of the concept of "principles of war," not in the early nineteenth century when it was written but at the end of the nineteenth century when the existence of principles was widely accepted and when Clausewitz's influence was rising in higher schools of war.

Early in the memorandum, Clausewitz warned against a reliance on principles.

> These principles, though the result of long reflection and a continuing study of the history of war, have none the less been drawn up hastily and thus will not stand severe criticism with regard to form. . . . They will not so much give complete instruction to Your Royal Highness as they will stimulate and serve as a guide for your own reflection.[37]

But later theorists who were seeking to condone a terse list of immutable principles ignored the warning. The first part of the memorandum was devoted to "principles for war in general," but the three numbered sections of this introduction contained concepts totally alien from modern operational principles of war. Here, Clausewitz was too philosophical, too ethereal, and too impractical for most participants in and students of war; hence, these principles have been ignored by advocates of the modern format of principles of war. Clausewitz's three "principles for war in general" were:

> 1. The theory of warfare tries to discover how we may gain superiority of physical forces and an advantage at the decisive point; when this is not possible, the theory also instructs us to consider the moral dimensions. . . .
>
> 2. Naturally, the probability of success is sought by gaining either physical or moral advantages, but since this is not always possible,

something else must be undertaken against the probability of success when nothing better can be done. If we despair here, we abandon our use of reason just where it is most necessary. . . . We must never lack the calmness and firmness that is so difficult amidst the danger of war. . . . We must familiarize ourselves with the thought of a creditable failure. . . .

3.  In all operations . . . there is always a choice between the most daring and the most careful solution. . . . Theory would advise the most decisive solution that is also the most daring. . . . Never forget that no commander has become great without audacity.[38]

The philosophic, the moral, the pragmatic, and the realistic dimensions of war were all included in these brief principles, but they have been passed over, along with his enumerations of general tactical principles for the offensive, principles for the defensive, and principles for the use of terrain, which all appeared in the didactic memorandum, in order to arrive at the general principles of strategy, which appeared to later writers to be more congruent with the more definitive concept of principles that evolved from Jomini's writings.

In Clausewitz's discussion of strategy, each paragraph was numbered as a method of organization. If Clausewitz ever intended to enumerate principles in the Jominian sense of a few fundamental operational considerations, the resulting list would be found in paragraphs 5 through 8 of his discussion of strategy. In paragraph 5, Clausewitz wrote, "The first and most important principle [*Grundsatz*] . . . is: to mobilize all of our forces with the greatest energy." Paragraph 6 read, "The second principle is: to concentrate as much as possible where the main effort is to be made." Paragraph 7 began, "The third principle is: to waste no time," and paragraph 8 read in part, "Finally, the fourth principle is: to follow up the successes that have been achieved with the greatest energy."[39]

The final section of Clausewitz's memorandum confirmed that the list was never intended as an all-inclusive rendering of the principles of the art of war, for even in this didactic work, he considered the principles of war to include all of the "principles" that he had discussed. Furthermore, he saw the most important object of the essay to be not the illustration of principles but rather the demonstration of the difficulty of executing any "principles that can be laid down." His purpose was not to present a list of considerations upon which success in war depends but to illustrate the rudiments of the operational branches of war and to demonstrate the difficulty of applying even these rudiments. Even though he used the word *principle,* his concept of it differed markedly from Jomini's and more modern definitions. In *Vom Kriege* he defined *principle* at length:

> *Principle* is also a law for action, but not in its *formal definitive meaning;* it represents only the spirit and the sense of law: in cases where the diversity of the real world cannot be contained within the rigid form of law, the application of principle allows for a greater latitude of judgment. Cases to which principle cannot be applied must be settled by judgment; principle thus becomes a support, or lodestar, to the man responsible for the action.[40]

Jomini argued against the "yokes of pedantry," but if his definition of principle had been as rigorous and if he understood the limits and qualifications of this Clausewitzian definition, the charge of pedantry might well have escaped the concept of the principles of war that lay at the base of Jomini's theory.

In the final analysis, Jomini, far more than Archduke Charles or Clausewitz, laid the foundations for the modern concept of the principles of war. Jomini did not present a list that purported to include all of the principles of war, and he did not use the titles common to modern lists. He did, however, insist upon the existence of a few fundamental principles, and he provided a brief list of tersely expressed truths, derived from the study of successful military operations and intended to guide future commanders with the requisite knowledge of their profession. And though the influence of Archduke Charles and Clausewitz was considerable, Jomini's influence upon the military institutions of the nineteenth and early twentieth centuries has been far greater, for it was in "Jominian terms" that soldiers were trained.

Jomini's theory of principles was used, revised, rewritten, sometimes rejected, but rarely ignored, in nineteenth-century military schools. By examining the courses that dealt with the theory of war and with military history—the study of military history has often been a euphemism for the study of a theory of war—in the leading military schools, the development of Jomini's ideas on the principles of war can be traced. Of the military educational institutions that existed in the half-century after Napoleon's defeat, those that taught the most senior officers generally provided an accurate expression of the nation's military thought. These include the Kriegsschule (war college) in Prussia, the French Ecole d' application de l'artillerie et du génie (the artillery and engineer school of application), the Royal Military College in Great Britain and the military academy in the United States. Although the last two schools taught candidates for commissions, their instructors were recognized as the highest authorities on the theory of war—at least until staff colleges were established in these countries later in the century. Writers remote from these and other schools also contributed to the growing belief in the existence and efficacy of principles of war, and their writings were an integral part of the development of the modern principles. Through the schools and through the literature, a belief in the existence of principles of war spread to savants, teachers, and soldiers.

Jomini's chapter on the general principles of the art of war that was published in 1808 in the German military journal, *Pallas,* was read by influential military theorists. Among them, Georg Heinrich von Berenhorst, a former adjutant of Frederick the Great and an important writer on military affairs,thought that the concept of principles had some merit.[41] Others, notably Clausewitz, found the idea arid and one-sided. At the Prussian war college, where Clausewitz served as director from 1818 until 1830, the theory of principles was ignored until the appointment of Wilhelm von Willisen as instructor of the history of war in 1832. Military instruction at the war college made up a relatively small part of a highly technical curriculum, and every course was based upon highly practical considerations. Typical examination questions in the tactics course, for example, asked students to draw up the defenses of Berlin in the face of three advancing enemy corps or to describe the position needed to halt an enemy pursuit.[42] The course on the history of war also had a practical goal: to provide "a finished picture of the characters of great military leaders and of the troops which they commanded."[43]

In 1840, von Willisen published the first volume of his *Theorie des grossen Kriegs* (Theory of war), which attempted to simplify the study of history for the students at the school. The book examined the Russo-Polish campaign of 1831, and like Jomini's lengthy essay on the Seven Years War, it sought to present general conclusions that were illustrated by the historical narrative. Like Jomini, too, von Willisen used the concepts of bases and lines of communications, and in his study of the offensive, he proposed a single fundamental rule, which was founded on the observation that the flanks are the weakest parts of an army and that the front represents the strength. The rule was expressed as, "The application of strength against weakness, front against flank, masses against a weak front, and superior power against lesser power."[44]

Von Willisen's writings, however, did not lead to a lasting acceptance in Prussia of a theory or doctrine of war based upon a few fundamental principles, partly because of his ill-fated career. In 1848 he failed to crush a Polish uprising in Posen by either political or military means. He was recalled by his superiors and resigned from the service the following year. When Jomini's most influential follower in the Prussian service withdrew to private life, Jomini's influence on German military thought declined. But more fundamentally, Jomini's concept of principles waned in Prussia because of the growing Clausewitzian tradition that emphasized freedom of decision and the uniqueness of each event.

The influence of Jomini's belief in the existence of a few fundamental principles of war was far more profound in France. Although the many lists of principles and maxims that appeared from time to time cannot always be traced directly to the example that he provided in his chapter on general principles of war, the format that he used was frequently adopted and the substance of his thought often repeated.

One of the routes to a commission in the French cavalry and infantry was through study at the Ecole royale spéciale militaire, which had been established at Saint Cyr in 1808. An early instructor of the course in military art and history, Jean T. Rocquancourt, stated the benefit to be derived from the study of principles of warfare:

> The study of principles must precede their application. It is necessary in all things that principles, founded upon experience and reason, indicate the route of thought; the genius himself . . . can then use for action the time he would otherwise use in the search and discovery of the means to success.[45]

And in a chapter on strategy, Rocquancourt provided a list of aphorisms that appeared in ten numbered paragraphs (see appendix 12). One of the paragraphs claimed to be derived from the writings of the seventeenth-century Habsburg general, Raimondo Montecuculli; one was a maxim; others were presented as principles. Their content was typical of Jomini's theory: the predominance of the single line of operations, the advantage of interior lines, and the importance of anticipating the enemy's actions. The sixth was strongly reminiscent of Machiavelli.

Men who sought a commission in the French artillery or engineer corps encountered Jominian ideas on principles in their special schools too. Their first professional training took place at the Ecole polytechnique where they studied along with contemporaries destined for positions in civilian technical fields, such as the roads and bridges service, the hydrographical corps, the tobacco department, and the telegraph department. Little instruction in the art of war was offered at the Ecole polytechnique, but the method of instruction demonstrated a proclivity toward fixed rules and systematic knowledge. The method was called the repetitorial method, a very able "combination of professorial and tutorial teaching," that united "the well-prepared lecture of a German professor with the close personal questioning of a first-rate English school."[46] Briefly, students in vast numbers attended professorial lectures. They immediately retired to study rooms where *répétiteurs* assisted them with the reconstruction of their lecture notes until the lecture was very nearly repeated verbatim. Frequent reviews and examinations ensured that the "professorial knowledge" had been properly digested. Little opportunity existed for the students to question or even augment the information they received in lectures; knowledge was thus reduced to fixed, definitive quantities.

After leaving the school, those students pursuing commissions attended the artillery and engineer school at Metz. The theoretical knowledge gained at the polytechnic school in subjects such as mathematics, physics, and chemistry was here applied to the practical concerns of the military profession. A course in the military art was included in the curriculum, and at the end of the second and final year, the study of strategy was undertaken. In 1832, the course was taught by Professor G. F. Français, whose notes paralleled entire paragraphs from Jomini's published works. Like Jomini's discussion of the fundamental principle, for example, Français's notes read, "The fundamental principle of war consists in operating, with superior forces, in a combined effort, at the decisive place."[47] He continued, "the means of applying this principle reduce themselves to about the following," and he then listed in numbered paragraphs seven of the twelve maxims included in Jomini's 1816 version of his chapter on general principles (see appendix 14).

Students at Metz were not the only French students in schools of application to be exposed to Jomini's concept of principles of war. At the staff school in Paris, whose students came from Saint Cyr and the polytechnic school, Jean-Baptiste Koch established the chair of military art and history. Throughout his long life, he wrote historical and strategical works that were profoundly influenced by Jomini, whom Koch had served as aide-de-camp in 1813.[48] Koch was succeeded at the staff school by Jules Vial, whose teaching continued to reflect a strong Jominian imprint. The only list that Vial provided was the one taken from the writings of the duke of Rohan in the seventeenth century (appendix 3), but early in the course Vial displayed other tendencies toward Jomini's theory. He stated, for example, that he had assembled the principles that appeared "the simplest, the clearest, the most useful and the best."[49] After long chapters on the myriad activities in war, however, it was clear that Vial had stressed not the existence of a few fundamental principles that focused on operations but rather the idea that principles exist throughout the realm of war. Still, many of Jomini's ideas about the principles of war persisted. Vial concluded, "The principles are taken from the examples of the greatest generals. . . . They are easy to comprehend, but they are difficult to apply," and reminiscent of the conclusion of Jomini's *Précis,* he added, "It is in the study of military history that students will find the source of true military instruction and the true principles of the art of war."[50]

It would be remiss to leave a discussion of the principles of war in post-Napoleonic France without mentioning Marshal Marmont's *L'Esprit des institutions militaires.* Marmont's military exploits— he had been with Napoleon at Toulon, Marengo, and Ulm and had lost an arm in a cavalry charge in Spain—suggested that his influence might have been great, but his betrayal of Napoleon in 1814 and of the Bourbons in 1830 limited his influence, especially in France. In Great Britain, however, he was included with Jomini and Archduke Charles as one of the great contributors to the concept of principles of war. The popular British journal, the *Quarterly Review,* reported:

> Nobody with the works of Jomini, the Archduke Charles and Marshal Marmont before him can pretend to say anything that is absolutely new in explanation of the great principles on which the art of war is founded.[51]

Marmont claimed that he disliked Jomini and his theory, but their thought on the principles of war was strikingly similar. Marmont wrote, for example, "General principles for the conduct of armies are not very numerous. . . . I will lay down, as principles, certain rules of which a general should never lose sight."[52] He offered no list, but his work discussed many of the dictums included in Jomini's list of maxims. Marmont stated, "It is thus seen how important it is for a general to assume the initiative." On other occasions he differed slightly from Jomini: "Numerical superiority, at the very instant of combat, is of extreme importance. Doubtless, the quality of troops is more to be considered than their numbers." And in the conclusion to his chapter on bases, lines of operation, and strategy, Marmont summed up the "double aim" of strategy:

> 1.   To unite all the troops, or the greatest number possible, on the field of action, when the enemy has only a part of his own there; in other words, to cherish a numerical superiority for the day of battle.
>
> 2.   To cover and insure our own line of communications, while threatening those of the enemy.

The continental schools paid some attention to the study of the conduct of war or at least to the study of military history. In Great Britain and the United States, however, the so-called scientific basis upon which nearly all military schools were founded allowed little opportunity for the study of other than formal scientific subjects.

Courses in military history and strategy were almost unknown in British military schools in the early nineteenth century. Hence, Jomini's ideas had little impact within the curricula, but they were discussed by influential British soldiers. In July 1821, for example, William Napier lavishly praised Jomini's *Traité* in an article published in the *Edinburgh Review.* He wrote that Jomini's work was "unquestionably one of the most profound, original, and interesting, that has appeared in our day," and he referred to Jomini as "the first to give a complete exposition of the principles of war"—a claim Jomini himself denied.[53] Napier's praise continued throughout the article, and he credited Jomini with the creation of both the principles of war and the art of war:

> Candour must force us to confess, that this wonderful man, whose genius first thoroughly perceived and developed all the principles on which the success of Strategy depends, has himself furnished the most glorious and brilliant examples of an art which he may be said to have created.[54]

Two years after this article was published, Napier began his monumental *History of the Peninsular Wars.* The object of this six-volume history was "to erect a fitting monument of British glory as achieved by British arms," but it was also a tribute to Jomini, whose ideas were often evident.[55]

Napier's admiration of Jomini was shared by many British soldiers. Perhaps the most influential among them was Patrick Leonard MacDougall. MacDougall had been educated at Edinburgh and at the Royal Military College, which he left in 1842 with special commendation; two years later he married one of Napier's daughters. In 1854 MacDougall was assigned as superintendent of studies at the Royal Military College. Although called "the most neglected of all British military theorists," his impact on British military thought belies the epithet.[56]

Before MacDougall's appointment to the Royal Military College, military education had played a relatively unimportant role in preparing the British army for war. The duke of Wellington, whose victory over Napoleon at Waterloo helped give the duke considerable and justified influence in the British army, "thought all military education nonsense."[57] He believed that nothing was more likely to lead to the "lowering of the social qualifications" of the officer corps. The Royal Military Academy, Woolwich, and the Royal Military College, Sandhurst, continued to provide extensive precommissioning studies in scientific topics—primarily to sons from well-founded families—but little emphasis was placed on advanced military education or on the formal study of military topics until after Wellington's death in 1852.

In spite of the inattention paid to military education during Wellington's ascendancy after Waterloo, the duke was responsible for the publication of a treatise on war, *The Principles of War, Exhibited in the Practice of the Camp; and as Developed in a Series of General Orders of Field-Marshal the Duke of Wellington, K.G. etc., etc., etc. in the Late Campaign on the Peninsula.* The editors of this study sought to retain and to call to the attention of its readers those ideas gleaned from the orders issued during the peninsular campaign that contributed to the British success. But unlike Jomini's attempt to divine the essence of Frederick's and Napoleon's conduct of war, the British editors dealt with details rather than with the sublime. Some aphorisms appeared in the British volume. For example, the chapter on forage emphasized "Forage of Country recommended," and the chapter entitled, "Before the Enemy," admonished, "Corps to be as strong as possible"; "Unnecessary Men to be Left with Baggage"; "Every man must have a good flint, and the dust must be well cleaned from the locks and touchholes."[58] Whether the advice offered in the book served to educate the British army is not known, but the disasters that befell the British in the Crimea just after the duke of Wellington's death confirmed that changes in British views toward military education were long overdue.

MacDougall had served in the Crimean War. After his return to the Royal Military College in 1856, he published his *Theory of War,* the first modern treatise on war by an English soldier. He dedicated the book

> to the young officers of the British Army, in admiration of their courage and constancy, and in the hope that they may be induced to study the principles of that profession which they have so nobly illustrated by those qualities.[59]

From the start, MacDougall accepted the existence of fundamental principles. In this respect he was wholly in accord with Jomini. In fact, MacDougall made no claim to originality in his work:

> The first four chapters are compiled from the writings of Napoleon, Frederick, the Archduke Charles, and Jomini, and from the only classical military history in our language, Napier's "Peninsular War." In those chapters there can, obviously, be nothing new except the method of arrangement.[60]

But the new arrangement was significant. The first chapter, "The Principles of War," presented three specific principles. Like Jomini's fundamental principle, MacDougall's "Principle No. 1" held a position superior to all other principles. According to MacDougall the "Leading principle of war" was "to place masses of your army in contact with fractions of your enemy."[61] "Principle No. 2, To operate as much as possible on the communications of your enemy without exposing your own," and "Principle No. 3,

To operate always on interior lines," were secondary. Just as Jomini had written that every maxim can be deduced from the fundamental principle, MacDougall wrote, "Every true maxim in war can be deduced from the above given principles," and he provided a list of thirty such maxims (see appendix 18). MacDougall defined neither *principle* nor *maxim,* but his thirty maxims were consistently subordinate to his three principles. Hence his discussion of principles and maxims was clearer than Jomini's, who used the words *principle* and *maxim* interchangeably. MacDougall was also more explicit regarding the application of the principles of war:

> These three principles supply an infallible test by which to judge of every military plan; for no combination can be well conceived, no maxim founded in truth, which is at variance with them.

MacDougall's *Theory of War* was significant. It reinforced the Jominian idea of the existence of a few fundamental principles, and along with Napier's writings, it extended Jomini's concept of principles to the British military world.

In the year after MacDougall published *Theory of War,* other changes significantly affected British military educational institutions. In April 1857, the duke of Cambridge issued instructions that set forth new qualifications for staff officers. Among these was the requirement that every staff officer "be thoroughly acquainted with military geography and military history, especially as related to the campaigns of ancient and modern commanders."[62] Second, the report of the commission to consider the best mode of reorganizing the system for training officers found the existing system of military education to be lacking in regard to "encouragement and superintendence."[63] And finally, MacDougall published "The Senior Department of the Royal Military College," which drew attention to the lack of proper instruction for staff officers. These three developments were in part responsible for the founding of a British staff college in 1858 and for the appointment of MacDougall as its first commandant. Mathematics still held a prevalent position in the curriculum, but military theory, military history, and geography were also included. An institutional path now existed along which the theory of Jomini and MacDougall's interpretation of Jomini could enter the corporate mind of the British army.

Lying outside the mainstream of the development of British military thought and education in this period was an obscure work that also demonstrated the acceptance and extension of the Jominian concept of principles to the British military world. James John Graham, remembered almost solely for his 1873 translation of Clausewitz's *On War,* published *Elementary History of the Progress of the Art of War* in 1858. He wrote, "The existence of fundamental principles by which all operations of war should be conducted, has been placed beyond a doubt by the researches of Jomini and other military writers."[64] He claimed to be quoting Jomini when he wrote:

> All combinations in war, to be good, must be governed by the following principles:
>
> First, To bring by strategical combinations, the mass of an army successively on the decisive points of the theater of war, and, as far as possible, on the communications of the enemy without endangering our own.
>
> Second, To maneuver so as to engage fractions only of the enemy's force in succession with the mass of our own.[65]

The ideas were certainly from Jomini's chapter on strategy in the *Précis,* but the form of presentation was more similar to Mac-Dougall's. By 1860 the belief that a few fundamental principles govern the conduct of war had reached a wide audience in Great Britain. Since then the belief has rarely been questioned even though the principles inherent in the belief have markedly changed in form and in content.

The first significant introduction of the Jominian concept of principles to the United States occurred in 1817 when John Michael O'Connor appended an edited translation of Jomini's chapter on general principles to his translation of Simon Gay de Vernon's *Traité élémentaire d'art militaire et de fortification* (Elementary treatise on the military art and fortifications). The English title read, *A Treatise on the Science of War.* Ironically, the author considered that his book dealt with the art of war, but the translator interpreted the same book as a treatise on the science of war. Perhaps war was viewed more scientifically in 1817 when the translation appeared than it had been in 1805 when the original French edition was published, or perhaps American society was simply more scientifically and less artistically oriented than French society in the early nineteenth century. Perhaps, too, the translation required the portents of science to be accepted as a text at the United States Military Academy, the nation's only military school at the time. And possibly the addition of Jomini's chapter on principles gave the work a more scientific cast.

This last explanation was suggested by the translator's introductory comments to Jomini's chapter: "General Jomini has transcended all writers on war. . . . [He] has reduced the hitherto mysterious science of war to a few self-evident principles and maxims."[66] O'Connor referred to Jomini's principles and maxims as the "grand principles of the science," but he went beyond Jomini, who in 1816 had subordinated twelve maxims to the fundamental principle (appendix 10) by listing thirteen (see appendix 11). The O'Connor translation was used at West Point until Dennis Hart Mahan, whose influence at the academy extended nearly from the day of his arrival in 1820 until his death in 1871 had it replaced by his own texts.[67] The chapter adapted from Jomini was especially repulsive to Mahan. He found it too abstract and too lengthy, bordering "upon the pedantry he abhorred."[68]

Like the curricula of the cadet school at Sandhurst, the program at West Point paid little attention to the study of military history and strategy in the early nineteenth century. This omission was surprising because both Sylvanus Thayer and Mahan had extensively observed military schools in France where military history and strategy were both taught. Mahan spent four years in Europe, and in his sixteen months at the artillery and engineer school at Metz, he probably heard or read Français's lectures on Jomini's principles. Together Thayer and Mahan brought many continental ideas and books on the theory of war to West Point, but military history and strategy courses were for the most part ignored.

Although Mahan admired Jomini, he did not develop a fondness for Jomini's chapter on principles; yet Mahan maintained an almost dogmatic belief in the existence of principles for the conduct of war. This faith was probably more an expression of his age than of Jominian influence.

It is true that he believed there were certain principles important to the successful waging of war, and he adopted some of Jomini's ideas; but he also insisted upon injecting common sense, the practical approach, into the practice of the art. And he decried the blind application of foreign methods under suitable adaptation to American ways.[69]

It was the duty of instructors to reduce the complex to the simple, and principles were ideally suited to this task. In a curriculum dominated by scientific subjects, principles were the basis for the solution of most academic problems. In 1836, Mahan wrote one of his first texts, *A Complete Treatise on Field Fortifications,* and it contained not only general principles of permanent fortifications—such as, "No point within enemy cannon range shall afford shelter to the enemy"; "Works shall enclose the greatest space with the smallest perimeter"; and "Works shall be secure from attack by storm,"—but also a list of nine "principles regulating the plan and profile of intrenchments" (see appendix 15). The tendency to enumerate was not confined to the study of scientific or engineering subjects, for an examination of the titles alone of the texts used at the military academy in the period between its founding in 1802 and 1860 reveals that nearly one-quarter of the titles of texts used in humanities courses claimed to present the "elements of" or the "principles of" some particular subject. In the sceinces, nearly 30 percent of the titles of texts claimed to present "principles" or "elements."[70]

In 1860 a committee chaired by Jefferson Davis on the organization, system of discipline, and course of instruction at the academy noted the scant attention given to the study of military history and strategy. Mahan taught these subjects at the end of his course on military and civil engineering, but he spent so much time on the engineering that history and strategy were mentioned just briefly.[71] The tactics department taught the theory of strategy and grand tactics for a short time and used a translation of Jomini's *Précis* as a text, but amid the changes at the academy in the early months of the Civil War, Mahan "quietly brought strategy back into the engineering course."[72] Interest in the study of strategy by the Davis committee, by cadets, and by events of the war, however, contributed to Mahan's decision to enlarge his celebrated text, *Advanced-Guard, Outpost, and Detachment Service of Troops,* by adding "a concise statement of the Principles of Strategy and Grand Tactics."[73] He provided no lists in this addendum, but as Jomini suggested in his fundamental principle, Mahan concluded, "the only chance of success lies in concentrating all we can."[74] And like Jomini Mahan viewed military history as the laboratory in which the rules of strategy could be discovered:

> It is in military history that we are to look for the source of all military science. In it we shall find those exemplifications of failure and success by which alone the truth and value of the rules of strategy can be tested.[75]

The schools of war became the centers of military thought in the nineteenth century, but occasionally a writer, who was usually a soldier, of significance emerged who was not on the faculty of one of the formal schools. Examples of such individuals are the Russian, Nikolai Okunev, and the American, Henry Wager Halleck.

Okunev was a major-general and an aide to Czar Nicholas when his four-part treatise on war was published. The first part was entitled *Considérations sur les grandes opérations de la campagne de 1812 en Russie* (Discussion of the great operations in the campaign of 1812 in Russia); the second, *Mémoires sur les principes de la stratégie* (Memoirs on the principles of strategy); the third, *L'Examen raisonné des propriétés des trois armes* (Systematic examination of the characteristics of the three arms); and the fourth, *Un Mémoire sur l'artillerie* (A memoir on artillery). Throughout these independent studies, Okunev acknowledged his respect for and reliance on Jomini. For example, in the section on the principles of strategy, Okunev wrote with reference to lines of operations that it is impossible to give more complete definitions or more satisfactory explanations than those provided by Jomini in his *Traité*.

That Okunev knew Jomini well is certain since Jomini remained an adviser to the Russian czars from 1813 until his death in 1869. After 1825, however, Jomini spent much of his time in Paris and Switzerland because the climate in Saint Petersburg was less favorable to his health. Okunev also accepted Jomini's ideas concerning the existence of principles of war. He spoke in a general sense about principles and also provided a list of ten considerations that he called maxims (see appendix 17). He introduced this list by stating, "In summary, all the general principles that we have discovered for the relationship that exists between the three arms . . . enable us to pose the following series of maxims."[76] He listed maxims, and he spoke of the existence of general principles, which he claimed to have enumerated. But like Jomini, he was imprecise in identifying the principles.

Henry Wager Halleck was also a disciple of Jomini. Known as "Old Brains" because of his proclivity toward intellectual pursuits, he translated Jomini's *Vie politique et militaire de Napoléon* (Political and military life of Napoleon) to pass the time while sailing from New York to California in 1846. In the same year, he published a series of lectures that he had written. Entitled *Elements of Military Art and Science,* he relied heavily on Jomini's *Traité* and made no pretension

> to originality in any part of the work; the sole object having been to embody, in a small compass, well established military principles, and to illustrate these by reference to the events of past history, and the opinions and practice of the best generals.[77]

Halleck presented terse principles, rules, and maxims and used the terms interchangeably. For example, he stated, "The first and most important rule in offensive war is, to keep your forces as much concentrated as possible. This will not only prevent misfortune, but secure victory."[78] On the next page, he added, "If, as we have seen, it be the first great rule for an army acting on the offensive principle, to keep its forces *concentrated,* it is no doubt, the second, *to keep them fully employed.*"[79] He then referred to these "great rules" as the "leading maxims for conducting offensive war." In referring to Jomini's *Précis* in highly complementary terms, Halleck claimed that its chapter on strategy embodied the principles of that branch, and in referring to Napoleon's memoirs, he claimed that they contain "all the general principles of military art and science." He added with regard to Napoleon's memoirs:

> No military man should fail to study them thoroughly. The matter is so condensed, and important principles are embodied in so few words, that they are not easily understood by the ordinary reader, and probably will never be popular with the multitude.[80]

Halleck's volume proved to be a popular guide for American soldiers, but it did not achieve the fame of Jomini's *Précis.*

In the wake of the Napoleonic experience, two significant changes occurred in the realm of military thought. First, Napoleon's success led many students of war to the conclusion that a few simply stated principles or rules or maxims are fundamental to victory. Second, the significant books on the theory of war were written more by teachers in military schools than by successful high-ranking commanders as had tended to be the case before Napoleon. The term *principle* was emerging to describe the most important considerations for commanders seeking success in war, but the idea of myriad general principles persisted. To those who accepted that a few simply stated principles could be identified, the one most commonly stated was some form of Jomini's great principle, "To be strong at the decisive point." Jomini, however, acknowledged that Lloyd convinced him of the truth of "strength at the decisive point." Few lists were compiled in this period, and the dictums in the lists that were compiled were generally called maxims. The trends were all quite Jominian, and on the eve of the American Civil War, it appeared that Jomini might well become not only the prophet but the god of that war.

*NOTES*

1. Gouvion de Saint Cyr, *Mémoires pour servir à l'histoire militaire, sous le Directoire, le Consulat, et l'Empire,* Vol. I, quoted in France James Soady, *Lessons of War as Taught by the Great Masters and Others,* pp. 8-9.
2. Napoleon I, *Correspondence,* X, no. 8209 (Au général Lauriston, Paris, 21 frimaire an XIII), from Ernest Picard, ed., *Précepts et jugements de Napoléon,* p. 209, my translation.
3. Napoleon I, in L. E. Henry, trans. and ed., *Napoleon's War Maxims with His Social and Political Thoughts,* p. 39.
4. Antoine-Henri Jomini, *Précis de l'art de la guerre,* I, pp. 26-27, my translation.
5. Gaspard Gourgaud, *Sainte-Hélène: Journal Inédit de 1815 à 1818,* I, p. 20, my translation.
6. Michael Howard, "Classical Strategists," in Michael Howard, *Studies in War and Peace,* p. 154.
7. Antoine-Henri Jomini, *Traité de grande tactique,* I. pp. 5-6, my translation. Later editions of Jomini's *Traité de grande tactique* are often cited elsewhere in this book because the content of the editions varied. See John I. Alger, *Antoine-Henri Jomini: A Bibliographical Survey,* for a detailed discussion and listing of Jomini's publications.
8. Jomini, *Précis,* I. pp. 23-24.
9. Jomini, *Traité de grande tactique,* I, p. 125.
10. Ibid., pp. 533-34.
11. Ibid.
12. Ferdinand Lecomte, *Le Général Jomini, sa vie et ses écrits,* 3d ed., p. 61, my translation.
13. Antoine-Henri Jomini, "L'art de la guerre," *Pallas: Eine Zeitschrift für Staats = und Kriegs = Kunst* 1 (1808):32, my translation. This article appeared within weeks of the publication of the Glogau pamphlet and is probably identical with it.
14. Ibid., pp. 32-40.
15. [Archduke Karl], *Grundsätze der höherer Kriegskunst für die Generäle der österreichischer Armee,* p. 2, my translation.
16. Ibid., pp. 2-3.
17. Ibid., p. 90.
18. Antoine-Henri Jomini, *Histoire critique et militaire des guerres de Frédéric II,* I, p. x, my translation.
19. Archduke Karl, *Grundsätze der Strategie* in *Ausgewählte Schriften*

*weiland seiner kaiserlichen Hoheit des Erzherzogs Carl von Oesterreich,* p. 237, my translation.

20. Ibid., pp. 239-40.

21. Ibid., p. 240.

22. Ibid., p. 235.

23. Antoine-Henri Jomini, *Tableau analytique des principales combinaisons de la guerre,* pp. 63-64, my translation.

24. Jomini, *Précis,* I, p. 158.

25. Jomini, *Tableau,* p. 64.

26. Jomini, *Précis,* I, pp. 157-58.

27. Jomini, *Tableau,* p. 64.

28. Jomini, *Précis,* I, p. 190.

29. Ibid., pp. 26-27.

30. Ibid., II, p. 401.

31. Ibid., I, p. 26.

32. Edmond Bonneau du Martray, *Maximes, conseils et instructions sur l'art de la guerre,* 36th ed., pp. 3-9, my translation.

33. Peter Paret, *Clausewitz and the State,* p. 149.

34. Bernard Brodie, *War and Politics,* p. 446.

35. Frederick Maurice, *British Strategy,* p. 28.

36. United States Military Academy, Department of History, *Jomini,* p. 25.

36. United States Military Academy, *Jomini, Clausewitz, and Schlieffen,* 162-63, my translation. An edited translation, by Hans W. Gatzke, of the memorandum appeared as *Principles of War* in 1942.

38. Ibid., pp. 163-64.

39. Ibid., pp. 186-87.

40. Carl von Clausewitz, *On War,* trans. Michael Howard and Peter Paret, p. 151.

41. *Aus dem Nachlasse von Georg Heinrich von Berenhorst,* II, pp. 281-84.

42. Henry Barnard, *Military Schools and Courses of Instruction in the Science and Art of War,* rev. ed., p. 331.

43. Henry Vizetelly, *Berlin under the New Empire,* I, p. 408.

44. Wilhelm von Willisen, *Theorie des grossen Krieges angewendet auf den russisch-polnischen Feldzug von 1831,* I, p. 81, my translation.

45. Jean T. Rocquancourt, *Cours élémentaire d'art et d'histoire militaires à l'usage des élèves de l'Ecole royale spéciale militaire,* Vol. I, 2d ed., p. 7, my translation.

46. See Barnard, *Military Schools,* pp. 73-76; and Great Britain, *Report of the Commissioners Appointed to Consider the best Mode of Re-*

*organizing the System for Training Officers for the Scientific Corps Together with an Account of Foreign and Other Military Education,* p. 27.

47. G. F. Français, "Cours d'art militaire, à l'usage des élèves de l'Ecole d'application de l'artillerie et du génie," p. 6, my translation.

48. Musée de Payerne, *Général Antoine-Henri Jomini, 1779-1869,* p. 54, my translation.

49. Jules Vial, *Cours d'art et d'histoire militaires,* I, p. v.

50. Ibid., p. 420.

51. "Operations of Modern Warfare," *Quarterly Review* 120 (October 1866):513.

52. The Marmont quotations are from Auguste Marmont, *The Spirit of Military Institutions; or Essential Principles of the Art of War,* trans. Henry Coppée, pp. 37, 38, 48.

53. "Traité des grandes opérations militaires . . .," *Edinburgh Review* 35 (July 1821):377. The article appeared anonymously, but the *Dictionary of National Biography* attributes it to Napier.

54. Ibid., p. 391.

55. *London Times,* 14 February 1860, p. 5.

56. A. W. Preston, "British Military Thought, 1856-1890," *Army Quarterly* 89 (October 1964):65. See also Jay Luvaas, *The Education of an Army: British Military Thought, 1815-1940,* p. 102.

57. Hugh Thomas, *The Story of Sandhurst,* p. 80.

58. Arthur Wellesley, duke of Wellington, *The Principles of War, Exhibited in the Practice of the Camp,* pp. 246, 265, 266.

59. Patrick L. MacDougall, *The Theory of War Illustrated by Numerous Examples from Military History,* 2d ed., dedication.

60. Ibid., pp. vi, vii.

61. Ibid., p. 51. The discussion of principles and maxims is found on pages 51 and 52, and all subsequent quotations of MacDougall are from these pages.

62. Brian Bond, *The Victorian Army and the Staff College, 1854-1914,* p. 71.

63. Great Britain, *Report of the Commissioners,* p. xl.

64. James John Graham, *Elementary History of the Progress of the Art of War,* p. 5.

65. Ibid., pp. 23-24.

66. John M. O'Connor in Simon Gay de Vernon, *A Treatise on the Science of War and Fortification,* II, p. 386.

67. United States Military Academy, *Annual Report of the Superintendent,* 1896, p. 160.

68. Thomas E. Griess, "Dennis Hart Mahan: West Point Professor

and Advocate of Military Professionalism, 1830-1871" (Ph.D. diss., Duke University, 1968), p. 219.

69. Ibid., p. 290.

70. These statistics (23.4 percent and 29.2 percent) were compiled from a bibliography of textbooks that appeared in the *Centennial of the United States Military Academy at West Point,* I, pp. 439-66. In the period 1860-1902, only 4.8 percent of the humanities titles claimed to be "elements" or "principles of . . . ," and 32.5 percent of the science titles made such a claim.

71. Stephen Ambrose, *Duty, Honor, Country: A History of West Point,* p. 137.

72. Lieutenant R. Williams in Jefferson Davis, *Report of the Commission,* 13 December 1860, p. 85; and Ambrose, *Duty, Honor, Country,* p. 137.

73. Dennis Hart Mahan, *Advanced-Guard, Outpost, and Detachment Service of Troops, with the Essential Principles of Strategy and Grand Tactics,* p. iv.

74. Ibid., p. 203.

75. Ibid., p. 217.

76. Nikolai A. Okunev, *Considérations sur les grandes opérations de la campagne de 1812 en Russie; des mémoires sur les principes de la stratégie; de l'examen raisonné des propriétés des trois armes; et d'un mémoire sur l'artillerie,* p. 295, my translation.

77. Henry W. Halleck, *Elements of Military Art and Science,* p. 5.

78. Ibid., p. 40.

79. Ibid., p. 41.

80. Ibid., p. 59.

# 3

# THE AMERICAN CIVIL WAR AND THE CONTINENTAL FORMALIZATION OF MILITARY THOUGHT

THE AMERICAN CIVIL WAR affected American military institutions in much the same way as the Crimean War affected British military institutions. The civilian leaders of both governments were shocked that their armies had had to relearn the art of war and questioned the means of preparation for and the accepted theories of war. In times of peace or at least of relative peace, armies are beset by requirements that obscure their *raison d'être* and detract from their capability to fight effectively in a major conflict. For example, armies have been frequently involved in civil construction projects and in quelling civil disturbances. The Indian Wars and the Mexican War, which involved the U.S. Army, brought experience to a few of the leaders responsible for the conduct of battle in the Civil War, but the benefits derived from this experience were often difficult to discern. Two fundamental problems, inherent in armies that must expand their numbers when major wars unfold, emerged. First, many whose recent experience lay wholly outside the realm of war were recalled to active duty. Second, those who had remained with the colors almost without exception found themselves in positions of responsibility far greater than any they had dreamed of in times of peace. Their experience was hence of limited value except where certain fundamentals transcended the echelons of command. To know what those fundamentals were was a great relief. To be ignorant of the fundamentals was not only a potential source of embarrassment but of defeat and danger as well. The fundamentals, in whatever guise they existed, were eagerly sought by all who faced the burden of leadership in battle. Hence during the Civil War, the legend grew that a copy of the Holy Bible and a copy of Jomini's *Art of War* were carried in the knapsack of every successful general.

When the war ended, however, reassessment of Jomini seemed necessary. War had changed dramatically, at least in a technological sense, and new concepts of military thought heralded by Prussian success in three major European wars added to the challenge of the belief that a few simply expressed principles formed the foundation of success in war. During the American Civil War, however, Jominian ideas about war in general and about the principles of war in particular dominated both books on war and events on battlefields.

For example, in 1862 a translation of Marmont's essay on military institutions appeared in Philadelphia. The translator wrote in his preface, "My object in translating this work is to offer to the patriotic soldiers in the field . . . a summary of the great practical principles of the art of war, which they may daily apply." The book's English subtitle, *Essential Principles of the Art of War,* promised to present the fundamentals that commanders needed.[1] The translation was also published in Columbia, South Carolina, in 1864 with a new translation of Jomini's chapter on the general principles of the art of war. And in Philadelphia in 1862, Emil Schalk, who was born in Mainz, Germany, educated in Paris, and had no close connection with American military institutions, brought Jomini's ideas on the principles of war to the public attention in his *Summary of the Art of War.* He wrote,

There are three great maxims common to the whole science of war; they are—

1st—Concentrate your force, and act with the whole of it on one part only of the enemy's force.

2d—Act against the weakest part of your enemy—his center, if he is dispersed; his flank or rear, if concentrated. Act against his communications without endangering your own.

3d—Whatever you do, as soon as you have made your plan, and taken the decision to act upon it, act with the utmost speed, so that you may obtain your object before the enemy suspects what you are about.[2]

In the following year Schalk published his second book, *Campaigns of 1862 and 1863 Illustrating the Principles of Strategy,* which summarized the theory of his earlier work. The wording of the three maxims was slightly changed, and they were now called the "principles belonging to the entire science of war."[3] Schalk acknowledged his debt to Jomini by referring to him as the writer of the "most complete discussion of the principles of strategy," but since Jomini's work required "considerable knowledge of military history," Schalk decided to reduce the Jominian ideas to a compact and easily understood form.[4] Schalk used Jomini's theory to further his understanding of the Civil War and to point out ways in which the conduct of war might be improved. His discussion of the theory of war concluded, "We will apply the different principles, maxims, and rules just laid down to the present war; and thereby give a more exact idea of the mode in which wars of conquest ought to be conducted."[5]

During the Civil War Jomini's theory was not only discussed by civilians like Schalk, but it influenced such experienced commanders as P. G. T. Beauregard. In 1863, General Beauregard published a pamphlet on the art of war for the instruction of the officers of his command. The origins of the pamphlet are interesting in the light of his background. He was born in Louisiana of French parents and read and spoke French fluently. He attended the United States Military Academy where he was exposed to Mahan's ideas on war and where he also had access to the French editions of Jomini's writings. But in spite of these opportunities, Beauregard took his ideas and words from MacDougall's *Theory of War.* He wrote, nearly verbatim from MacDougall,

The whole science of war may be briefly defined as the art of placing in the right position, at the right time, a mass of troops greater than your enemy can there oppose to you.

Principle No. 1—To place masses of your army in contact with fractions of your enemy.

Principle No. 2—To operate as much as possible on the interior lines of your enemy without exposing your own.

Principle No. 3—To operate always on interior lines (or shorter ones in point of time).[6]

Beauregard concluded verbatim from MacDougall, "These three principles supply an infallible test by which to judge of every military plan; for no combination can be well conceived, no maxim founded in truth, which is at variance with them."[7] Beauregard also presented thirty-four maxims, which differed only slightly from the thirty maxims MacDougall presented. Perhaps Beauregard felt that the ultimate truths of war were very nearly defined by MacDougall and that his addition of four maxims might lead to the perfect theory of war. Regardless, Jomini's ideas on the conduct of war were spread through the South by a French-American who had borrowed them from an Englishman.

Many other civil War leaders also admired Napoleon and Jomini, but there is little evidence that any of them significantly advanced the concept of principles of war. George McClellan and Robert E. Lee were both enthusiastic members of the Napoleon Club at West Point, but neither articulated a theory of war that influenced subsequent thought. Ulysses Grant frowned on all theory, had no military library to speak of, and demonstrated in 1864 through his series of costly attacks from the Wilderness to Cold Harbor that he tended toward goatskin traditions. Ironically, Nathan Bedford Forrest, who had but a single year of formal education, is occasionally cited as a contributor to the popularity of terse aphorisms that express the highest truths of the military art. Any mention of either Forrest or military fundamentals brings to mind the advice associated with his name: "Git thar furst with the mostest." This phrase is an astute, albeit homey, rewording of Jomini's fundamental principle to be strong at the decisive point, but Forrest undoubtedly conveyed more military theory to his Tennessee farmboys turned cavalrymen than most of them cared to know in a lifetime. The American Civil War was fought by practical men with practical means. A comprehensive theory of war was unknown to its generals, untested in its conduct, and uninfluenced by its results. Europeans remained the most prolific and the most profound writers on war. American generals, unwilling perhaps to reflect on the war against their own, quietly went into retirement or turned their attention to the nation's continued westward expansion.

By the end of the American Civil War, Jomini's concept of the principles of war had been variously interpreted and had reached wide audiences in Prussia, France, Great Britain, the United States, Russia, Spain, and many other countries. A few British and American publications identified the fundamental principles that Jomini claimed were the foundation of the theory of war. But of greater importance to the development of the modern concept of principles of war was the nearly universal acceptance of the belief that the conduct of war was indeed subject to regulating principles. An influential soldier reported in 1864, and incidentally, the exact words were reprinted in another source in 1891:

> In our days we no longer believe in . . . "heaven-born generals."
> It is agreed that modern warfare is the offspring of science and
> civilization—that it has its rules and its principles, which it is
> necessary to thoroughly master before being worthy to com-
> mand, and that it is wiser to profit by such lessons of history . . .
> than to purchase experience by the blood of battlefields.[8]

This belief dominated the study of war in the newly created staff college in Great Britain and spread to higher schools of military education in the United States and France. And in each of these schools, military history assumed the role of "a great quarry of principles and examples to be judiciously selected to bolster pre-conceived ideas on traditional doctrines."[9] In Prussia the focus of military education remained upon the study of individual cases, but in France, Great Britain, the United States, and Russia, the struggle between Jominian principles and the study of individual cases persisted for half a century—when a major war again altered institutionalized beliefs about the nature of war and its guiding principles.

As a result of the overwhelming Prussian success in the Danish

War of 1864, the Seven Weeks War of 1866, and the Franco-Prussian War of 1870 and 1871, the model of military professionalism shifted from the memory of Napoleon to Prussian realities. The shift had enduring consequences for the development of the principles of war, for every theory was confronted by German pragmatism. At the war academy in Berlin, practical instruction was stressed over abstract theory; theory was subordinated to the study of the concrete case. In the schools of war where a theory based on principles had been used extensively, its impact with the Prussian method occurred in a variety of ways, but the belief in the existence of principles was rarely forsaken. In the light of the Prussian method, which stressed unique solutions to specific problems, and Prussian success on the battlefield, charges of pedantry were frequently bestowed upon attempts to teach the conduct of war in the classroom. But many factors, among them the persistent encroachment of science into people's daily lives, suggested that the proper conduct of war was controlled by simple, natural, and rational laws. On the other hand, the advance of time and the insistent claim that with time, there is change and that change reflects progress rather than immutable principles suggested that all theory is temporal and that there are no enduring principles.

By the turn of the century, two extremes of thought could be identified: on the one side, the rejection of all rules and principles and on the other, the acceptance and identification of a few specific principles of war. Instruction in most schools fell between these extremes. The applicatory system, which brought practice or "application" to the war colleges and academies, was universally relied upon, and it was often used to demonstrate specific principles or, more usually, "general principles."

The merit of the applicatory system, which stressed the practical application of theory through historical reenactments, field exercises, staff rides, map problems, or war games was expressed by General von Peucker, the director of Prussian military education, in 1868:

In war actions speak louder than words, practice surpasses theory. It is not enough to memorize certain truths, certain abstract rules; one must apply one's intelligence to discover by mature deliberation the fundamental principles which underlie them all.[10]

These ideas were endorsed by Helmuth von Moltke, chief of the Prussian, and later the German, general staff from 1858 until 1888 and architect of the Prussian victories in the Seven Weeks War and in the Franco-Prussian War, but he denied the value of principles. In his instructions for senior commanders, he wrote, "The doctrines of strategy do not go beyond the rudimentary propositions of common sense; they can hardly be called a science; their value lies almost entirely in their application to the concrete case."[11] On another occasion, he wrote, "Strategy is a system of expediencies. . . . In war, as in the arts, there is no general standard, in neither can talent be replaced by a rule."[12]

Throughout the late nineteenth century, German military thought and German military education adhered to these Moltkean precepts. The schools and the general staff focused primarily on the contingencies for war against each of the many combinations of powers that might oppose Germany in a future war. While Otto von Bismarck, the great chancellor of Germany, sought protection in the form of political treaties, Moltke's general staff formulated its plans to thwart every possible threat. No other great power was as intent or as thorough in its pursuit of the pragmatic solution to potential international problems. In spite of Moltke's influence, however, the German military world was confronted by the concept of principles of war.

In the year following the defeat of Austria by Prussia in the Seven Weeks War, the Austrian Field Marshal Heinrich von Hess published *Allgemeine praktische Grundsätze der Strategie und höheren Taktik* (General practical principles of strategy and grand tactics); it was written for army, independent corps, and division commanders and sought to update the writings of Archduke Charles by modifying and amplifying his instructions. Hess presented principles for mountain warfare, principles for diversions and for demonstrations, and terse instructions for many other operations in war. Three "strategic basic rules [*Grundregeln*] for offensive and defensive war" were also included. The first expressed the importance of the initiative and of the necessity "to gain superiority of power through the offensive."[13] The second pointed out the advantages of striking the flank of the enemy and of cutting the enemy line of communications. The third dealt with interior lines and the manner in which a united main force can defeat an enemy force separated from the main army. The central ideas in these basic rules had changed little since the writings of Archduke Charles and Jomini in the early nineteenth century, but their form was considerably different. They were enumerated as three separate and fundamental rules in the manner used by Jomini's followers in Great Britain and the United States.

The enumeration of principles rarely occurred in German military schools and literature in the late nineteenth and early twentieth centuries because of the prevalence of ideas held by Moltke and other influential German military writers. Wilhelm von Verdy du Vernois, a prolific didactic German writer of the period, expressed these ideas as follows:

> As to *rules,* we can accord them only limited importance, for we are able to apply them only so far as we can overlook and absolutely control existing conditions. There may be rules (or rather principles) for the arrangement of marches . . . ; rules for the establishment of outposts; or rules determining upon what visible objects a battery should fire under various circumstances; but for conducting an engagement on a large scale no rules can be given—there they simply become phrases, for we can neither overlook all conditions nor absolutely control them.[14]

The conviction that war, like the rest of life, can never assume rigid and immutable attributes became a fundamental belief of the German army.[15] As much as, if not more than, von Peucker and von Moltke, Verdy du Vernois was convinced of the inanity of rules applicable to all circumstances; "the method of concrete cases never had a more fervent apostle."[16]

Another significant German military writer of this period was Wilhelm Friedrich Rüstow. Unlike Verdy du Vernois, who rejected the existence of fundamental principles, Rüstow was "a staunch adherent of Jomini-Willisen's system."[17] The first edition of his *Feldherrnkunst des neunzehnten Jahrhunderts* (The art of field service in the nineteenth century), which was intended to be "a handbook for consultation, for self-study and for instruction in advanced military schools," concluded with a chapter on the "fundamental laws of strategy." Rüstow wrote the chapter "only because of the special desire of the publisher," who maintained that a positive conclusion was needed for his historical review of strategy.[18] The feeling of Rüstow's publisher toward the necessity for a definitive conclusion to a historical-theoretical work is reminiscent of Berthier's criticism of the first two volumes of Jomini's *Traité*. In both cases the authors added a chapter that summarized rules or maxims of war.

In the third edition of Rüstow's book, which appeared in 1878 and 1879, just over twenty years after the first edition, Rüstow wrote that he had become aware in these years of many and various views concerning the existence of fundamental laws in the conduct of war. He decided, however, that since the laws included nothing detreimental, he would allow them to remain at the conclusion of the third edition. His remarks were not a convincing endorsement of the existence of basic laws within the realm of strategy, but he did attempt to summarize the basic laws. He also listed his laws in twenty-seven numbered paragraphs, whose content and general format reflected Jominian ideas. In the sixth paragraph, for example, Rüstow wrote, "Concentration of our force is the most important rule of war." In the seventh paragraph he wrote, "Detachments should never be made without a clear objective," in the thirteenth, "Victory is completed by pursuit," and in the twenty-fifth, "The first characteristic of every war plan is the greatest possible simplicity."[19] The content of Rüstow's thought on war influenced subsequent military thinking, but his enumeration of aphorisms had little enduring effect.

In 1887, Prince Kraft zu Hohenlohe-Ingelfingen published *Strategische Briefe* (Notes on strategy) in which he stated, "There are . . . certain strategical axioms which must always be adhered to in war."[20] He listed five (see appendix 19). The axioms did not relate directly to operational considerations in war but addressed the relationship between national policy and military plans. Unlike most writers who accepted the existence of principles in war, Hohenlohe made no claim concerning the immutability of his axioms; he wrote that they would remain valid only as long as "present conceptions of war and peace, policy and strategy" remain valid.[21] For these reasons, his axioms did not significantly contribute to the evolution of the modern concept of principles of war. They did, however, parallel the development of the principles in a closely related field. Hohenlohe-Ingelfingen's enunciation of axioms further illustrated the propensity of modern thinkers to use the accumulated knowledge of one discipline in the search for knowledge in other fields. The laws of motion, of planetary movement, and even of human evolution had been reduced to simple propositions. The study of social activities, like war, was inspired by the advances in the study of natural phenomena, and the Newton, Kepler, or Darwin of war could surely discover its essence and reduce its essence to simple and infallible axioms or principles.

Von Moltke and Verdy du Vernois rejected the existence of principles, and Rüstow and Hohenlohe contributed little to their development. But one German writer of the late nineteenth century significantly influenced their further history. He was Colmar von der Goltz, whose military and diplomatic career included assignments with foreign armies and five years as a lecturer in military history at the war academy in Berlin. His early historical writings established him as a significant military writer, and *Das Volk in Waffen* (Nation in arms), first published in 1883 and translated into more than a half-dozen languages, extended his reputation to the world's major military powers. His popularity resulted in part from his able combination of Clausewitzian and Jominian thought. In his introduction to *Das Volk in Waffen,* he acknowledged his admiration for Clausewitz: "A military author who writes on war after Clausewitz is in the same danger as the poet who tries to write on Faust after Goethe or on Hamlet after Shakespeare."[22]

Von der Goltz's proclivities toward Jomini were apparent. For example, the Jominian belief in the existence of principles was as evident in the following remark as the Clausewitzian insistence on the importance of friction in war: "Even though the fundamental laws of the conduct of war may be eternal, the phenomena that have to be considered and resolved are subject to perpetual change."[23] Von der Goltz's acceptance of guides to success in warfare was confirmed when he acknowledged that he could not enumerate "all the conditions of success in war" but that he could point out "a few of the most important."[24] The discussion that followed this pronouncement dealt largely with national policy, but von der Goltz did not ignore operational considerations entirely. He wrote that "economy of forces" was one of the conditions of success. The words *economy of forces* were emphasized. The next emphasis was given to the phrase that von der Goltz called "the highest principle of modern warfare": make every effort as strong as possible at the decisive point." Throughout the concluding part of his discussion on the conditions of success, he emphasized other key words, such as, *morale, confidence,* and *fighting formations.*[25] In the fourth and longest section of *Das Volk in Waffen,* "Maneuver and Battle," von der Goltz continued to emphasize key words and phrases that he occasionally introduced as truths, occasionally as rules, occasionally as principles, but usually without any such label. Like Jomini, von der Goltz accepted the existence of principles and definitively identified the highest principle of war. Like Clausewitz, he saw war as an inseparable part of social life and recognized the difficulty of applying rules in the midst of human interaction. He presented no lists, but he emphasized words and phrases to describe complex truths.

In 1895 von der Goltz published his second major study on modern war. Entitled *Kriegführung, Kurze Lehre ihrer wichtigsten Grundsätze und Formen* (The conduct of war, a short study of its true principles and forms), and like *Das Volk in Waffen,* its popularity and influence were attested to by the numerous translations and editions that appeared. This book, like the first, demonstrated von der Goltz's acceptance of principles of war, but unlike the first, he now specifically referred to two "principles of modern warfare." The first was, "The enemy's main army is the primary objective against which all efforts must be directed."[26]

After a brief discussion of this principle, he wrote that from the first principle "follows a second general principle of modern warfare, namely, to concentrate if possible, all power for the hour of decision."[27] These two principles were by no means intended to be the only principles of war, for throughout the book von der Goltz included numerous apothegms that were surely among the true principles as he conceived them. In his conclusion, he wrote, "All the principles explained and forms described here are simple and capable of being understood without difficulty."[28] Two principles would hardly be referred to as "all the principles," especially when this reference was nearly two hundred pages removed from the mention of his first and second principles.

Like von der Goltz, Rudolf von Caemmerer implicitly accepted the existence of principles in the conduct of war. And like von der Goltz, he identified some of the principles but allowed his readers to guess which of his other observations on the conduct of war might be properly termed a principle. In *Die Entwickelung der strategischen Wissenschaft im neunzehnte Jahrhundert* (The discovery of strategical science in the nineteenth century), von Caemmerer reviewed the strategical thought of the nineteenth century and identified the principles that resulted from his review. He wrote, "The barring of the enemy's line of retreat, we may be sure, is one of the eternal principles that have been effectively tried for ages," but few other principles were so readily identifiable.[29] In his biography of Clausewitz, however, which appeared in 1905, von Caemmerer enumerated four basic truths (*Grundwahrheiten*), which he claimed that Clausewitz regarded as obvious.[30] The first of these truths, which according to von Caemmerer were "valid not only for the present but probably forever," was, "War is nothing more than a continuation of politics by other means." The second read, "The annihilation of the enemy force is the main principle of war," and the third, "The defense is the stronger form of warfare but with negative purpose, and the offensive is the weaker with a positive purpose."[31] The final truth discussed the dual nature of war. Von Caemmerer did not provide a list of principles that purported to include the ingredients of success in war. He did, however, accept the existence of principles and enunciate four "basic truths," which in form adhered to Jomini's belief that the principles of war were few in number and could be easily stated.

German military schools continued to emphasize the solution of practical problems, but in German military literature, some theoretical works recognized the existence and usefulness of principles within the realm or war. In the nations that sought to emulate the German military system in its entirety, some confusion concerning the value and domain of principles naturally resulted.

In spite of Jomini's long association with the Russian army, a variety of opinions concerning principles of war appeared in the writings of Russian soldiers. Major General N. Medem, a professor of strategy and military history at the imperial military academy, attacked the concept of fixed principles: "Constant, absolute rules for actions themselves cannot exist."[32] Colonel P. A. Yazykov, on the other hand, accepted Jomini's basic principle even though Yazykov felt that the principle was limited by conditions and hence was not eternal. General M. I. Bogdanovich accepted without qualification that there are eternal principles and that their existence was proven by military history and practice.

In the 1890s, General G. A. Leyer, a professor at the general staff academy from 1858 until 1889 and head of the academy from 1889 through 1899, presented a series of "basic principles."[33] In his list, he referred to many of the principles by title, such as the principle of economy of forces, the principle of concentration of forces on the decisive point, the principle of surprise, the principle of security, and the principle of initiative and dominance over the enemy's will and mind (see appendix 21). Leyer resolved the German preference for the uniqueness of the individual event with the acceptance of the existence of principles by stating that actions in war had to be substantiated "on the one hand, on a deep respect for the fundamental principles, and on the other, on just as deep a respect for the situation."[34] The most widely known Russian military theorist of the late nineteenth century was General M. I. Dragomirov, who denied the existence of principles in war: "At the present time, it will enter no one's head to assert that there can be a military science; it is just as unthinkable as are the sciences of poetry, painting and music."[35]

Jomini died in the year preceding the Franco-Prussian War.

His death, his legacy, and the disasters that befell the French throughout the war slowly turned French theoretical thinking from the Jominian concept of principles toward the German method of the concrete case. For a time after the war, there was more imitation in France than creation, and one of the first institutions established in the German image was the Ecole supérieure de guerre, the French war college. General Lewal, who was assigned as the commander of the new school, began "a necessary reaction against Jomini's theory" by establishing practical instruction in tactics for officers of all arms, but after Lewal a retreat to methods of the old staff school occurred.[36]

French texts, however, retained their affinity for Jominian concepts. In 1884, Henri Constant Fix, a Belgian officer, published a text, *La Stratégie appliqué* (Applied strategy), which sought "to unite, in as complete a synthesis as possible, the rules and principles that should govern the direction of armies."[37] He proposed three "precepts" that differed little from MacDougall's list of principles, which he in turn had based upon Jomini's fundamental principle as stated in the *Précis*. Fix's precepts read:

No. I.    Engage your masses with fractions of the enemy's forces, or your large fractions with his small ones.

No. II.    Always operate on interior lines.

No. III.    Operate as far as possible upon the communications of the enemy without exposing your own.[38]

His work was widely read in schools of war, and it enforced the Jominian concept of principles, which was being threatened by German pragmatism.

Other influential writers maintained Jominian ideas in their works, and they often discussed the dichotomy that existed between Jominian and German concepts. Victor-Bernard Derrécagaix, second in command to General Lewal at the Ecole supérieure de guerre, pointed out the continuing influence of Jomini's concept of principles as well as new tendencies toward Teutonic pragmatism. In his text, *La Guerre moderne* (Modern war), he "avoided the extreme views of those partisans who on the one hand contend that there are absolute rules of war incapable of the least vibration, and of those on the other who deny that there is such a thing as an 'art of war.' ''[39] In the preface to his volume, Derrécagaix spoke of another profound influence upon late nineteenth-century French military thought. He wrote that his purpose was to "analyze, probe to the bottom, and expound, the methods that have given victory to our enemies," and from these methods he hoped to establish general principles that would fix the methods of success in the mind of the French army.[40] Throughout the work, he referred to specific principles by title; for example, he spoke of the principle of compulsory service, the principle of unity of command, the principle of combining arms, and the principle of lines of operations. He did not, however, summarize the principles or specify the number of principles in existence. He extended the concept of principles beyond the operational field that Jomini addressed but still recognized his debt to Jomini. He acknowledged, for example, that Jomini was the author of the principle to "first seize the enemy's communications, and then turn upon his army."[41] He also presented four rules pertaining to lines of operations that reflected Jominian thought:

1st.    The aim in selecting lines of operations should be to *direct upon decisive points a stronger force than the enemy is able to bring to bear;*

2d.    *This selection depends upon the form of bases, the configuration of the ground, and the positions of the enemy;*

3d.    Simple and interior lines of operations are always to be preferred;

4th.    *The most advantageous lines of operations are those that lead an army upon the enemy's communications without endangering its own.*[42]

Derrécagaix did not question Jomini's belief in the existence of principles in warfare, but he apparently discarded the further Jominian belief that a composite list of all the basic principles that lead to success in war consisted of possibly not more than three or four principles. In content, Derrécagaix offered little that was original, but his use of titles was representative of the trend toward the form of the modern lists.

In 1891, Colonel L. Maillard, who had been a professor of general tactics and infantry at the Ecole supérieure de guerre, published *Les Eléments de la guerre* (The elements of war). The book dealt with tactics more than with strategy but discussed principles as an accepted part of both branches of the theory of war. In his discussion of maneuver, Maillard wrote that although maneuver had different characteristics for different types of operations, it was still subject to the application of certain principles, which he listed as

1st.   To discover the decisive point [in a theater of operations].

2nd.   To have the determination to march on this point.

3rd.   To choose the direction that leads to the point.

4th.   To move there rapidly.

5th.   To insure security.

6th.   To assure unity of forces at the desired moment and on the decisive point.[43]

These apothegms, according to Maillard, would guide commanders in the proper conduct of war. Maillard also listed "principles of the leadership of armies from the experience of the past":

superiority of the offensive, which encourages high morale . . .; security, which guarantees liberty of action . . .; economy of forces, which permits concentration of the greatest efforts at the decisive place.[44]

Twenty years after the French defeat at the hands of Prussia, principles, few in number and easily expressed, returned to French military thought. Maillard was a staunch supporter of the "method of the concrete case," but he also maintained the faith in principles that had long enraptured teachers in French military schools.

One of Maillard's successors at the Ecole supérieure de guerre was Henri Bonnal, who served as professor of military history, of strategy, and of general tactics from 1887 until he was succeeded by Ferdinand Foch in 1896. Bonnal returned to the school as commandant in 1901 but was relieved after sixteen months because his religious views were too tolerant for his superiors, who were embroiled in the Dreyfus affair. Bonnal was, however, reinstated in 1905. Having graduated from Saint Cyr in 1863, been captured at Sedan in 1870, and through his assignments at the war college, he had the experience and the opportunity for the study, reflection, and exposition of a doctrine of war. In 1892, he wrote,

> Ideas have little by little formed themselves into groups about a few great principles of experience that have formed the basis of a doctrine aiming at discipline of the mind. . . . A doctrine of war does not impose itself; it is born of the unanimous concurrence of understandings under the empire of convictions *progressively* acquired.[45]

A decade later Bonnal wrote "De la méthode dans les hautes études militaires en Allemagne et en France" (On the form of military theory in Germany and in France), which denied the validity of general principles like Jomini's and yet attempted to present great general principles of experience. The difference between Jomini's principles and principles of experience was that the former did not recognize the importance of the "sense of battle." To Bonnal, Jomini's principles ignored the human element in war and hence overlooked "the precious faculty of making decisions appropriate to the particular goal and means available." Bonnal continued, "nevertheless, there are a certain number of facts of experience, established by the most eminent men of war, which form the points of doctrine to which can be accorded the value of scientific truths."[46] The points of doctrine were not very numerous according to Bonnal, and they were needed to guide the mind through the study of complex concrete cases. He did not state the total number of such points of doctrine, but he presented the three most essential:

1. Maintain your own liberty of action and limit that of the enemy.
2. Impose your will on your adversary and do not submit to his.
3. Economize your forces in order to concentrate at a point suitably

chosen and at the favorable time with a view toward producing a
decisive result.[47]

Although Bonnal denied the principles presented by Jomini,
similarities between these points of doctrine and several of Jomini's
dominant ideas remained. Bonnal made distinctions even more
obscure by later referring to the points of doctrine as general
principles. By rejecting Jominian principles and then identifying
points of doctrine that later became general principles, Bonnal
was able to clothe French principles in the guise of the German
concrete case. He concluded, "The method of the concrete case
occupies by far the first place among the methods of education and
instruction in use in Paris as well as in Berlin for the teaching of
the higher subjects of war."[48] For Bonnal the principles no longer
existed as purely operational mandates; however, they retained the
Jominian characteristics of being few in number and easily expressed. The new general principles attempted to embrace the
metaphysical as well as the material components of war, and they
attempted to bring French principles closer to German pragmatism.

Like his predecessors at the French war college, Ferdinand
Foch relied heavily upon the historical method and upon the
method of concrete cases. He had received his formal education at
the Ecole polytechnique and at the cavalry school of application
at Saumur, where staff rides and field exercises provided practical
instruction for the students.[49] Foch had learned Napoleon's
maxims by heart, but upon his appointment as instructor of
military history, strategy, and applied tactics at the Ecole supérieure
de guerre, he placed little emphasis upon rote training and dogma.
Foch was never loquacious, and perhaps this personal characteristic
explained his fondness for tersely expressed ideas. As a strategical
writer, he has been labeled a "propagandist and a vulgarizer of
his greater predecessors," but his contribution to the development
of the modern principles of war was far-reaching and original.[50]

In a collection of his lectures published as *Des Principes de la
guerre* (The principles of war), Foch presented principles that were
not the purely operational principles of Jomini but rather a blend
of the moral and material like those expressed by Bonnal. Like

Bonnal and like Clausewitz, Foch believed that the theory of war had to consider the "human factor, with its moral, intellectual and physical aspects."[51] In his published lectures, he quoted Jomini only in reference to war's being a "terrible and passionate drama." The principles, as Foch interpreted them, were not directly inspired by Jomini except that the fundamental belief in the existence of a few simple principles, a key element of nineteenth-century military thought, was largely attributable to Jomini. Foch wrote that the theory of war "is made up in the first place of a number of principles":

The principle of economy of forces;

The principle of freedom of action;

The principle of free dispostion of forces;

The principle of security, etc.[52]

Foch did not hesitate to suggest Napoleon's endorsement of these principles; he simply concluded his listing by stating, "Napoleon believed in principles of war."

Foch's presentation of principles has been referred to as the first of the modern lists. It has been labeled a vulgarization of earlier thought on war, and it has been chided for the inclusion of "etc." at the end of the list. These observations each merit examination. First, Foch's list was unlike the modern lists because it went beyond operational considerations by attempting to include the moral aspects of war. Second, his thought paralleled that of Bonnal both in time and in substance and also relied heavily upon Clausewitz and even on von Peucker and the Russian, Dragomirov, but none of these writers used a list of titles as the basis upon which their thought rested. Finally, "etc." expressed better than any word the general state of every theory of war that embraced fundamental principles in the late nineteenth and early twentieth centuries. No writer of this period presented a list that purported to include all the principles of war. MacDougall had presented three after the Crimean War, and Schalk and Beauregard insisted on three during the American Civil War. But toward the end of the century and in spite of the identification of some specific principles by various authors, no one attempted to enumerate all the principles of war. Foch provided a list, but it was still not a definitive one. He identified four principles, and his "etc." suggested that there were others that he was not able to identify. The impact of his format on subsequent thought concerning the principles is difficult to assess, but in France, the terse list was quietly forgotten, at least for a time. The theoretical compendiums published in the years after Foch's *Des Principes de la guerre* returned to more general references to principles, in the manner of von der Goltz and Derrécagaix.

In 1907, Gabriel Darrieus, a professor of strategy and naval tactics at the French naval war college, published *La Guerre sur mer, stratégie et tactique* (War on the sea, strategy and tactics). It contained the substance of the ideas that he had presented to naval war college students and sought "to make at least one seaman's voice heard, in the passionate debate . . . about the principles of naval warfare."[53] Like his counterparts in the army, Darrieus viewed naval education as one of the requirements necessary for the proper preparation for the next war, and he also used the historical approach to aid the study of strategy. He wrote, "The great captains of all times have owed their victories to some general rules, some wise dispositions, which we may well hope to apply to modern wars. . . . We shall seek in history for the ensemble of those general principles of the military art."[54]

Darrieus presented no list, but in his historical narrative, he italicized the words and phrases that illustrated the higher dictums related to the conduct of war. In his discussion of Alexander the Great, he wrote, "To maneuver his troops so as to be stronger at *one point* of the field of battle than those who opposed him *at that point,* such is the great principle of war which the King of Macedonia constantly applied and to which he owed his persistent triumphs."[55] In his discussion of Frederick the Great, Darrieus wrote that Frederick's marching "ten hours a day, to fight and then to rest" postulated the "immutable principle of rapidity, accepted by all great leaders as an article of faith of the military gospel throughout all ages."[56] In other discussions Darrieus spoke of the principle of concentration, the principle of prevision, the principle of command of the sea, the principles of mutual confidence and self-trust in battle, the principle of specialization in warfare, and the principle of the objective. He identified many principles, and in his chapter, "The Resume of the Lessons of History," he wrote:

> It certainly cannot be a mere coincidence that we always find identical principles underlying the ways of acting of all the great captains; for that reason alone we already have the right to believe that their successes have been due precisely to their agreement in the application of these principles.[57]

And he concluded, "Throughout this book I have tried to bring out the small number of fundamental principles without which victory cannot be hoped for."[58] The ideas expressed were reminiscent of Jomini. The titles used to identify the principles were a harbinger of twentieth-century doctrine.

In the early twentieth century, French doctrine continued to reflect conclusions drawn from the victories attained a century earlier. The existence of principles of war was widely accepted in spite of their rejection by prominent Prussian and Russian soldiers, and the enduring lesson gained by French military writers from the Franco-Prussian War was not that principles were anathema to sound doctrine but that principles somehow had to include human parameters. The psychological dimension of war, which had been so poignantly presented in Ardant du Picq's *Etudes sur le combat* (Battle studies), shaped the entire nation's military theory.

The Continental experience pertinent to the development of the principles of war in the nineteenth and early twentieth centuries included two noteworthy developments. First, some brief lists of principles or laws appeared, for example, in the writings of Leyer and Hohenlohe-Ingelfingen and earlier in the courses of instruction at Saint Cyr and at the school of application at Metz. Second, specific principles were identified by title, a trend that was most pronounced in the writings of von der Goltz and Darrieus. The titles gave soldiers and teachers a shorthand for discussing the conduct of war that has persisted to the present day. The two dominant characteristics of the form of the modern principles— their appearance in a brief list and their identification by titles— were combined in Foch's list of four principles of war, but no one claimed to present an all-inclusive list of operational principles. For these reasons, neither Foch's list nor any other nineteenth- or early twentieth-century compendium of military thought could claim to be the sole predecessor of the modern "principles of war."

## NOTES

1. Henry Coppée in Auguste Marmont, *The Spirit of Military Institutions; or Essential Principles of the Art of War,* trans. Henry Coppée, p. vi.

2. Emil Schalk, *Summary of the Art of War,* p. 11.

3. Emil Schalk, *Campaigns of 1862 and 1863 Illustrating the Principles of Strategy,* p. 11.

4. Ibid., p. 10.

5. Ibid., p. 32.

6. Pierre Gustave Toutant Beauregard, *A Commentary on the Battle of Manassas of July 1861 Together with a Summary of the Art of War,* p. iv.

7. Ibid., pp. 160, 161. See Patrick MacDougall, *The Theory of War,* p. 52.

8. George Cullum, "Jomini's Life of Napoleon," *United States Service Magazine* 2 (August 1864):128. The same quotation appeared in the preface to Cullum, *Biographical Register of Officers and Graduates of the United States Military Academy and Early History,* 3d ed., I, 1891.

9. A W. Preston, "British Military Thought, 1856-1890," *Army Quarterly* 89 (October 1964):60.

10. Quoted in Charles D. Rhodes, "How Best to Instruct Our Officers in Tactics," *Journal of the Military Service Institute* 43 (September-October 1908):211.

11. Quoted in Rudolf von Caemmerer, *The Development of Strategical Science during the Nineteenth Century,* trans. Karl von Donat, p. 214.

12. Helmuth von Moltke, "Strategie," in "Moltkes Kriegslehren, Die Schlacht," *Moltkes militarische Werke,* IV, p. 1, my translation.

13. [Heinrich von Hess], *Allgemeine praktische Grundsätze der Strategie und höheren Taktik,* p. 13, my translation.

14. Wilhelm von Verdy du Vernois, *Studies in the Leading of Troops,* trans. William Gerlach, p. vii.

15. Eugène Carrias, *La Pensée militaire allemande,* p. 262.

16. Henri Bonnal, "De la méthode dans les hautes études militaires en Allemagne et en France," *Minerva: Revue des lettres et des arts* 1 (1 October 1902):29, my translation.

17. Von Caemmerer, *Development,* p. 22.

18. Wilhelm von Rüstow, *Die Feldherrnkunst des neunzehnten Jahrhunderts,* 3d. ed., II, p. 602, my translation.

19. Ibid., pp. 603, 604, 607.

20. Kraft zu Hohenlohe-Ingelfingen, *Letters on Strategy,* trans. Walter James, I, p. 9.

21. Ibid., p. 10.

22. Colmar von der Goltz, *Das Volk in Waffen,* 4th ed., p. 1, my translation.

23. Ibid.

24. Ibid., p. 123.

25. Ibid., p. 132.

26. Colmar von der Goltz, *Kriegführung, Kurze Lehre ihrer wichtigsten Grundsätze und Formen,* p. 12, my translation.

27. Ibid., pp. 13-14.

28. Ibid., p. 203.

29. Von Caemmerer, *Development,* p. 25.

30. Rudolf von Caemmerer, *Clausewitz,* in D. von Pelet-Narbonne, ed., *Erzieher des preussischen Heeres,* 2d ed., p. 102, my translation.

31. Ibid.

32. N. Medem, *Obozreniye izvestneyshikh pravil i sistem strategii,* p. 168, quoted in Vasili Ye. Savkin, *The Basic Principles of Operational Art and Tactics (A Soviet View),* trans. and published under the auspices of the United States Air Force, p. 29.

33. G. Leyer, *Metod voyennykh nauk,* pp. 53-54, quoted in Savkin, *Basic Principles,* p. 31.

34. G. Leyer, *Korennyye voprosy,* p. 122, quoted in Savkin, *Basic Principles,* p. 32.

35. M. Dragomirov, *Ocherki,* p. 48, quoted in Savkin, *Basic Principles,* p. 33.

36. Dallas D. Irvine, "The French Discovery of Clausewitz and Napoleon," *Military Affairs* 4 (1940):150-51. In 1878 the former staff school became the Ecole militaire supérieure. In 1880 the name was changed to Ecole supérieure de guerre.

37. H. C. Fix, *La Stratégie appliqué,* p. 6, my translation.

38. Ibid., pp. 11-12.

39. C. W. Foster, translator's preface to Victor-Barnard Derrécagaix, *Modern War,* p. iii.

40. Victor-Barnard Derrécagaix, *Modern War,* trans. C. W. Foster, p. viii.

41. Ibid., p. 244.

42. Ibid., p. 293.

43. L. Maillard, *Les Eléments de la guerre,* p. x, my translation.

44. L. Maillard, quoted in Jean Dany, "La Littérature militaire d'aujourd'hui," *Revue de Paris* 2 (April 1912):614, my translation.

45. Henri Bonnal, quoted in Gabriel Darrieus, *War on the Sea, Strategy and Tactics,* trans. Philip R. Alger, p. 253.

46. Bonnal, "De la méthode," p. 334.

47. Ibid., pp. 334-35.

48. Ibid., p. 351.

49. George Gray Aston, *The Biography of the Late Marshal Foch,* pp. 56-57. The discussion that follows is also from Aston.

50. Bernard Brodie, "Strategy," *Encyclopedia of the Social Sciences* 15 (1968):284.

51. Ferdinand Foch, *Des Principes de la guerre: Conférences faites à l'Ecole supérieure de guerre,* 2d ed., p. 3, my translation.

52. Ibid., p. 8.

53. Darrieus, *War on the Sea,* p. 5.

54. Ibid., pp. 12, 13.

55. Ibid., p. 29.

56. Ibid., p. 40.

57. Ibid., p. 196.

58. Ibid., p. 322.

# 4

# BRITISH AND UNITED STATES REACTION TO CONTINENTAL THEORY

IN GREAT BRITAIN and the United States in the half-century after the U.S. Civil War, military thought and military education were both altered by the Prussian belief in the uniqueness of the individual event and its manifestation in the applicatory method. But the validity of principles as a basis for the study of the proper conduct of war remained a major article of faith in both nations.

Just as the professors at the French war colleges provided the evidence of the development of the principles of war in that country, the professors at the British Staff College and the Royal Naval College provided the evidence of the development in Great Britain. At the Staff College, the first professor of military history was Edward Bruce Hamley. He had been present at every major battle in the Crimean War, and his later assignments as professor of history (1859-1865), member of the council of military education (1865-1870), and commandant of the Staff College (1870-1877) gave him experience and influence that profoundly affected the course of British military thought and education. The essence of his thought on war was contained in *The Operations of War,* a text that "received an altogether unmerited acclamation"; in substance and style it closely followed Jomini's *Précis de l'art de la guerre.*[1] Hamley stated that the purpose of the book was to select "*representative* operations, each involving and illustrating a principle or fact, which, when elicited and fully recognized, will serve for future guidance."[2] His reliance on Jominian thought and on the format used by MacDougall in his *Theory of War* was evident from Hamley's introduction:

> In the following chapters strategical movements will be considered as having the following objects: 1st, *To menace or assail the enemy's communications with his base,* 2d, *To destroy the coherence and concerted action of his army, by breaking the communications which direct the parts;* 3d, *To effect superior concentrations on particular points.*[3]

These three objects bore a striking resemblance to the three principles offered by MacDougall, but Hamley had a rather different view of the principles of war. He did not confine the principles to "three or four" as Jomini had suggested; his statement of purpose asserted that a principle would be illustrated by each of the representative operations discussed. Specific references to principles were rare, but in his lengthy historical narratives, he spoke of the "principle of concentration," "the principle of the strategic offensive," the principle of surprise and of pursuit.[4] He accepted the existence of principles, confined them to operational considerations, sought them in the past, and suggested their validity in the future. But he provided neither a summary nor an indication of the total number of principles in existence.

In spite of his success as a lecturer and his positions of influence in the British military educational system, Hamley was a pedant. He "expected his pupils to accept his deductions as well as his facts, and did not encourage original research."[5] Furthermore, "a cursory glance at almost any of the examination papers from these years reveals the pedantic or unrealistic nature of the questions put to mature men who were supposedly training to be staff officers."[6] The difficulties plaguing the British system of military education did not escape official notice; in 1869 a royal commission, much like the commission appointed in 1857, was tasked "to inquire into the present state of military education and into the training of candidates for commissions in the army." Testimony heard by the commission confirmed the existence of pedantry and also found that the emphasis on competitive examinations encouraged "cramming," a practice that was detrimental to the retention of knowledge and to the attainment of understanding and that possibly contributed to the ready acceptance in Great Britain of the modern "principles of war."

The education commission also noted the dearth of practical instruction at the Staff College and recommended, "The instruction in all subjects should be made more strictly practical than at present, and should have a direct bearing on the duties of Staff officers in the field."[7] But the pedantic atmosphere at the Staff College persisted for decades, and cramming remained the standard means of preparation for the many examinations that confronted British officer candidates and officers. Even though practical instruction was increased in the 1880s by the initiation of tours to battlefields in western Europe and by the elimination of mathematics from the curriculum, cramming remained a problem. J. F. Maurice, professor of military art and history in the late 1880s complained, "Even now, in the Staff College, the greatest thing against which I have always to fight is the natural tendency of students to cram for their examinations, and I look upon that as the greatest enemy that there is."[8]

Examinations were used to determine qualification for commissioning, promotion, and for entrance into the British military schools. Although the use of competitive examinations had been long established in France, in Great Britain their extensive use had more pervasive effect. For example, it fostered a group of masters known as "crammers" and the arid knowledge that they proffered. It also contributed to the wide acceptance of and reliance upon "enumerable facts." The crammers offered no guarantee that any given examination would be passed, but their success was as well known as their methods were pernicious to the education of the officer corps. Captain Lendy, a Sunbury crammer and military author of some repute, concentrated on the memorizing of facts; under his tutelage, "the first four books of Euclid were learnt by heart with no attempt at understanding them."[9] Winston Churchill, with typical wit, related his cramming experience prior to his acceptance to the Royal Military College at Sandhurst:

When I failed for the second time to pass into Sandhurst, I bade farewell to Harrow and was relegated as a forlorn hope to a "crammer." . . . It was said that no one who was not a congenital idiot could avoid passing thence into the Army. The Firm has made a scientific study of the mentality of the Civil Service Commissioners. They knew with almost Papal infallibility the sort of questions which that sort of person would be bound on the average to ask on any of the selected subjects.[10]

In spite of the changes recommended by the commission on military education, the cramming industry continued to thrive, and in support of the industry, a raft of literature was published that categorized the most esoteric knowledge and provided extensive lists fit for memorization. The problems attendant upon rote memorization of subjects that deserve attention, study, and understanding also found their way into other military educational institutions. Cramming encouraged pedantry at its worst, and furthermore, Maurice maintained that only pedants "could believe in an 'art of war' that could be reduced to systematic 'rules.' "[11] In place of the dogmatic recitals of Hamley and the crammers, Maurice wanted his students to gain an understanding of history. His efforts were largely in vain, for in the 1890s, Colonel Henry Hildyard, commandant of the Staff College, was still compaining, "We want officers to absorb, not to cram."[12]

The belief in the existence of a few principles that underlay the conduct of war was threatened along with the efforts to remove pedantry and cramming from military instruction at the Staff College. But in December 1892, the popular colonel, G. F. R. Henderson, was appointed professor of military art and history. In his early lectures at the college, he revealed his close theoretical bonds with Jomini. "There are certain principles," he stated, "which serve as guides; and it will be seen that they are all accessory to a rule of strategy . . . viz., *the concentration of superior strength, physical and moral, on the field of battle.*"[13] Henderson went beyond

Jomini by including moral strength as well as physical strength in this leading principle of strategy. Moral strength, a topic much in vogue in France, was also a consideration in Henderson's "two great principles which are the foundation and crown of all strategical methods." He claimed that his American Civil War hero, Thomas "Stonewall" Jackson, was the originator of these two principles, "which strike heavily and directly at the *morale* of both the hostile commander and of the troops he commands." The principles were:

1. *Always mystify, mislead and surprise the enemy.*

2. *Never give up the pursuit so long as your men have strength to follow, for an army routed, if hotly pursued becomes panic stricken, and can be defeated by half their numbers. To move swiftly, strike vigorously, and secure all the fruits of victory is the secret of successful war.*[14]

Henderson presented other lists of principles in his lectures at the Staff College. In 1897, for example, he expanded the ideas contained in Jackson's two principles to make a list of five:

Always endeavour to mystify and mislead your enemy, whether you are attacking or defending; if you can surprise the enemy's general his army is already defeated.

Always attack at that point where the moral effect will be greatest. Strike the enemy's flank in preference to his front, enfilade his line, and threaten his retreat.

Never fight except on your own ground and at your own time.

Never attack unless you are superior in numbers.

Never knock your head against a strong position.[15]

These principles, like Henderson's others, reflected the moral considerations in the conduct of war that were accorded a high regard in the contemporary German and French military literature. This list also illustrated Henderson's homely style, which in all probability contributed immensely to his popularity as a teacher and to the popularity of his courses as well.

Although Henderson explicitly and tersely enumerated principles, he warned of the difficulty in their application:

> It is not to be assumed that they are merely theoretical and pedantic formulae. A general who was an absolute slave to them . . . would probably fail to achieve decisive success; but a general who acted in defiance of them would, to put it in mildest form, run an enormous risk.[16]

This warning was similar to Jomini's and to the warnings of nearly every other serious student of the conduct of war who believed in the existence of principles of war. Unlike Jomini and most other writers, however, Henderson claimed on one occasion that he had presented "all those [principles] that are absolutely essential in the field."[17] He did not say how many existed and did not clearly identify every principle in his discussion, but he nevertheless claimed to have presented all of the essential ones. He admitted in another lecture that he could not identify every principle of war but that he could certainly direct attention to the very prominent ones.[18]

The changing attitudes toward the place of principles in British military thought since the publication of Hamley's *Operations of War* was aptly stated by Henderson in 1898. He wrote that Hamley's book was not a good practical guide to strategy in the field because little was written of great principles. He stated, "I do not say that such points as the objective, as the action of a defending army, as the importance of concentration, are not alluded to in Hamley, but they are not to my mind sufficiently impressive."[19] A complete checklist of principles was also unsatisfying to Henderson. He continued, "A list of principles, unaccompanied by examples, is not of itself of much value. To have such by heart would be of little service to a general in the field." These comments typified the state of the principles of war in Great Britain in the early twentieth century. The existence of principles was accepted, and the identification of the principles derived from the study of the past and from practical experience was believed to be possible. The principles were not enumerated; they were, however, often identified by titles consisting of a single word, such as *concentration* or *pursuit;*

or of a short phrase, such as *unity of command* or *economy of forces*. The trend in Great Britain was toward specificity in both content and form.

Military thought relative to the development of the principles of war in the United States was an amalgam of the thought expressed in both the continental and British schools and literature. The French example, which had been carefully and energetically emulated in the United States before the Civil War, was slowly augmented by German methods and by British ideas.

In the years immediately following the Civil War, the curriculum at the United States Military Academy was subjected to scrutiny and concomitant change. The need for a course in the theory of war had been suggested by the requirements placed upon graduates of the academy during the war, and since Dennis Mahan had included lessons on strategy at the conclusion of his military engineering course before the war, his engineering department was expanded to include instruction in the "Science of War." Notes published by this department in the 1870s pointed out the close links connecting the conduct of war, the experimental sciences, and military history:

> The general principles of war are deduced from the rules and methods used by those generals who are known as great and eminent in the practice of the profession. In the "art of war," as in all the experimental sciences, observations made upon the actual occurrences precede the theories. It is therefore evident that an intimate connection exists between the history of military operations and the "art of war," and that a course of military history is indispensible as an introduction to the teaching of the "science of war."[20]

The distinction between the science of war and the art of war was more clearly drawn with reference to the principles of war:

> It will be more proper, from the previous definitions, to use the term, military art, as applying to the practical application of the rules of war, or when the general subject is under consider-

ation; and to use the term, science of war, when the scientific principles upon which the art is founded are considered.[21]

But during the instruction in this course, no specific principles were revealed in any readily identifiable form. There were no lists or even terse phrases to suggest what some of the principles might be. Like the principles of morality or the principles of Christian ethics, their existence was inherently accepted.

In 1879 Junius Wheeler, Dennis Mahan's successor as professor of engineering and the  science of war, published *A Course of Instruction in the Elements of the Art and Science of War* to enable students at the academy to gain a general knowledge of the theory of war. Wheeler wrote, "The plan of the book required brevity and condensation. The constant endeavor has been to state principles and rules intelligently and as concisely as possible."[22] He added, "Although the number of known facts is steadily increasing, the number of general principles upon which the theories of the science are based is constant, if not decreasing."[23] Clearly Wheeler accepted the existence of principles, but apparently he did not accept the belief of a few immutable principles. His text used military history as the laboratory for the science of war, but for him and his students, the science of war had no terse expressions of principles or lists to guide the military commander.

After thirteen years as department head, Wheeler was succeeded by James Mercur, who also published a text for his course. He spoke of the existence of principles but did not list them or suggest that they were enumerable. Mercur did, however, emphasize the idea contained in Jomini's fundamental principle. He wrote that the commander must be able to make himself *"stronger than the enemy at the time and place of actual combat."*[24] Such strength could "only be accomplished by preserving *unity of command, concentrated action and mobility, with the least exposure of the men to loss."* Mercur rarely referred to general principles, but he stated that the same general considerations govern the details of every campaign plan and that the best writers have summed up those considerations in a single rule: *"Strike and cut your enemy's communications and protect your own."*[25] He also presented a list of seven "principles of mounted tactics of cavalry" (see appendix 20). Why there should be a list of principles for cavalry and not for the other arms is not known, but the list was indicative of the tendency to enumerate terse rules that simplified the teaching of complex activities of war.

The belief expressed by the professors at the academy that war was a science and hence that its conduct was subject to regulating principles was also expressed in late nineteenth-century American military literature. The *Elements of Military Science and Tactics,* a handbook authorized by the War Department, distinguished between war as an art and war as a science. War was a science "because a general must decide upon the principles to govern his operations"; the practical application of the principles pertained to the art of war.[26] At the department of military science at Yale University, the affinity of war with other natural sciences received perhaps its strongest endorsement. In 1894, Captain James S. Pettit, an instructor in the department, published *Elements of Military Science for the Use of Students in Colleges and Universities,* and on the first page he asserted that war "is as truly a science as chemistry or philosophy."[27] But since the principles of chemistry or of philosophy were not definitively enumerated, there was little reason to expect that Pettit would provide a list of principles of war. He did not; he merely stated that his subject was scientific and hence dependent on principles that could be deduced from a proper examination of facts and elementary ideas.

Little original thought on the theory of war existed outside of the courses that addressed the science of war in U.S. military schools. Indeed, little original thought on war originated anywhere in the United States with the possible exception of the higher schools of war established by the army at Fort Leavenworth, Kansas, and by the navy at Newport, Rhode Island.

The impetus for the establishment of these higher schools of war came in part from Emory Upton, a respected 1861 graduate of West Point who was promoted to brevet brigadier general in 1864. In 1875 and 1876, he made an official tour of the world's major military powers at the behest of General William T. "War is Hell" Sherman, the commanding general of the army. Upton's observations on the state of military education were especially pertinent to the future role of the principles of war in American strategy and military education. Upon his return to the United States, he concluded that the military academy at West Point was "far superior to any academy abroad for the prepatory training of officers. But once in service," he observed,

> we have nothing to compare with the war academies of Europe. . . . you know how ignorant our generals were, during the war, of all the principles of generalship. . . . We cannot Germanize, neither is it desirable, but we can apply the principles of common sense.[28]

Upton's recommendation for a higher school of war was realized in part by the establishment of the School of Application for Infantry and Cavalry at Fort Leavenworth in 1881, but until its closing at the outbreak of the Spanish-American War, it contributed little to the field of military thought and doctrine. Arthur L. Wagner, one of the early instructors in the art of war at the school, wrote a popular text, *Organization and Tactics,* but the book as well as the instruction at the school were based predominantly on foreign sources and upon the applicatory system. When the school was reopened in 1903 as a result of Secretary of War Elihu Root's reevaluation of the U.S. military educational system, Wagner returned as an instructor and published a short work, *Strategy,* that presented two "principles of all strategy":

> The soldier like every other human being needs food, clothing, and medicine, that in addition to these common wants of mankind, he needs an unfailing supply of ammunition. . . .
> All other things being equal, two or three men are able to beat one.[29]

The first of these principles was reminiscent of Lloyd's "first of all the principles," and the second was a rewording of Jomini's fundamental principle. Wagner's principles were an enumeration in the midst of an era when principles were rarely enumerated. At the conclusion of his remarks on strategy, Wagner also presented a paragraph that tersely and simply attempted to outline the requirements for the proper conduct of war. Wagner called this paragraph "the correct rule of strategy":

> Remember that your objective is to meet and defeat the enemy and endeavor to take the most direct means to accomplish this end. Look carefully to the supply of your army; protect your flanks and guard your communications; aim, if possible, at the flanks and communications of your adversary; remember that the enemy has as much cause to worry about you as you have to feel anxiety about him. Having made your plan, stick to it unless compelled to change. Plan carefully and deliberately; then move quickly and strike hard.[30]

The supply problems that the U.S. Army encountered in the Spanish-American War undoubtedly had some influence on this paragraph as did some of Jomini's ideas. Wagner's presentation, however, was apparently too pedantic for the Leavenworth school, for in 1906 the assistant commandant reported:

> The text book on strategy has taken much time and attention. It is the study of strategy which more than any other exposes the military student to the charge of pedantry. . . . We have early adopted a comprehensive study of military history and confidently left the strategy as a logical result of the former.[31]

The school dropped the Wagner text and used von der Goltz's *Conduct of War,* a translation of *Kriegführung,* to fill the gap, but the teaching of strategy floundered. Attempts to elicit the rules of strategy were viewed as pedantic, and attempts to teach strategy during practical instruction in the field were thwarted by the comprehensive nature of the topic. Military history, as the surrogate laboratory for the study of war, provided the only solution.

Matthew F. Steele, one of Wagner's successors at Leavenworth, revived the teaching of strategy when he opened the course in military art in 1907 by stating, "One cannot learn the art of war . . .

unless one is sufficiently acquainted with the principles of war."[32] He continued that Jomini, Clausewitz, and Hamley are the professors in the academy of war and that their books hold the principles. Jomini's belief in the simplicity of the principles was also revived by Steele when he stated, "The principles of war which history has proved to be sound are simple, and can be stated in a few words."[33] But Steele did not conceive that their total number could be three or four, or even fewer than twenty. By stating that Napoleon's maxims contained "most if not all of them," he admitted that he either did not know all of the principles of war or that he did not know all of Napoleon's maxims. The former was probably the case. Steele did, however, mention some of the principles. In his opening lecture he stated that it was still a principle of strategy to conceal one's movements and intentions from the enemy and take him by surprise. He wrote that one principle of strategy had undergone no alteration either real or apparent and quoted von der Goltz: "Be stronger at the decisive point."[34] Other lectures on the art of war discussed the principle of concentrating within the region controlled by the enemy, the principle that the union of two corps should never take place near the enemy—despite the Prussian success with this technique against the Austrians at Königgrätz in 1866—"secrecy," "celerity," and "preparedness."

Evidence concerning Steele's concepts of principles is also found in his lectures on military history, which were originally published in 1909 as War Department Document Number 324 under the title, *American Campaigns;* the published lectures were used as a text in military schools for nearly a half-century. Most of the text is concerned with the military history of the Civil War, and in this section, where Steele's stated purpose was "to get at the exact truth" and "to appreciate the causes of success on the one hand, and of failure on the other," Steele presented a potpourri of principles from a variety of sources.[35] He spoke of McDowell's plan at First Bull Run, which proposed to "turn the enemy's position and force him out of it by seizing or threatening his communications"; he spoke of "the mistake of having two armies with independent commanders in the same theater of operations" during his discussion of the action around Forts Henry and Donel-son; he quoted a note of General Sherman that "generals in chief-command generally worry more about things which never happen than about real campaigns"; and in criticizing the Battle of Shiloh, he quoted two of Napoleon's maxims.[36] Steele also presented a list of a "few of Stonewall Jackson's maxims" that he claimed were "as worthy of a place in the student's notebook as Napoleon's were worthy of room in Jackson's saddle pockets" (see appendix 25).[37] Steele claimed that Jackson carried the Bible, Webster's dictionary, and Napoleon's maxims with him rather than the Bible and Jomini's *Art of War* as other sources claim. Regardless, the message that Jackson had a fondness for the terse expression of principles was conveyed.

Steele presented an excellent history that served well as an introduction to the theory of war, but his inconsistent use of terms like *principle, strategic principle, maxim,* and *general rule* and his selection of such fundamentals illustrated the general confusion concerning such concepts that existed throughout the theory of war in the early twentieth century. Steele, like Jomini, stated that only a few simple principles existed, and like Hamley, he referred to specific principles in his narratives of historical events. On occasion he used titles to identify key principles, but in the tradition of his day, he neither summarized nor definitively enumerated all of the principles of war.

Von der Goltz's study of the most important branches and guiding rules for the conduct of war was translated into English for use at the Fort Leavenworth school by Joseph T. Dickman, one of Steele's contemporaries. Dickman was hence exposed to von der Goltz's and Steele's concepts and comments concerning principles, but he attempted to resolve the problem of the teaching of principles and the concomitant charges of pedantry by providing a list of general principles to be considered during tactical rides. He combined the teaching of theory with the applicatory method by posing general principles that he expressed in the form of questions:

1.  Does the situation permit or demand an attack, or is a defensive attitude indicated?

2.  (a) The attack having been chosen, against what objective should
it be directed? What can the enemy do, and what means are available
to defeat his plans?

(b) In case a defensive solution of the problem is demanded,
what can the enemy do? What suitable position is available, or where
and how can we oppose the enemy's undertakings?

3.  Does the ground favor our intentions? Are there obstacles, and
how can we utilize or overcome them?

4.  Are our communications secure? Can we threaten those of the
enemy?[38]

Dickman tried to resolve one of the fundamental questions in
military education; can any benefit be derived from theoretical
principles? Many converts to the applicatory method might have
answered no, but theory was not easily dismissed.

The debate between practice and theory was especially intense in
the navy, for the "school of the ship" was the only one recognized
by many naval officers. Alfred Thayer Mahan sought to combat
this prevalent view, and in spite of differences with officers in
his own country and service, his thought precipitated and guided a
revolution in American naval policy, provided a theoretical
foundation for Great Britain's determination to remain the dominant sea power in the world, gave impetus to German naval
development, and affected the character of naval thought and
practice in France, Italy, Russia, Japan, and among many of the
lesser powers. One of Mahan's major objectives was to derive
from a study of naval history certain fundamental and immutable
principles of naval strategy that would be comparable to the
principles of land warfare suggested by Jomini.[39]

Mahan was born at West Point. His father, Dennis Mahan,
and his environment provided ideal opportunities for his early
exposure to the study of war and to the books written on war.
The elder Mahan's respect for Jomini was shared by his son, but
decades passed before the full impact of Alfred Mahan's admiration of Jomini became evident. Mahan attended Columbia University for a time, was graduated from the United States Naval
Academy in 1859, and participated in the Union blockade of

southern ports during the Civil War. He subsequently served in the Atlantic and the Pacific, at the Boston Naval Yard, at the New York Naval Yard, and as an instructor at the naval academy, but until his special talents as a thinker were recognized by Rear Admiral Stephen B. Luce, his career was not extraordinary.

Admiral Luce contributed more than any other individual in the navy to the establishment of naval professionalism in the United States. He was the commandant of midshipmen at Annapolis from 1865 until 1869, a founder and president of the United States Naval Institute, and was primarily responsible for the establishment of the Naval War College. When the college admitted its first students in the fall of 1884, he was its president, and as one of its instructors, Luce chose Alfred Mahan.

Luce was a staunch believer in the existence of principles in warfare. During the siege of Charleston late in the Civil War, General Sherman had told him that the garrison would fall when its line of communications was cut, and Luce later reflected that he had realized at that moment "that there were certain fundamental principles underlying military operations which it were well to look into; principles of general application, whether the operations were conducted on land or at sea."[40] Alfred Mahan lectured on naval history and tactics at the war college, and for nearly a year prior to teaching his first students, he researched and prepared lectures. He began teaching at the college in 1886, and in 1889 he succeeded Luce as president of the college. Luce's belief in the existence of principles was endorsed and expanded upon by Mahan, and this belief became one of the cornerstones of Mahan's reputation as an internationally known writer and theorist.

That Mahan was influenced by Jomini cannot be questioned. Mahan called Jomini his "best military friend," and in a public address at the war college in 1892, Mahan stated that Jomini's works "if somewhat supplanted by newer digests, have lost little of their prestige as a profound study and exposition of the principles of warfare."[41] Mahan also insisted upon the Jominian idea that the fundamental principles are few in number and a necessary asset to the understanding of war. He lectured that the principles of the art of war "are dear and not numerous" and that "the

search for and establishment of leading principles—always few—
around which considerations of detail group themselves, will tend
to reduce confusion of impression to simplicity and directness of
thought, with consequent facility of comprehension."[42]
    Mahan's insistence upon the value of theoretical instruction
brought vociferous objections from those who adhered to the
dictum that the only proper naval school was the school of the ship.
He inveighed against these critics:

> Is this neglect to master the experience of the past, to elicit,
> formulate and absorb its principles, is it practical? Is it "practical"
> to wait till the squall strikes you before shortening sail? If the
> object and aim of the College is to promote such study, to
> facilitate such results, to foster and disseminate such ideas, can
> it be reproached that its purpose is not "practical," even
> though its methods be at first tentative and its results imperfect?[43]

    The spread of Mahan's influence was not checked by the ob-
jections to his theory, to his principles, and to his college. Yet
he proceeded cautiously in his presentation of the principles in
which he believed. He recognized two possible methods of using
principles to facilitate the study of war. The first, to state them and
then give illustrations of their application or violation in recorded
events, was compact and systematic with its certain brief rules,
but it supplied the student with "digested knowledge." Mahan
chose the second method: a consecutive narrative, utilized as a
medium for illustrating the principles—a method that allowed the
student to assimilate the principles in his own mind.[44]
    If Mahan had chosen the first method, he might have presented
a list of principles or at least a summary of the principles. His
narratives, however, sufficiently revealed the identity of many of
his principles. He spoke of the principle of striking at the enemy's
line of communication, of the "principles of concentration, of
central position, and of interior lines," of the necessity of cooperation, and of the "bearing of communications upon military tenure
and success."[45] In spite of these scattered references to specific
principles, Mahan believed that it was only in recent years "that

these principles have been so digested and systematized, so demonstrated and established, as to form a code recognized by all in theory, however badly applied in practice."[46] In fact, the codification of the principles was in its infancy, but Mahan correctly recognized the trend toward specificity in their number, form, and content.

Mahan was led to his belief in the existence of a few fundamental principles of war by several forces: his father's influence and both his father's and his own scientific proclivities, the availability of books on science and on the theory of war, his early introduction to the French language and to Jomini's works, his scientific education at Columbia and at the naval academy, and the legacy of Luce at the Naval War College. Beyond these explanations, Mahan provided other clues that suggested reasons not only for his interest in and acceptance of principles in warfare but for principles of his profession and for his age as well.

First, the introduction of steam power gave navies, and through the railroads the army, too, an aspect of certainty that did not exist in an earlier age. Navigation and the conduct of battle could be more methodically planned and hence needed to be more systematically studied. Mahan stated, "Now the turns of the screw can be counted upon better even than the legs of the soldier. . . . If possible we must get hold of the principles which, throughout all changes, underlie naval war."[47] Second, a "principle" had a far-ranging influence and a vast scope of application for Mahan and such nineteenth-century philosophers as Herbert Spencer. For Mahan, a principle was applicable to a wide range of activities. He stated, for example,

It is, I think, a distinct gain for a man to realize that the military principle of concentration applied to the designing of a ship, to the composition of a fleet, or to the peace distribution of a navy, as effectively as it does to the planning of a campaign or to an order of battle.[48]

This wide range of applicability arose from the belief that the principles belonged to the "Order of Nature, of whose stability so much is heard in our day.''[49] The stability of nature in turn implied that regulatory principles must exist.

The wide range of applicability of Mahan's principle of concentration brought him and his concept of principles to political and even to national prominence. Mahan believed that the principle of concentration was "the ABC of naval strategy," and when the Senate passed the recommendation to divide the battle fleet between the Atlantic and the Pacific coasts, Mahan successfully urged President Theodore Roosevelt to veto the proposal. When Roosevelt left office in 1909, he wrote to his successor, William Howard Taft, "Keep the battle fleet in one ocean or the other.''[50] When the Taft administration was succeeded by the administration of Woodrow Wilson, Theodore Roosevelt wrote to Franklin Delano Roosevelt, the new assistant secretary of the navy, "There ought not to be a battleship or any formidable fighting craft in the Pacific unless our entire fleet is in the Pacific.''[51] The operative idea was Mahan's principle of concentration, and in 1914 Mahan again argued for adherence to that principle in view of the "conditions consequent upon the completion of the Panama Canal.''[52]

For Mahan the principle of concentration was applicable even for historians. In his address before the American Historical Association during his tenure as its president, he stated:

> So again "concentration" the watchword of military action . . . reminds [the historian] that facts must be massed as well as troops if they are to prevail against the passive resistance of indolent mentality, if they are to penetrate and shatter the forces of ignorance or prejudgment.[53]

Mahan believed that history and principles were intimately connected. He wrote, "Each is a partial educator; combined you have in them a perfect instructor. . . . Master your principles then ram them home with the illustrations that History furnishes.''[54] Mahan combined the merit of historical example as cited by von Peucker with the Jominian belief in the existence of a few fundamental and immutable principles. But Mahan was too great a scholar to believe that the principles that he enunciated were completely formulated and unchangeable. He maintained constantly that new light might be shed upon the principles either by restatement or by experience in war.[55]

Throughout the late nineteenth and early twentieth centuries, the principles of war were a significant part of broader themes in military education, in the conduct of war, in other disciplines, and in other human activities. The fact that they existed became widely accepted, but they were rarely enumerated. Individual principles, however, were increasingly identified by title and spoken of with high regard. Their total number was still indefinite but tending toward the few that Jomini insisted upon. The trend toward their formal and definitive exposition was apparent.

The half-century that followed the American Civil War was a formative period in the development of the modern "principles of war." On the one hand, it was marked by the ascendancy of the German military system and the denial of the existence of principles of war by Germany's most prominent soldiers and military theorists— generally men of high position and vast experience. Beyond Germany higher schools of war were established and refined in order to facilitate the conduct of and to insure success in war. The teachers in these schools, who often were the nation's martial theorists as well, were generally younger than their German counterparts, and they tended to view war in a more predictable manner.

In France the defeat at the hands of Prussia caused military thinkers to conclude that in their preparation for war they had neglected its moral aspects, and formerly accepted, operationally oriented principles were discarded in favor of a doctrine of war that placed greater emphasis upon the moral, the psychological, and the human dimensions of war.

In Great Britain the existence of principles in warfare went largely unquestioned. The ubiquitous enemy was pedantry. But examinations for promotion, for commissioning, and for entrance to and exit from the military schools demanded tangible and identifiable banks of knowledge among the officer corps. Where hard and sure facts were difficult to confirm, as in the study of strategy, surrogate subjects, like military history, were relied upon. Terse and enumerable principles fit well in this environment; they bridged the gap between the known past and the unknown future.

There was little original thought on a theory of war in the United States in the decades after the Civil War with the exception of Alfred Mahan's extensive application of principles—to war, to history, and to life itself. As the United States grew from the selective immigration from many nations, the schools of war tried to glean the best from many systems. To most U.S. service school instructors, "the best" included the acceptance of the belief in the existence of principles and the belief that they could be tersely stated.

Schools of application, spawned from German models, flourished in the late nineteenth century, and theory struggled to find its place in an environment dominated by practical methods and practical men. But the very existence of higher schools of war meant that officers assigned as instructors were obligated to think about war, about its conduct, and about the best method of teaching war. At the one extreme principles provided the solution, if they could be accurately and simply stated. On the other hand principles were a restraint to learning, if they were regarded as models to be slavishly followed.

The debate concerning principles—their existence, form, content, and usefulness—continued into World War I, and the new forces and requirements that beset the services influenced the development of military thought in general and the principles of war in particular. To some the continuing quest for principles appeared quixotic, but for many twentieth-century thinkers and writers, the task was undertaken with the seriousness, assiduousness, and zeal that characterized the efforts of all professionals. The profession demanded such devotion. It also demanded clarity, conciseness, and completeness in its doctrine. These demands seemed to some to be fulfilled when "principles of war" were codified and sanctified.

*NOTES*

1. A. W. Preston, "British Military Thought, 1856-1890," *Army Quarterly* 89 (October 1964):68-69.

2. Edward Bruce Hamley, *The Operations of War Explained and Illustrated*, 5th ed., p. 6.

3. Ibid., p. 60.

4. Ibid., p. 92. See also Brian Bond, *The Victorian Army and the Staff College, 1854-1914,* p. 87.

5. As quoted in Jay Luvaas, *The Education of an Army: British Military Thought, 1815-1940,* p. 136.

6. Bond, *The Victorian Army,* p. 92.

7. Great Britain, *First Report of the Royal Commission Appointed to Inquire into the Present State of Military Education and into the Training of Candidates for Commissions in the Army,* p. 51.

8. Bond, *The Victorian Army,* p. 137.

9. Ibid., p. 89.

10. Winston S. Churchill, *My Early Life, A Roving Commission,* p. 42-43.

11. Bond, *The Victorian Army,* p. 136.

12. Ibid., p. 154.

13. George Francis Robert Henderson, *The Science of War, A Collection of Essays and Lectures, 1891-1903,* p. 40.

14. Ibid., p. 42.

15. Ibid., p. 102.

16. Ibid., p. 43.

17. Ibid.

18. Ibid., p. 103.

19. G. F. R. Henderson, "Strategy and its Teachings," *Journal of the Royal United Service Institution* 42 (July 1898):775.

20. United States Military Academy, "Science of War. Introductory," p. 1. These notes were found in a copy of Dufour's *Strategy and Tactics,* a text used at the academy in the 1860s and 1870s. "Woodward" was handwritten at the top of the first page of the notes. Charles Woodward graduated from the academy in 1877.

21. Ibid., p. 2.

22. Junius B. Wheeler, *A Course of Instruction in the Elements of the Art and Science of War,* p. v.

23. Ibid., p. 7.

24. James Mercur, *Elements of the Art of War,* 2d ed., p. 20.

25. Ibid., p. 290.

26. Hugh T. Reed, *Elements of Military Science and Tactics,* 7th ed., p. 519.

27. James S. Pettit, *Elements of Military Science for the Use of Students in Colleges and Universities,* p. 1.

28. Emory Upton in Peter S. Michie, ed., *The Life and Letters of Emory Upton,* p. 418.

29. Arthur L. Wagner, *Strategy,* p. 9.

30. Ibid., pp. 54-55.

31. United States War Department, *Annual Report of the Commandant, U.S. Infantry and Cavalry School, U.S. Signal School and Staff College,* p. 116.

32. Matthew F. Steele, "Conduct of War," *Journal of the Military Service Institution* 42 (January-February 1908):23. This article was originally presented as the opening lecture for the course in the conduct of war at the Army Staff College, Fort Leavenworth, Kansas, in 1907.

33. Ibid., p. 24.

34. Ibid., pp. 30-31.

35. Matthew F. Steele, *American Campaigns,* I, p. 62.

36. Ibid., pp. 65, 79, 81, 88, 89.

37. Ibid., p. 115.

38. Joseph T. Dickman, "Tactical Rides," p. 35.

39. Margaret Tuttle Sprout, "Mahan: Evangelist of Sea Power," in Edward Mead Earle, ed., *Makers of Modern Strategy,* p. 429.

40. Alfred Thayer Mahan, *Naval Strategy Compared and Contrasted with the Principles and Practice of Military Operations on Land,* p. 15.

41. Ibid., p. 107, and Alfred Thayer Mahan, "The Practical Character of the Naval War College," *United States Naval Institute Proceedings* 19 (1893):163.

42. Alfred Thayer Mahan, *Lessons of the War with Spain and Other Articles,* p. 13, and Mahan, *Naval Strategy,* p. 118.

43. Mahan, "The Practical Character," p. 162.

44. Mahan, *Lessons,* pp. 6-7, 15.

45. Alfred Thayer Mahan, *The Influence of Sea Power upon History, 1660-1783,* 7th ed., p. 11, and Mahan, *Naval Strategy,* pp. 61, 8, 25.

46. Mahan, *Naval Strategy,* p. 112.

47. Ibid., p. 115.

48. Ibid., p. 62.

49. Mahan, *Influence,* p. 88.

50. William L. Neumann, "Franklin Delano Roosevelt: A Disciple of Admiral Mahan," *United States Naval Institute Proceedings* 78 (July 1952):713.

51. Ibid.

52. Alfred Thayer Mahan, "The Panama Canal and the Distribution of the Fleet," *North American Review* 200 (September 1914):406.

53. Alfred Thayer Mahan, "Subordination in Historical Treatment," *American Historical Association Annual Report,* 1902, p. 60.

54. Mahan, *Naval Strategy,* p. 17.

55. Ibid., p. 2.

# 5

# MARTIAL PRINCIPLES
# IN TOTAL WAR

WAR HAS CONSISTENTLY caused and made possible the reappraisal of military institutions. Changes sought and denied in times of peace because of the lack of funds or the lack of experience or because of latent conservatism bound to the methods of the last war occur rapidly and often without the bureaucratic awareness or approval necessary at other times. In the era of World War I, principles related to the conduct of war were often found useful by military teachers and commanders. These principles tended to be tersely and simply expressed, for the virtue of simplicity—that it reduces the probability of accident and misfortune—cannot be ignored in war. The desire for simplicity placed practical limits on the number of principles enunciated in wartime orders and in instructional books. And even though simply expressed principles often conflicted with the prevailing concept of principles stated in such official publications as field service regulations, wartime orders were often terse, and their major subdivisions were often enumerated and sometimes introduced by a catchword or brief title.

Before World War I, military literature contained a variety of ideas about the nature of principles of war. Some lists were presented, but in most publications and in the field-service regulations, principles were the general truths or considerations necessary for the proper understanding of the many activities of war. Each of these activities had its own collection of "general principles." A review of selected books on the theory of war written in the early twentieth century and a review of the field-service regulations that were in effect in the same period and at the start of the war reveal the divergent ideas about the principles of war. The acceptance of the existence of principles remained a fundamental tenet in books on the theory of war throughout the Western world, and occasional lists of principles relating to the proper conduct of war continued to appear. More often, however, the listing of principles was viewed with disdain, especially in scholarly works.

In Germany, General Friedrich von Bernhardi, a veteran of the Franco-Prussian War, published *Vom heutigen Kriege* (On today's war) in 1912. In the first section, the "Principles and Elements of Modern War," he stated, "The fundamental principles of war certainly remain the same, whenever it is waged."[1] His principles were not enumerated; rather, they existed in his narratives. And he warned of the danger of identifying principles in a way that might lead to dogmatic interpretations:

> The constancy manifesting itself in a variety of ways in war and in all that concerns war is thus in every direction the determinant for the doctrine of war. *But we must guard against* wishing to coin it into definite *laws of acting* and into binding *rules for practical conduct of war,* which are only too apt to be used as thumbrules, and then become fetters to freedom of action. We must rather remain constantly aware that from such constancy nothing but general principles and norms of acting can be deduced which nowhere restrict freedom of action, and, in so far as they are not of a nature to apply generally, must in their application always appear in different forms in compliance with the changes in armaments and in the conduct of war.[2]

Similar notions appeared in France. Jean Colin, a gifted member of the French historical section of the War Ministry and later professor at the French war college, wrote in his *Les Transformations de la guerre* (The transformations of war), "Napoleon laid down the principles and gave us the models of modern war," but aside from occasional references to principles in general, he did not identify specific principles for the conduct of war.[3] Colin did, however, emphasize a variation on Jomini's fundamental principle. Colin's wording was also reminiscent of von der Goltz's "highest principle of modern warfare": "*Victory is above all a matter of force;* that *to win, we can never be too strong*; that as many men as possible must be employed; that *for the battle itself as many troops must be concentrated as possible,* none must be neglected."[4] Colin presented no lists, and only an occasional "principle" could be identified in his lengthy narrative.

In London, too, the notion that an indefinite number of principles exists prevailed. For example, in 1908, J. Bürde published *Tactical Principles,* which he claimed presented a new rather than an exhaustive treatise, and its title confirmed his belief in the existence of principles. He did not enumerate all of the principles of war or even all of what he called tactical principles, but he did list seven of the "chief tactical principles" (see appendix 24).[5] Other works spoke of principles generally but included no lists. Major General Edward Altham's *The Principles of War Historically Illustrated* was one of these. But Altham's stated purpose revealed that all of the principles of war would not be specifically identified in this work either. He wrote that he intended to illustrate "the principles set forth in *Field Service Regulations,*" and he recognized that he could discuss only "a comparatively small proportion" of the principles presented in the regulations.[6] Neither Altham nor the British *Field Service Regulations* of 1909, to which he referred, attempted to enumerate the principles of war in a brief list or even to identify the most important principles.

In the United States, principles were discussed by Gustave J. Fiebeger, professor of civil and military engineering at the military academy from 1896 until 1922. He published a text, *Elements of Strategy,* which was frequently revised and reprinted during his long tenure at the academy, and even editions written well before World War I contained a list of twenty-one "military principles" (see appendix 23). Many of the principles were taken from Napoleon's writings, some from Moltke's, and some from Jomini. Fiebeger explained:

Correct military principles are learned from a study of the important campaigns of history, and from comments and criticisms of those campaigns by their participants, or by able military students. Military principles are to the art of war what the principles of mechanics are to the art of engineering.[7]

He did not claim that his list of twenty-one items included all of the principles governing the conduct of war, but for his students, the list was undoubtedly from a high enough source to purport to be correct and complete.

Official doctrine and handbooks similarly reflected differing views concerning the nature of principles of war in the era before World War I and similarly presented no definitive lists of principles. The attitude presented in the 1900 German *Felddienst = Ordnung* (Field service regulations) concerning outposts applied to the conduct of war in general and throughout the doctrinal handbooks of the world's major powers. The German regulations stated, "The diversity of situations, purposes, and country, makes it impossible to lay down rules for outposts which would be suitable to all occasions. In every single case the distribution of the outposts and of their commands, and the routine of duty must be arranged to suit the special circumstances."[8] Adherence to the uniqueness of events prevailed.

In 1908 the revised German *Felddienst = Ordnung* briefly discussed the "general principles of written communications" but had no other sections on "principles." The regulations were conceived in a broad spirit that did not allow them to be definitively interpreted.[9] However, the foreword to this edition, which was signed by Emperor William II, authorized the minister of war to make modifications to the regulations except in regard "to the principles that it consecrates."[10]

An earlier unofficial German handbook, *Handbuch für den Truppenführer* (Handbook for the troop leader), which was frequently revised and republished in the decades before World War I, not only recognized the existence of principles but presented some very practical guides. Eight numbered paragraphs, for example, were included in the section, "General Principles" for the offensive tactics of the combined arms.[11] The first stated, "Whoever seeks decisive results must attack." The fifth paragraph claimed to be the "main principle": "Every attack is prepared for by fire (infantry and artillery), and after gaining fire superiority or the disruption of the enemy, the attack must be continued by fire."[12] This handbook also presented three general principles for the defensive. None of the principles claimed to be immutable, and none of the lists claimed to be complete. Throughout German official and unofficial sources, the "principles" tended to be more descriptive than prescriptive.

The field-service regulations for the French army in the years preceding the war were descendants of the *Décret du 18 mai 1895 portant réglement sur le service des armées en campagne* (Decree of 18 May 1895 which sets forth guidance for armies on campaign), and like other French military works of the prewar period, the decree did not include a list of general operational principles. Principles were referred to only in a very broad sense, for the purpose of the regulations was not to provide specific principles but "to set forth certain proper general principles in order to establish in the army the unity of doctrine that concerns the indispensible conditions of success."[13] The earlier *Décret du 26 octobre 1883* also contained general principles, which were included in a chapter entitled "A Summary Instruction on Combat." The word *principle* was used throughout this chapter but not in conjunction with the advice "to attain superiority of numbers and fire at the decisive point."[14]

The French regulations current at the start of the war included *La Conduite des grandes unités du 28 octobre 1913* (The command of large units, dated 28 October 1913), *Le Décret sur le service des armées en campagne du 2 décembre 1913* (The decree on the field service of armies, dated 2 December 1913), and *Le Réglement de manoeuvre de l'infanterie du 20 avril 1914* (Infantry drill regulations, dated 20 April 1914). The importance of the offensive dominated these regulations, but no "principle of the offensive" was referred to. In *La Conduite des grandes unités,* however, the statement was offered that "the French army . . . no longer recognizes any law in the conduct of operations except the offensive."[15] Ironically, the "absolute principle" that was stated in the field-service decree concerned the defensive: "the division must hold until it is completely sacrificed."[16] The infantry drill regulation was also explicit in its statement concerning the defensive: "An infantry unit that has the mission to hold a piece of ground must never abandon it without an order. It resists to the end; each man will die rather than give up the ground."[17]

There was relatively little emphasis on the existence of fundamental principles of war in the continental regulations of the prewar era, but in the British *Field Service Regulations* of 1909, the enunciation of a few specific principles appeared to be from some remarks, the foundation upon which the regulations were based. The first chapter discussed the application of general principles to the leading of troops:

> The principles given in this manual have been evolved by experience as generally applicable to the leading of troops. They are to be regarded by all ranks as authoritative, for their violation in the past has often been followed by mishap, if not by disaster. They should be so thoroughly impressed on the mind of every commander that, whenever he has to come to a decision in the field, he instinctively gives them their full weight.[18]

The discussion concluded with a Jominian remark concerning the principles: "The fundamental principles of war are neither very numerous nor in themselves very abstruse, but the application of them is difficult." The remainder of the regulation, however, seemed to deny that there was a small number of principles. It did not include a summary of a few principles but rather lengthy sections consisting of general principles for quarters, for billets, of protection, for the flank guard, for outposts, for information, for the attack, for defense, for the encounter battle, for the attack of fortresses, for night operations, for warfare against an uncivilized enemy, for mountain warfare, for convoys, and for ammunition and supply.

"General rules" were presented for other topics of field service, and the numbered paragraphs in the sections on general rules and general principles totaled more than one hundred. Some familiar ideas were stated. Jomini's fundamental principle, for example, was among the general principles of the attack: "It is seldom either possible or desirable to attempt to overwhelm an enemy everywhere. The object will usually be to concentrate as large a force as possible against one decisive point."[19] But Jomini's belief that the number of principles was small, and even the claim in the regulations themselves that the principles were not very numerous, appeared to have been forgotten or overlooked. The principles of warfare stated in the British *Field Service Regulations* had a much greater scope than Jomini's or the later official lists. Perhaps it was in part due to this expanse of principles and rules that when reflecting on the British army's state of preparedness in 1914, Lloyd George complained, "It is not too much to say that when the Great War broke out our Generals had the most important lessons of their art to learn. Their brains were cluttered with useless lumber, packed in every niche and corner."[20]

Service regulations in the United States in the early twentieth century also reflected the wide use of general principles as an introduction to the various activities of field service. In the 1905 edition of the regulations, "general principles" of orders, information, security, marches, and subsistence were presented. Ironically, the section on combat was introduced by "general considerations." The Japanese, too, in their attempts to Westernize their army in the late nineteenth century, mirrored the use of "general principles" and "general rules" as the terms were used in the manuals of the Western world's major military powers. Japanese traditions were added to an organization and thoughts that were strikingly Western.

In spite of the widely shared belief that the principles of war were composed of myriad truths associated with the many activities that make up the whole practice of war, a few official publications in the United States began to enumerate imperatives that purported to contribute to success in war. *Infantry Drill Regulations* of 1911, for example, included a summary of imperatives at the conclusion of the section on combat (see appendix 26). This list of fourteen items was not presented as a list of principles, except that the introduction to the section on combat stated that only the "basic principles of combat tactics as applied to infantry and to special units, such as machine guns and mounted scouts" would be discussed.

The U.S. *Field Service Regulations* were revised in 1913, and the "general considerations" contained in the section on combat in the 1905 regulations were expanded upon and entitled "General Principles." The statements in the section were more positive than they had been in earlier regulations. The first paragraph of the revised section read, "In combat, troops act either on the offensive or on the defensive. *Decisive results are obtained only by the offensive.*"[21] The first principle for offensive tactics in the German *Handbuch* made the same claim, and the first paragraph of the section on battle in the British *Field Service Regulations* read: "Considerations which influence a commander in offering battle. 1. *Decisive success in battle can be gained only by a vigorous offensive.*"[22] It followed from each of these sources that the dictum that decisive results are obtained only by the offensive could properly be called a "principle." The general principles section of the U.S. regulation, however, continued with six additional paragraphs that did not appear to carry the imperative force of a principle. They were captioned: Advantages of the Offensive, Advantages of the Defensive, Preliminaries, Fire, Ranges, and Intrenchments. Their content was informational rather than directive in nature, and because they served more to inform than to guide or to cause, they were not principles of war in the later official sense.

The U.S. *Field Service Regulations* were revised and published again in 1914. In this edition the regulations were divided into three parts—organization, operations, and administration—with six articles in the section on operations: information, security, orders, marches and convoys, combat, and shelter. Each article was introduced by a section on "general principles," except the article on combat, which was now introduced by the title, "combat principles." The characteristics of these principles differed from the general principles included elsewhere in the *Regulations* of 1914 and from the general principles on combat in the 1913 edition. "Combat principles" were apparently quite different from "general principles." Ten paragraphs of "combat principles" were presented, and each was stated as an imperative rather than as an item of general information.

Some of the ideas expressed were reminiscent of ideas that had earlier been referred to as principles. For example, Jomini's fundamental principle was suggested in the statement that "every man that can be used to advantage must participate in the decisive stage of combat." The phrase *unity of command* and the thought associated with the term were a prevision of the "principle of unity of command," and the mention of the benefit of simple and direct plans suggested the "principle of simplicity," which like "unity of command" became an official U.S. "principle of war" less than a decade later. The imperatives summarized in the 1914 *Regulations,* however, were not called the principles of war, they were not identified by titles of one or a few words, they were not immutable, or at least no claim was made that they were immutable, and the claim was not made that their application would ensure success in war. Nevertheless, the enumeration of ten imperatives, referred to as "combat principles," demonstrated the official acceptance of the belief in the existence of principles and a proclivity to enumerate definitive principles for the conduct of war in official doctrine.

The official as well as unofficial military literature of the prewar period contained disparate views on the nature of principles of war, but the belief in the existence of such principles was widely held. Terse labels, like those assigned to specific principles in the writings of Hamley, Mahan, and Foch, were not used extensively in the military literature, however, until after the war began. Concomitantly, the dominant view of the nature of principles of war shifted from the idea that they were descriptive considerations to the idea that they were few in number and could be simply and tersely expressed.

Two factors contributed to this shift. The first was general and has often been overlooked; the second can be attributed to the efforts of a single individual. The first factor was the necessity to transmit basic information to masses of people whose backgrounds and training differed widely. Technological, pedagogical, and

security considerations often required that information be trans-
mitted tersely and simply. On the battlefield, wireless and other
means of communication required simply stated messages. On the
drill field, terse and simple commands facilitated the instruction of
large groups of soldiers. In the classroom courses shortened by
the urgent need for trained combat leaders, staff officers, and
soldiers allowed time for the presentation of only the most immediately useful subjects. Instructors and the writers of handbooks
quite naturally responded to the reduced opportunities for study
by selecting and stressing fundamental elements, characteristics,
or principles of their respective topics.

The second force that gave impetus to the idea that the principles
of war were few in number and capable of being simply expressed
was generated by the didactic efforts of John Frederick Charles
Fuller, unquestionably the most influential contributor to the
modern concept of "principles of war" in the twentieth century.
He has been called the "discordant trumpet" because of his in-
dividualistic and freely spoken views regarding mechanization in
the British army in particular and the prevailing conservative
nature of British military institutions in general.[23] But since he
blew his own trumpet too loudly over the use of "his principles"
in the postwar British *Field Service Regulations,* his contribution
to the development of the modern "principles of war" has been
misinterpreted and often overstated. The shift in the view of the
principles of war from an innumerable summary of truths of war
to a short list of aphorisms on war by military men during World
War I occurred quite independently of Fuller's views. Fuller's
ideas were indicative of the shift and undoubtedly contributed to
it in some circles, but the principal causes were far more pervasive than Fuller's influence.

In Germany, France, Great Britain, and the United States,
imperatives few in number and tersely expressed appeared in an
assortment of wartime orders, manuals, and handbooks. A list
of such imperatives was included for the conduct of defensive
operations in a German order of 1915 (see appendix 29). The
order sought to call attention, "in the form of a general summary,
to the essential principles which must be observed in the defense of

our positions."[24] Eleven numbered paragraphs followed, the last containing administrative information. Some key words and phrases, such as, *first line* and *always occupy the same trenches* were emphasized, and each of the first ten paragraphs expressed imperatives for successful defensive actions.

Combat instructions in the German army also reflected a belief in the efficacy of principles. The German manual of position warfare listed four "principles of command" (see appendix 34), and in the section of the manual entitled "The Attack in Position Warfare," eight principles appeared (see appendix 38). In the latter list, each of the principles was given a brief title—for example, command, liaison, surprise, and flanking action. The acceptance of principles was new to German doctrine, and their terse and enumerated format was particularly unusual when viewed against the theory of von Moltke, von Peucker, and Verdy du Vernois, which was based on the uniqueness of individual events and on a general dislike of dogmatic rules. World War I changed many traditional German beliefs.

In France the term *principles of war* was used in the terser sense by Marshal Louis Hubert Lyautey. He was minister of war in Paris for a short time during the war but spent the bulk of his mature years as military governor of Morocco. In a section entitled, "Response to Possible Objections," of a report dealing with the actions of the French forces in Morocco, Lyautey wrote that he had invented nothing new concerning the methods that he had used in Morocco and that he merely made "application of the eternal principles of war, which are demonstrated by all the great masters since the beginning of time and from which the most modest students have gained inspiration." Lyautey continued his report by listing five terse principles:

The passive defensive leads only to ruin.

The attack alone anticipates the attack.

Whoever does not progress recedes.

He who does not impose his will submits to the enemy's will.

Complete success comes only to those who can control ideas, imagination, active minds and the initiative of movement.[25]

Lyautey's principles were unlike the imperatives contained in orders and in many of the manuals of the war period, but they demonstrated the extent to which the belief in the existence of a few basic principles had spread, for Lyautey, one of France's most distinguished soldiers, discussed them almost matter of factly.

At the other extreme of the French officer rank structure, a *Manual for Commanders of Infantry Platoons* (1917) presented four "principles, which should be known to all." Like Foch's four principles, they were introduced by very brief phrases— energy, unity of action, surprise, and security—but unlike Foch's list no "etc." indicated the possible existence of additional principles. Each title was explained by a short paragraph (see appendix 35). The first paragraph spoke of "soldierly qualities," the human characteristics necessary for success in battle, but the remaining three paragraphs discussed operational imperatives. The list thus had nearly all of the characteristics of the modern "principles of war." It contained a small number of principles, the principles were stated as imperatives for the proper conduct of war, and each principle was given a brief title. In content, these imperatives were intimately associated with dictums past and future that had been or would be identified as "principles of war."

Late in the war, the French army published directive number 5 (12 July 1918), which according to one source

definitively established all the principles resulting from the experience obtained during four years of war:

—principle of gaining strategic and tactical surprise;

—principle of maneuver, the basis of every operation;

—principle of exploitation of success;

—principle of compromise between care in preparation and rapidity and continuity in execution.[26]

In summary form, the French had presented a list of principles, referred to by titles and based on the lessons of the past.

In 1917, the same year that the French list of principles for platoon leaders appeared, the British army published a pamphlet that also contained a short list of principles. Entitled *British Tactical Notes,* it had five numbered paragraphs that were entitled "principles of training," and like the French principles for platoon leaders, each was given a brief title: concentration, vitality, the offensive spirit, bullet and bayonet, and fire and movement. The format resembled the French list for platoon leaders and most modern lists, but except for the "principle of concentration," which had long been established in the military lexicon by such influential writers as Hamley and Mahan, the content of this 1917 British list was quite different from the French and other contemporary lists. It pertained to training soldiers for action rather than to the operational considerations of war itself (see appendix 36). Other British wartime statements, however, spoke tersely of operational considerations. For example, a British order issued in 1917 directed attention to

principles which underlie all the enemy's instruction:—

　(i)　The constant insistence on the supreme importance of a spirit of determination to endure and to conquer at all cost.

　(ii)　Although this spirit of determination is the main factor in success, no material precaution which skill and foresight can provide is to be neglected.

　(iii)　The defeat and destruction of the hostile infantry is the aim to be held constantly in view.

All means available, and all methods employed, must be directed toward this end.[27]

The order continued, "These three fundamental principles do not differ from those on which we also rely. It is on applying them more thoroughly than the enemy that we must primarily depend for success." Fundamental principles, few in number, thus were a part of British army doctrine during World War I. No claim was made that the content of any given list of principles had been generalized to encompass all the dominant operational considerations that lead to success in war, but the format of the later offical lists of principles was widely employed.

The ten paragraphs of "combat principles" that appeared in the U.S. Army's *Field Service Regulations* of 1914 demonstrated further acceptance of the belief that a few fundamental principles regulate the conduct of war. This belief was also evidenced by a list of sixteen numbered paragraphs claiming to be the general principles for the employment of cavalry (see appendix 28), which appeared in the U.S. *Cavalry Service Regulations* (1914). The paragraphs were both informational and instructional, and some contained imperatives for the successful conduct of cavalry operations. The importance of the initiative, security, and mobility was pointed out.

Terse expressions of imperatives for combat also appeared in U.S. handbooks. In 1916, Colonel V. A. Caldwell wrote an instructional booklet, sanctioned by the War Department, entitled, *Five Tactical Principles and Uniform Tactical Training.* Caldwell identified the five principles as: "Get a correct grasp of the tactical situation as a whole, act according to the circumstances and the nature of the terrain, team work, fire superiority, and simple and direct methods."[28] The principles were so terse and so general that their meaning and usefulness were questionable without further explanation. Caldwell stated, too, that the five principles applied extensively: "They govern the tactical actions of the general and of the private, of the army and of the squad." Neither the identification nor the range of applicability of principles related to the conduct of war had ever been so definitively expressed.

Caldwell's five principles reappeared in 1918 in *Catechism of Uniform Tactical Training,* another of his booklets sanctioned by the War Department. The principles were listed in five numbered paragraphs in response to the rhetorical question, "Are there any tactical principles that state just *WHAT* you should do in any and every fight?"[29] The answers were:

1.  Get a correct grasp of the situation as a whole.
2.  Act according to the circumstances, and the nature of the terrain.
3.  Plan team work.
4.  Get fire superiority.
5.  Use only simple and direct methods and plans.

Caldwell added, "Tactical principles are the only things in tactics that do not change."

Another handbook, *Technique of Modern Tactics,* contained fourteen paragraphs of imperatives, which were called "General observations on combat" (see appendix 30). Each imperative was tersely expressed; for example, the fourth paragraph stated, "All movements should be simple," and the seventh, reminiscent of Jomini's fundamental principle, stated, "Put into the main fight all available forces."[30] Although these observations on combat were not identified as principles, the handbook discussed the concept of principles of war at length:

> The rules and principles of war or tactics, such as they are, are common sense based upon experience and precedent. It has been found that a certain method or procedure has repeatedly given good results in similar situations. . . . Accordingly, the principles of the art of war are usually stated in very general terms, accompanied by the cautions that the proper procedure "depends upon circumstances," that we "must keep aloof from rigid forms or models," and that "there is no such thing as 'normal' formation," etc.[31]

Another handbook of this era, *Fundamentals of Military Service,* published in both the United States and England, discussed concepts of principles at length:

> There are a few principles for handling men and situations in the presence of the enemy, so fundamental and yet simple, that I have thought they could be grouped here together, and so thoroughly learned that they might become to the military man what the multiplication table is to the mathematician. They may strike you as almost too simple to bother with; yet we have seen one or another violated again and again at maneuvers, while our history teems with instances where officers have met disaster through non-observance of these simple rules.[32]

In comparison with the relatively short lists presented in other handbooks of this period, the twenty-five paragraphs of "tactical rules" presented in this work were quite lengthy (see appendix 31). They were not expressed as boldly or as tersely as others had been, but they did provide a further demonstration of the belief that rules or principles existed and that they could be readily enumerated.

Yet another handbook, *Applied Minor Tactics,* appeared in the United States during the war, and it included a brief list of operational principles. The text claimed to be "simplified for beginners" and especially well adapted to the instruction of noncommissioned officers and privates. Seven paragraphs of operational imperatives were included under the heading, "A Few General Principles" (see appendix 37). These principles were called the key to the study of minor tactics:

> There is nothing difficult, complicated or mysterious about applied minor tactics—it is just simply the application of plain, everyday common, horsesense—the whole thing consists in familiarizing yourself with certain general principles based on common sense and then applying them with common sense.[33]

Principles were also enunciated in "Combat Instructions," a directive signed by General Pershing and issued in 1918 to division commanders assigned to the American Expeditionary Forces. The principles were expressed in twenty lengthy paragraphs that dealt with both methods and materiel, but the idea that a few fundamental principles existed was apparent. The opening sentence read, "It is necessary . . . to repeat once more a few fundamental principles which must be impressed upon all concerned."[34]

In 1918 a manual, which was translated from a French document and published by the U.S. War Department, *Instructions for the Offensive Combat of Small Units,* continued the trend toward the definitive enumeration of fundamental imperatives or guides necessary for the proper conduct of the war. The manual stated, "An analysis of the present German methods of defense therefore demands no essential modifications in our offensive tactics. It does make clear, however, the extreme importance of certain fundamentals, which may be summarized as follows."[35] Nine paragraphs of terse imperatives comprised the fundamentals—one was referred to as a principle (see appendix 39). Another evinced the ideas associated with the principle of concentration.

Wartime literature did not eliminate the confusion surrounding the identity, the definition, or even the proper format for the presentation of principles of war. Some sources claimed to present general principles for the conduct of war; others presented principles that were applicable to a specific arm or to a specific activity of war, such as the offensive, the defensive, or position warfare. The enduring consequence of the various expressions of principles, however, was that the existence and efficacy of principles became widely accepted among military men. Also, because many of the wartime lists were officially sanctioned and because orders and instructions in war were positively stated, the different principles, whether of command, of the defensive, or of minor tactics, were generally stated definitively. Emphasis was placed on the known rather than upon the unknown. Henderson had claimed that he could present most of the important principles of war. Foch stated four principles and then added "etc.," but wartime literature tended to state boldly, "Here are THE principles to be observed."

After the war military doctrine was gradually reappraised in light of the experience gained during combat. Because the interest in and the need for military publications was greatly reduced in the postwar period, the war experience became largely concentrated in general reference books, like *Field Service Regulations.* New concepts of principles emerged from the war experience, and the new concepts were compatible with ideas that J. F. C. Fuller had been espousing since his days at the British Staff College.

After the adoption of a brief list of principles of war in the British *Field Service Regulations—Operations* (Provisional) of 1920, Fuller claimed that he had been the first to identify the true principles of war and that his first list had appeared in a pamphlet, *Training Soldiers for War,* which he had written in 1912.[36] Taken in context, however, the six principles identified in the pamphlet were merely a collection assembled from other sources. Furthermore, Fuller had stated that the six were only the most important of the principles of war. He wrote, "On searching for a doctrine our first task is to lay bare the principles of war, the chief of which are the principle of the Objective . . . the principle of Mass . . . the principle of the Offensive, and the principles of Security, Surprise and Movement (i.e., rapidity)."[37] These principles were not presented as a definitive list, nor was each presented as a title with a terse explanation of its meaning. Fuller simply offered an enumeration of some of the principles that were often spoken of in the military literature of the day.

Fuller next took up the principles of war during his student days at the British Staff College, but even before his arrival he became acquainted with the pedantry that permeated many prewar British military institutions. Fuller had failed in his first attempt to gain admission to the Staff College, but he succeeded in 1913, perhaps because he recognized that in the British army "success does not so much depend upon what you know as upon what the examiner knows." He further concluded that one should not study in order to become a staff officer, "but in order to pass the examination. Abide rigidly by the manuals and regulations; do not read books that are of value, but instead crammers' productions; for the average crammer is no fool."[38] Once established at the Staff College, Fuller continued to express his dissatisfaction with British military institutions, and he also maintained the concept of principles that was evident in *Training Soldiers for War;* that is, he believed that the important principles were few in number and that they could be referred to by titles. In his last essay written at the college before war interrupted the course, he compared the battles of Salamanca (1812) and Chancellorsville (1863) in the light of the principles cited in his pamphlet.

His essay began by noting that the *Field Service Regulations* of 1909 stated, "The principles of war are neither very numerous nor in themselves very abstruse," and he complained that not one principle was mentioned. In fact, many were, but Fuller's conception of principles differed from the view expressed in the regulations, which was that the principles were general truths associated with each of the many activities of war. He further believed that the principles, as he conceived them, "kept criticism on logical lines and supplied a skeleton to the illogicalities of war. Unfortunately his were not in the *Field Service Regulations*, therefore [according to his mentors] they were incorrect."[39] When he asked what the correct ones were, he was curtly told that it was not the business of the student to amend the regulations but to study them. In less than a decade, the principles as Fuller conceived them would find expression in the *Field Service Regulations,* but for the moment his instructors were unwilling to admit that a student's essay would be superior to the doctrine that they were required to teach. Fuller reflected on their plight: "They were just parts of a machine created to produce standardized thinking, and to think in a standardized way is a great relief to an instructor, for otherwise he might be caught out."[40] Fuller had the courage to be inquisitive and to differ from standardized and conventional responses, but his thinking was not so far afield that he could be dismissed as a charlatan.

For the British Army, 1914 and 1915 were years of disappointment on the battlefield, and Fuller used his conception of the principles of war to explain the causes of the problems. He admitted that he thought about war on a higher level than his duties warranted, but his efforts were rewarded when his article, "The Principles of War with Reference to the Campaigns of 1914-15," was published, though anonymously, in the *Journal of the Royal United Service Institution.* When Fuller appraised his contribution to the list of eight principles of war adopted in 1920 by the War Department, his recollection of the details of this article was again misleading, as his memory had been faulty in recalling his mention of principles of war in *Training Soldiers for War.* Concerning the journal article, he wrote in 1925, "This article was published in February 1916, and to the former six principles, I added two new ones—the principle of economy of force and the principle of co-operation."[41] The two "new" principles were certainly not new, but his statement was in error for another reason as well. His article did not discuss just the eight principles that were adopted with minor changes in the postwar *Field Service Regulations* but eleven principles of war.

The eight principles recalled by Fuller were included in the first part of the article, "Strategical Principles." These were: the objective, offensive, mass, economy of force, movement, surprise, security, and cooperation. Part two of the article was entitled, "Tactical Principles," and three such principles were identified: demoralization, endurance, and shock. Wartime literature and prewar literature often referred to principles in either the tactical or strategical branches of war, and Fuller similarly enumerated principles in both areas. Thus, he did not present a list of the principles of war in his 1916 article but rather one list of strategical principles and another of tactical ones. He stated that the latter list included the eight strategical principles, but it remained a list of the principles of tactics and not of war. He also recognized that some semantic difficulties existed with the terms *strategy* and *tactics* but attributed "all of these misunderstandings . . . not only to faulty use of words, but to cabalistic definitions studiously inculcated by army crammers and such-like illuminati" and did little to clarify distinctions between the two. Fuller further confused the proper sphere of the principles that he presented by stating that the eight strategical principles were the "leading ones in the science of war" and that the whole art of war was centered about the three tactical principles.[42]

Fuller also promoted his conception of the nature of the principles of war through a series of commanding officers conferences that he headed. Each course consisted of seven days of instruction in France, and the course was repeated five times, with twenty to thirty senior officers attending each weekly session. Fuller lectured twice a day but in his memoirs was able to recall only three lectures that he had given at the school; the opening lecture had been "Address on the Principles of War."

Fuller's proclivity to get to the heart of every subject and to lay bare its essentials was apparent in an article written during the war, "The Principles of Defense as Applied to Trench Warfare." It was not published, perhaps because, as Fuller explained, "It was considered that it might be of value to the enemy; consequently, I presume, the logic was that it could be of no earthly value to ourselves."[43] Another of his papers, "Plan 1919," did receive considerable exposure, for it was circulated among such senior British officials as Sir Henry Wilson, chief of the Imperial General Staff, and Winston Churchill, then secretary of war. In this paper,

Fuller mentioned only one of his principles. He wrote, "Irrespective of the arm employed, the principles of strategy remain immutable, changes in weapons affecting their application only. The first of all strategical principles is 'the principle of the object,' the object being 'the destruction of the enemy's fighting strength.' "[44]

The exposure of British soldiers and politicians to Fuller's ideas on the principles of war certainly had an impact upon British military thought, but even when the war ended, Fuller did not think of principles as a single list that purported to hold all of the truths necessary for the proper conduct of war. His writings indicated that he believed that there were a few fundamental principles for the various operational branches of war, that these principles could be expressed briefly, and that they could be identified by short titles. This concept of principles was evident in his widely read journal article, in his lecture at the commanding officers course, and in his papers, "The Principles of Defence as Applied to Trench Warfare" and "Plan 1919." He sought to identify the essential, and he accepted the efficacy of principles in the conduct of war:

> I believe that we, in common with all other nations, have erred by abandoning the rock of principle for the shifting sands of chance. If this be true, let us cease to stop our ears to the oracle of history, instead let us follow in the footsteps of the great masters of war whose successes are directly attributable to the maintenance of these principles.[45]

But a single list that could claim to be the true and complete enumeration of all the principles of war still had not been formulated. That task fell to the group of officers charged with rewriting the British *Field Service Regulations* for the postwar army.

*NOTES*

1. Friedrich von Bernhardi, *On War of Today,* trans. Karl von Donat, I, p. 14.

2. Ibid., p. 43.

3. Jean Colin, *France and the Next War,* trans. L. H. R. Pope-Hennesey, p. 191.

4. Ibid., p. 194.

5. J. Bürde, *Tactical Principles*, pp. 23-24.

6. Edward A. Altham, *The Principles of War Historically Illustrated*, I, p. viii.

7. Gustave J. Fiebeger, *Elements of Strategy*, p. 73. One copy of this text that was undated but carried a pencil entry, "1906," was substantially the same as other copies annotated "revised edition."

8. Germany, Army, *The Field Service Regulations of the German Army, 1900*, trans. H. S. Brownrigg, p. 45.

9. Marie Félix de Pardieu, *Critical Study of German Tactics and of the New German Regulations*, trans. Charles F. Martin, p. 6.

10. Germany, Army, *Réglement du 22 mars 1908 sur le Service en campagne dans l'armée allemande*, trans. General Peloux, foreword.

11. Friedrich Immanuel, ed., *Lehnerts Handbuch für den Truppenführer*, 21st ed., pp. 87-88, my translation.

12. Ibid., p. 89.

13. My translation from Eugène Carrias, *La Pensée militaire française*, p. 283. The text of the *décret* appears in *Bulletin officiel du Ministère de la guerre*, Partie réglementaire, Premier semestre (Paris, 1895), pp. 710-92.

14. France, Minister of War, *Décret du 26 octobre 1883 portant réglement sur le service des armées en campagne*, 7th ed., p. 187, my translation.

15. My translation from Pascal Marie Lucas, *L'Evolution des idées tactiques en France et en Allemagne pendant la guerre de 1914-1918*, p. 2.

16. *Le Décret sur le service des armées en campagne du 2 décembre 1913*, article 112, my translation from Lucas, *L'Evolution des idées tactiques*, p. 8.

17. *Le Réglement de manoeuvre de l'infanterie du 20 avril 1914*, article 337, my translation from Lucas, *L'Evolution des idées tactiques*, p. 8.

18. Great Britain, War Office, *Field Service Regulations, 1909* (amended 1914), p. 13. British *Field Service Regulations* are hereafter cited as Great Britain, *FSR* [year].

19. Ibid., p. 136.

20. David Lloyd George, *The War Memoirs of David Lloyd George*, VI, p. 339.

21. U.S. Army, *Field Service Regulations*, 1913, p. 158. U.S. *Field Service Regulations* are hereafter cited as United States, *FSR* [year].

22. Great Britain, *FSR*, 1909, p. 131.

23. See Jay Luvaas, *The Education of an Army*, chap. 10; and Anthony J. Trythall, *"Boney" Fuller, The Intellectual General, 1878-1966*, for biographical information of Fuller.

24. Germany, Army, "Essential Principles for the Defence of Positions as Laid Down in Instructions Issued by G. H. Q.," trans. Great Britain, General Staff, Intelligence (1 August 1915), p. 1.

25. Louis H. G. Lyautey, *Lyautey l'africain: Textes et lettres du maréchal Lyautey*, ed. Pierre Lyautey, III, p. 141, my translation.

26. Lucas, *L'Evolution des idées tactiques,* p. 259.

27. Great Britain, General Staff, *Instructions for Battle* (May 1917), p. 1.

28. V. A. Caldwell, *Five Tactical Principles and Uniform Tactical Training,* p. 8.

29. V. A. Caldwell, *Catechism of Uniform Tactical Training,* p. 172-73.

30. Paul S. Bond and M. J. McDonough, *Technique of Modern Tactics: A Study of Troop Leading Methods in the Operations of Detachments of All Arms,* 3d ed., pp. 204ff.

31. Ibid., p. 53.

32. Lincoln Andrews, *Fundamentals of Military Service,* p. 212.

33. James A. Moss, *Applied Minor Tactics,* p. 30.

34. United States War Department, *Combat Instructions,* 5 September 1918, p. 7.

35. United States War Department, *Instructions for the Offensive Combat of Small Units,* trans. from a French document at General Headquarters, Allied Expeditionary Force, France, p. 10.

36. John Frederick Charles Fuller, *The Foundations of the Science of War,* p. 14.

37. J. F. C. Fuller, *Training Soldiers for War,* pp. 41-42.

38. J. F. C. Fuller, *Memoirs of an Unconventional Soldier,* p. 21.

39. Ibid., p. 28.

40. Ibid., pp. 28-29.

41. Fuller, *Foundations,* p. 14.

42. [J. F. C. Fuller], "The Principles of War with Reference to the Campaigns of 1914-15," *Journal of the Royal United Service Institution* 61 (February 1916):3, 17, 18.

43. Fuller, *Memoirs,* p. 62.

44. Ibid., p. 324.

45. Fuller, "Campaigns of 1914-15," p. 40.

# 6

## CODIFICATION
## AND CONFRONTATION

THE TENDENCY TO enumerate and encapsulate principles of war was evidenced in the regulations, directives, handbooks, and manuals used by major Western powers throughout World War I. At the conclusion of the war, the role of the principles as doctrine, which refers to ideas that are sanctioned by recognized authority and promulgated to all who might profit from the ideas, entered its most important and consequential phase. As the lessons of the war were ferreted from tomes of operational reports in order to update earlier doctrine, the principles of war, in context and form, became a focal point of controversy. Some nations rejected the idea that a definitive list of principles of war could benefit doctrine. In others, however, the list form prevailed; the principles were codified. But in their guise as a definitive list of aphorisms, each identified by a brief title, the principles were confronted by critics who argued against not only their content and form but against their existence as well. For a time, it appeared that the confrontation was won by those who favored the rejection of a doctrine based on a list of principles of war. But the tradition and benefit of principles in any guise was long established. And once codified, the principles could not be stripped from the collective memory of armies that had sanctified them.

Official codification and sanction of "principles of war" first occurred in Great Britain as a result of the work of a committee of British officers under the direction of Colonel J. G. Dill. Appointed in 1919, the committee was charged to revise the *Field Service Regulations* in light of the experience gained in the war. The nature of the principles of war became a topic of debate among the committee at the request of J. F. C. Fuller. Dill, who had been a classmate of Fuller at the Staff College, was certainly aware of his writings on the principles of war, and other officers on the committee probably knew of Fuller's ideas on them through the article in the *Journal of the Royal United Service Institution,* the officer courses conducted by Fuller in France, or the course of instruction at the Commanding Officers School established at Aldershot after the war where Fuller's journal article was used extensively. Nevertheless, Fuller personally brought the idea of the brief list of principles for the conduct of war to the attention of the committee. He wrote in his memoirs:

> So far as my military work is concerned, one fragment only has endured, namely the insertion of the "Principles of War" into the *Field Service Regulations.* . . . At the time I pointed out that in the F.S.R. of that date mention was made that "The fundamental principles of war are neither very numerous nor in themselves very abstruse," and then no single principle was defined. Thereupon the C.I.G.S. [chief of the Imperial General Staff] decided that definition was necesary.[1]

The committee working on the revision of the *Field Service Regulations* set out to define the principles, and a draft of the proposed regulations was sent to the Staff College and to other agencies for comment. Fuller, assigned as an instructor at the Staff College, was appalled when he read in the draft manual that two principles of war had been identified: "Infantry never relinquishes captured ground," and "Infantry is never exhausted."[2] His astonishment at the content of these pronouncements was apparently shared by others who read the early draft, for on April 6, 1920, he received a letter from a committee member that began, "We have finished our labours on the first chapter of F.S.R., Vol. II, which begins with your principles of war."³ For the first time, an official publication identified a terse list of operational dictums, each identified by a title, that claimed to be the "principles of war." They were introduced by the simple sentence, "The principles of war may be summarized as follows."⁴ Eight sections, each headed by a boldfaced word or phrase, concluded the section of the chapter entitled, "The Principles of War." The "boldfaced" principles read:

    (i.)   Maintenance of the objective.—

    (ii.)   Offensive action.—

    (iii.)   Surprise.—

    (iv.)   Concentration.—

    (v.)   Economy of force.—

    (vi.)   Security.—

    (vii.)   Mobility.—

    (viii.)   Co-operation.—

With only minor differences, this list of eight principles corresponded to the eight principles of strategy that Fuller had identified in the journal article of 1916. But the 1920 *Field Service Regulations* did not claim that its principles were applicable to strategy or to tactics; they were rather "principles of war" or as they were referred to later in the manual, "principles applicable to the leading of troops." (See appendix 42 for the explanation of each of these eight principles.) The meaning of the word *principle* as used in the regulations, however, was shrouded in some doubt, for in explaining the application of the principles, the regulations read, "No two situations are identical, and therefore, the application of the principles cannot be made subject to rules."⁵ The regulations continued by discussing the importance of judgment and the usefulness of genius in the leading of troops, but by listing the "principles," pedants and parrots were given the material necessary to ply their trades. And in fact the "principles" in their new definitive guise were widely accepted—by teachers, writers, theorists, and professional soldiers in both Great Britain and abroad. The enthusiasm of the proponents was characterized in the letter that informed Fuller of the appearance of the eight-item list in the *Field Service Regulations:*

> What really matters is that they are in our Bible, and for that the whole Army should thank you, for I am convinced of the paramount importance of having them laid down in black and white as the "acid test" of our field training in peace and our operations in war. There is now no excuse for not knowing these principles, and therefore there is far less excuse, if any, for breaking them, with resultant failure.[6]

The claim of sanctity and the usefulness of a brief list of principles for use in war was not confined to the *Field Service Regulations— Operations.* In October 1920 Fuller published an article that identified eight principles, not of strategy or of tactics, but of war. He claimed that they were "eternal, universal and fundamental" and that they were applicable to "every scientifically fought boxing match" and to every battle.[7] In content they did not differ from the eight principles enunciated in the *Field Service Regulations.*

The official principles became widely accepted. For instance, in 1922 an article appeared that sought to confirm Fuller's and others' pronouncements that the principles were eternal. The article investigated the applicability of the eight principles at the battle of Kadesh, which occurred in 1288 B.C. The article concluded, "Viewing the campaign as a whole, it will surely be agreed that it goes far to substantiate the dictum that 'The principles of war are eternal.' "[8] In 1923 volume 1, *Organization and Administration,* of the *Field Service Regulations* followed the lead of volume 2, *Operations,* by enumerating terse principles. Five "general principles of war organization" were presented (see appendix 44). The propensity to enumerate and encapsulate the essence of complex subjects to facilitate the study and understanding of war was again evident.

After the adoption of the official list of "principles of war," Fuller wrote of the existence of eight principles of war in his book, *The Reformation of War,* but in *The Foundations of the Science of War,* published in 1926, he argued that there were nine principles in addition to "Economy of force," which was elevated to the position of the governing law of war. The nine remaining principles were: direction, concentration, distribution, determination, surprise, endurance, mobility, offensive action, and security.[9] The principles of maintenance of the objective and cooperation that had appeared in the *Field Service Regulations* were absent from this work, and the principles of direction, distribution, and determination were added. Nine principles resulted from Fuller's fascination with "threefold order." His nine were arranged in three groups of three. In *The Foundations of the Science of War,* Fuller attempted to establish the scientific basis of the principles, but even though one reviewer favorably compared the work to Clausewitz's *On War,* most commentators shared the opinion that its great danger was that "the young should take it seriously."[10] The book intensified and polarized the growing debate over the belief that a few fundamental and immutable principles, which can be simply and definitively stated, regulate the conduct of war.

The eight principles enunciated in the provisional *Field Service Regulations* of 1920 reappeared in the edition of 1924, but in the edition of 1929, the list was rearranged and shortened to seven by dropping the former first principle, "Maintenance of the objective." Throughout the 1920s British writers used the "principles of war" as an analytical tool to dissect battles of the past, and others used the principles to discuss the proper conduct of war. One author proposed a list that he thought clearer and more complete than the official list.[11] His principles had no titles, just bold Roman numerals (see appendix 47). Other authors merely suggested additions to or deletions from the official list, but in the early 1930s British military literature reflected "a growing reluctance to submit to a fixed set of principles."[12] For example, Sir Frederick Maurice, professor of military studies at the University of London, wrote, "The general conclusion . . . is that there are no fixed laws and rules of the art of war, and that even its principles are fluid and require constant reexamination in the light of changes which time brings."[13] The "entire elimination of those jewels 'three words long' which . . . masquerade as 'Principles of War' " was eventually called for.[14] In the 1935 edition of the *Field Service Regulations,* volume 2, *Operations,* the list no longer appeared, and only allusions to the formerly hallowed principles were made. The ideas behind the former "principles" were spread throughout the narrative in the revised regulations. Some of the old titles were italicized—surprise, mobility, concentration, security, cooperation, and offensive—but the term *principle* was totally avoided.

Fuller's influence on British doctrine had waned. The criticism of *The Foundations of the Science of War,* his resignation from the army in 1933, prompted by his refusal to accept an assignment in India, and flirtation with fascism were factors. The demise of the "principles," like their rise, was linked to Fuller, but the "principles" waned in influence primarily because of objections to the idea that "principles of war" can be definitively stated.

The British adopted the first official list of "principles of war" in 1920, and its appearance intensified the debate in other Western nations on the existence, nature, efficacy, and content of principles of war that began in the post-Napoleonic era. The British provided the codified model; it was on occasion emulated but at other times rejected by the military services of other nations.

> Before the First World War, Britain had produced no military theorist of note. . . . In the twenty years following, European military thought was dominated by Englishmen. It is unrewarding to speculate why this should have been. Perhaps it was that no other country saw the rise of the quality of Liddell Hart or J.F.C. Fuller; perhaps none offered its readers an audience.
>
> Not that Britain lent to either of its literary strategists a very ready ear; indeed both were read more widely abroad than at home and often in pirated editions.[15]

Even though Fuller and Basil H. Liddell Hart were widely read on the Continent, their concept of principles was not accepted by the authors of French and German doctrine. Liddell Hart, primarily remembered as a historian and strategic critic, himself never strongly endorsed the British list of eight "principles of war," but he nevertheless contributed to the spread of the belief that an enumerable list of principles can benefit military commanders. As early as 1919, he presented a list of principles, which he called the "ten commandments" of the combat unit (see appendix 40). He wrote, "It is suggested that if one can thoroughly imbue the commander of the Combat Unit, his section leaders and men, with these essential principles . . . a great advance will be made in the general efficiency of the infantry arm."[16] He later affirmed the existence of a few "general truths"—which he claimed differed from abstract principles—in his strategical writings; perhaps the criticism of the *Field Service Regulation*'s and Fuller's "principles" influenced his choice of the word *truth*. He first listed the "truths" in 1932 in *The British Way in Warfare: Adaptability and Mobility,* where they were expressed as eight "axioms expressed as maxims." Whether truths, axioms, or maxims, they were determined by examining the actions of a boxer and then likening the boxer's tasks to those of a commander in war (see appendix 49). Although his works undoubtedly influenced military thought in the interwar years, his concept of principles had little impact outside of Great Britain.

Fuller's writings, however, contributed to the debate concerning the existence of principles of war that was carried on in foreign military circles. In fact, at the conclusion of World War I, there were some indications to suggest that a short list of principles of war would soon appear in French doctrine. Foch, who as supreme commander of the allied forces during the war had considerable influence within the French general staff, wrote in the preface of his 1918 republication of *Des Principes de la guerre,* "The fundamental truths which govern this art remain immutable. . . . It is therefore still necessary to establish the principles of war."[17] Foch's quick departure from power, brought about largely because of his differences with Clemenceau over acceptable peace terms, severely limited his influence in the postwar army, but his belief that war was governed by a few basic principles nevertheless persisted and was repeated by a number of French military writers. In 1919, for example, Lieutenant-colonel Eugène Cholet, in his *A propos de doctrine, les leçons du passé confirmées par celles de la grande guerre* (Concerning doctrine, the lessons of the past confirmed by those of the Great War), concluded:

1st.   That fundamental principles of war certainly exist.

2d.   That they appear to be very few in number.

3d.   That they are immutable and have guided the actions of all the great leaders of war.[18]

No listing of the principles appeared in this work, but two years later, Fuller's article, "The Foundations of the Science of War," which presented the same eight "principles" that appeared in the 1920 British *Field Service Regulations,* was translated into French and issued to all units of the French army. General Henri-Victor Buat, chief of the French general staff, had ordered the translation; he declared that the article contained "an exact vision of the future."[19]

That the conditions that would lead to the adoption a list of "principles of war" in French military doctrine were present in France in the early 1920s cannot be denied, but when a board of distinguished officers, headed by Marshal Henri Philippe Pétain, convened to formulate new regulations for the training and operations in war of large units, the enumeration of fundamental principles was completely and explicitly rejected. The board expressed its views in the opening section of the regulations: "The commission has decided that the attempt to formulate principles capable of encompassing profoundly different situations is useless; it felt that the search would lead only to vague formulas, far removed from reality."[20] Although Fuller's concept of "principles" appealed to some senior French soldiers in the late 1920s and one of his articles on the "principles" was widely distributed in France, his "principles"—or indeed his concept of "principles"— were not adopted in French regulations until shortly before the outbreak of World War II.

Where in Great Britain the debate over the existence of enumerable principles was spurred by their elevation to doctrine, in France the debate proceeded in spite of the rejection of principles as doctrine. For example, in 1922 a French journal article concluded that von Kluck's application of proper principles led to his defeat in 1914 and that Foch's disregard of principles in 1918 led to victory.[21] By contrast, Major H. François argued on behalf of principles of war. He believed that since rules, laws, principles, or precepts existed in all areas of human activity, "It would be strange if war, the most violent expression of human activity, was an exception in this regard."[22] He concluded, "Principles of war exist; among the most important one can cite surprise, security, economy of forces, unity of purpose, superiority of the offensive, attack from strength or weakness, communications, destruction of enemy forces."[23] Another article, however, concluded that at least one of these principles, economy of forces, was not only inoperable during the greatest part of the war but that it was "only a procedure and not a principle."[24]

Books on the theory of war similarly took sides in the question of whether a few basic principles regulated the conduct of war. General Serrigny wrote in *Réflexions sur l'art de la guerre* (Reflections on the art of war):

> One is struck by the small number of principles which together regulate war: selection of an objective in accordance with the means, economy of forces, flanking action, rational employment of space and time, concentration, and successive decentralization of means. That is all![25]

In 1924 another French theoretical work spoke of principles "which do not assure victory . . . , but which if they are neglected considerably enhance the chances of defeat."[26] The principles were not listed, but many were identified, such as economy, unity, direction, security, and liberty of action. Each was discussed in turn.

Other works, however, were as clear in their rejection of the concept of principles. Emile Mayer argued in *La Théorie de la guerre et l'étude de l'art militaire* (The theory of war and the study of the military art) against the idea that while the methods of the military art vary incessantly, the principles remain immutable. In *L'Age des casernes* (The age of caserns), Colonel Dupuis claimed that the principles do not exist. Both of these works were challenged in an article entitled, "Hérésies stratégiques" (Strategical heresies), which came to the defense of principles and of Jomini. Jomini's association with the principles on this occasion was quite understandable, for the author of this article, H. Lecomte, was the son of Ferdinand Lecomte, Jomini's compatriot, disciple, and first biographer. The younger Lecomte wrote, "Jomini never tried to reduce war to formulas. He simply took from the comparative study of the campaigns of Frederick and Napoleon a few proper principles, which would not assure victory, but would make it more probable."[27]

Another study that focused on the evolution of tactical ideas during the war and that sought to evaluate the doctrine of the prewar period in order to further the understanding of postwar doctrine identified four principles for the offensive. In this study, *L'Evolution des idées tactiques* (The evolution of tactical ideas), each principle was given a title: the principle of mass, the principle of surprise, the principle of exploitation of success, and the principle of moral superiority. The conclusion stated, "The principles of our prewar offensive doctrine have been sustained in their entirety; the few modifications which have or may be made in them, will not change their general character, which for centuries has not varied." The four principles were then stated:

To increase the chances of success in the offensive, it is always necessary

—to have superiority of means, if not a total superiority over all the enemy's means, at least at the point chosen for the attack.

—to use surprise, to maintain the superiority for as long a time as possible.

—to know how to exploit to the extent possible the success attained, to gain the maximum benefit from the superiority gained by surprise.

—finally, to have a moral superiority over the enemy, without which the combatant would be discouraged by the suffering that he must endure before gaining victory.[28]

The author continued that the principles are always true and that only their method of application on the battlefield changes. He concluded by quoting an observation General Langlois made before the war: "One sees too easily a revolution in the art of war where there is simply an evolution of tactical methods."[29] The form of these principles was markedly similar to those established as doctrine in Great Britain. In content, the first was reminiscent of Jomini, the second was common to many enumerations, and the fourth reflected the high regard that the French maintained for moral forces in war, especially after their humiliation in the Franco-Prussian War.

The debate in France in the 1920s concerning the existence of principles of war involved another military writer, one whose name became well known in later decades. Charles de Gaulle indicated in his early writings that within prescribed limits, he too accepted the existence of principles in warfare. In 1925 he wrote, "The principles which govern the employment of methods: economy of forces, the necessity of proceeding by concentration . . . ; surprise for the enemy; security for ourselves, only have value when they are adapted to circumstances."[30] When his *Le Fil de l'epée* (The edge of the sword), a plea for changes in prevalent French military thought and methods, appeared in 1932, it contained the same advice.

French doctrine, which rejected the idea of principles in 1921, included principles in the 1936 revision of the instructions for the employment of large units. The reasons for accepting the principles were stated as follows:

The remoteness from war, the regular increases in the cadres of the army, and the adoption of new methods have induced the high command to ask the Commission to present an outline of offensive and defensive battle, a sort of collection of general principles for the leading of large units and for the combined use of all arms.[31]

Some "general principles" were included in the chapter on battle, but they were not presented as a definitive list. Elsewhere in the work, however, "directing principles" appeared, which "because of their general character and permanence," the regulation claimed, "are at the base of all the operations of war."[32] The next paragraph began, "These principles are the following," but the precise identity of the principles was not apparent. Three phrases appeared in boldfaced type—"impose your will upon the enemy," "maintain liberty of action," and "strict economy [of forces]"—but in the following paragraph, which was also part of the section on directing principles and which began, "Success in war is attained by:" italics were used for the words *surprise* and *anticipation of distant events.* All five of these items were preceded by a dash, and all five have been interpreted as the "principles of commanders."[33] Whether the list included five items or just three remains a matter of interpretation, but that a list, albeit a less definitive one than the British, appeared in French regulations demonstrated that the proclivity to enunciate and encapsulate the essence of the proper conduct of war into a few regulating principles occurred not only in Great Britain but also in France in the interwar period.

A definitive list of aphorisms known as the principles of war never became part of German military doctrine. Although writers like von der Goltz had identified specific principles before World War I and German wartime orders often included terse lists of principles on operational subjects, official doctrine in the immediate post-World War I period denied the existence of general principles of war. On some occasions, however, the concept of principles did appear in postwar military literature. General Friedrich von Bernhardi, who had written *Vom heutigen Kriege* (On today's war) before the war, wrote a sequel to the work in 1920. The former volume pointed out that the great fundamental laws of war remained the same at all times, and in the introduction to the latter volume, Bernhardi presented "great fundamental and vital principles which mean success in war." They appeared as a series of phrases:

Retaining the initiative; using the offensive as the decisive form of action; concentration of force at the decisive point; the superiority of the moral factor to purely material resources;

the proper relation between attack and defence; the will to victory; the unconditional dependence of policy on the requirements and results of strategy or military effort.[34]

His works were well received, but his enunciation of definitive principles had little impact on those responsible for the writing of German doctrine.

In spite of Bernhardi and in spite of the familiarity of German military men with the works of Fuller and Liddell Hart, the decimated German military force allowed by the Treaty of Versailles did not try to emulate the victors in their statement of principles. When the German field-service regulations were revised as the *Truppenführung* (The command of troops) in 1923, its authors recalled the advice of the elder von Moltke and an era of German glory. Von Moltke was quoted in the foreword: "In war, that which is demanded by each concrete case must be done, without binding oneself to unchanging general rules."[35] This idea dominated German military thought, but at the University of Freiburg in the 1930s, Gerhard Ritter, a historian with close contacts with the General Staff, stated in a lecture,

> Napoleon's strategy . . . can be outlined by mentioning a few, simple principles. First, the resolute concentration of all available force on the decisive point . . . Second, a determined advance on the center of enemy power. . . . Third, on the day of battle itself, concentration of the attack against the key sector of the enemy's position. . . . fourth, immediately after the decision, ruthless pursuit of the enemy until horse and man drop.[36]

Ritter's enunciation of principles probably had little influence beyond the academic atmosphere of Freiburg. However, the edition of the *Truppenführung* that appeared in the late 1930s contained a section on general principles for marches, and each of the sections on the encounter battle, the offensive against positions, the defensive, the pursuit, and the breaking of contact and withdrawal began with brief paragraphs of "leadership principles." Among the leadership principles for the encounter battle, for example, were four paragraphs, each introduced by a brief, emphasized phrase. The first read, "Surprise of the enemy," and the fourth was reminiscent of Jomini's fundamental principle: "Early recognition of the enemy's weak point and the formation of a strong point opposite him."[37]

Jomini's principle was also recalled in 1940 in Colonel Hermann Foertsch's *Kriegskunst heute und morgen* (The art of war, today and tomorrow): "In describing the general nature of attack and defense it was stated to be a fundamental principle of strategy that there must be superiority of forces, not only absolutely but also at the decisive point."[38] Foertsch continued by stating that a "second fundamental principle requires surprise," but like the German doctrine he presented no brief and encompassing list of principles of war. Pragmatism and judgment applied to individual cases remained a fundamental tenet in German military thought— even in the light of their victors' adoption of terse and immutable "principles of war."

After the Russian Revolution in 1917, acrimonious debate often characterized the formulation of military doctrine for the Red Army. One of the central issues in the debate concerned the nature and form of principles of war. The belief in the existence of principles had been firmly established in nineteenth- and early twentieth-century Russian doctrine, in part by the writings of Jomini, whose service to the Russian empire lasted nearly fifty-six years (from August 1813 until his death in 1869), Okunev, and Leyer. After the revolution, however, the question of whether "bourgeois principles" could apply in a proletarian state was one of the issues in the conflict between Leon Trotsky and Mikhail Frunze, who after serving as an army and front (a force of several armies) commander in the civil war succeeded Trotsky as commissar for military and naval affairs. Frunze proposed a unified military doctrine in which the proletarian principles of the offensive and of maneuver dominated. Trotsky disliked the emphasis placed on the "proletarian" principles, and in spite of an occasional reference to the principles of economy of forces and surprise, he stated in 1921, "War cannot have eternal laws."[39]

Some bourgeois ideas on principles of war were widely distributed in the Soviet Union in the 1930s. The source of some of these ideas was Britain's J. F. C. Fuller, whose *Lectures on F. S. R. III (Operations Between Mechanized Forces)* was issued in 30,000 copies to Russian troops; a subsequent distribution was increased to 100,000 copies.[40] In *F. S. R. III* Fuller wrote:

> A little study and reflection will lead us to realize that all past strategy and tactics has been governed, consciously or unconsciously, as it may be, by the principles of war, and we may deduce from this that this government will continue. Economy of force, surprise, security, offensive action, movement and cooperation hold good whether an army is composed of footsoldiers, horse soldiers or machine soldiers.[41]

Fuller's advocacy of enumerated principles apparently impressed the Soviets less than his advocacy of mechanized forces, for in the Soviet *Field Service Regulations* of 1936, no enumerated principles appeared.

The introduction to the 1936 Soviet *Field Service Regulations* stated, "These regulations do not purport to give any hard and fast rules; the instructions they contain should be applied with due regard to particular situations."[42] The first section, which was entitled "General Principles," of chapter 1, however, provided information similar in style to the principles listed in the field-service regulations of Western nations during the 1930s. The section on general principles contained seventeen numbered paragraphs, and many of its statements suggested that they carried the same force as the principles stated in U.S. and British regulations of the period. For example, several of the concepts expressed by the British or American 'named principles" were inherent in the following:

> The military operations of the Red Army will be conducted with a view to the annihilation of the enemy. Decisive victory and the complete crushing of the enemy will constitute the principal objectives of the Soviet Union in any conflict that may be forced upon it. . . .
>
> It is impossible to maintain uniformly strong forces at all points. In order to gain victory, it is necessary to concentrate

decidedly superior forces for the main effort by a regrouping of forces and combat means. In secondary areas sufficient forces are needed only to contain the enemy.[43]

Throughout the interwar period, however, neither a bourgeois nor a proletarian list of principles appeared anywhere in Soviet army doctrine.

Fuller's ideas on principles of war had little impact in the Soviet Union, but in the United States his views significantly influenced the adoption of the first definitive list of principles of war in U.S. Army doctrine. As in England, a large measure of the responsibility for this adoption can be attributed to a single individual, and also as in England, the individual was an officer of intermediate rank who was only a part of the formalization process. Unlike Fuller, however, the American did not provide the substance to be incorporated in the list; he merely introduced Fuller's ideas to the proper milieu. This man, Hjalmar Erickson, brought Fuller's list to the U.S. Army, but the acceptance of principles in warfare, the identification of specific principles, and even lists of principles for various activities of war were already part of the American military experience.

In the United States the trend toward the codification of general principles relating to the operations of war was apparent not only in prewar field-service regulations and in wartime handbooks and instructions but in publications, both official and unofficial, that appeared after the war as well. In the *Infantry Drill Regulations* (Provisional) of 1919, a list of twelve "general principles" was included in the section on offensive combat (see appendix 41). No titles were used in this list, but such familiar concepts as the offensive, morale, surprise, mutual support, and objective were discussed in the enumerated paragraphs. An article that appeared in the *Infantry Journal* in 1920 mentioned three principles that "have probably been emphasized more than any other by the experiences in the great war of 1914-1919":

1.  Movement must be combined with fire.
2.  Aggressive defense through the counterattack.

3.  Having been assisted to the enemy's position, the infantryman must alone be able to complete the success.[44]

The author of this article discussed David's encounter with Goliath to show that von der Goltz was correct in stating that "the principles of war are unchanging." The author also used titles, such as the "principle of firepower" and the "principle of the counterattack," to refer to his unchanging principles. In 1921, Colonel William K. Naylor, an instructor at the General Service School at Fort Leavenworth, published a book in which he presented two principles of strategy:

Make the hostile army the objective.
To have, if possible, all the forces assembled at the hour of decisive action.[45]

Naylor believed that

the art of war should be enunciated in the form of maxims, such as those of Napoleon, and doctrines, such as those of von Bernhardi, and should constitute an ensemble capable of informing with precision the mind of the student upon the various questions it embraces; so that having the formula the student merely applies it and gets the results prescribed.[46]

Naylor's views were shared by at least one other instructor, for Fuller's eight principles of strategy, which had appeared in the February 1916 article, were being espoused by Erickson from the platform of the army's highest military school.

The Army War College had been founded in 1902 while Elihu Root was secretary of war. Although its purpose was to "train officers to command in war," the students were more heavily involved with general staff functions than with training. The school closed as an academic institution when the United States declared war on Germany in April 1917 and reopened in 1919 as the General Staff College, a name used until August 1921 when the former name was restored. The General Staff College was to be a true training school rather than part of the General Staff as the earlier

War College had been, but the students continued to work closely with the various divisions of the War Department. Many War Department plans and proposals either originated at the college or were sent to the college for action and completion. Such was the institutional environment that Major Erickson encountered upon his reporting for duty as an instructor at the college on 24 July 1919.[47]

Hjalmar Erickson had many experiences that could have exposed him to the concept of principles in warfare, but his experiences were neither unusual nor particularly influential until his assignment as an instructor at the college. Born in Norway, he joined the U.S. cavalry at the age of nineteen. He was commissioned from the ranks during the Spanish-American War, graduated from the Infantry-Cavalry School at Fort Leavenworth in 1904, and served in France as an infantryman and logistician during World War I. He was awarded the Distinguished Service Medal and recommended for promotion to brigadier general by the American commander, General "Blackjack" Pershing. In June 1919 Erickson was invited to instruct at the General Staff College. He accepted the invitation and was assigned to teach part of the training course, which worked closely with the War Plans Division of the General Staff. During Erickson's first months at the college, he traveled extensively to study the courses, materials, methods, and problems of instruction at other U.S. Army schools: the Infantry School at Camp Benning, the Field Artillery School at Fort Sill, the Coastal Artillery School at Fort Monroe, the Cavalry School at Fort Riley, and many others.

In April 1920 Erickson presented his first lecture at the General Staff College. Entitled "Doctrine of War and of Training," it discussed eight principles of war, which he stated, "could well be incorporated into our Field Service Regulations as a guide for the young officer and as an aide memoir for the older officer."[48] Fuller's influence was clearly revealed in Erickson's conclusion about the principles:

Through ages of actual practice on the battlefields of the World certain principles of war have been evolved. . . . When reduced to their fundamentals, these principles are few and they do not change. . . . It seems, therefore, that it should be easy to find and examine them. But our text books do not list them, so the military student must search history, the reports of campaigns and the writings of military authorities for illustrations of their correct or incorrect application.[49]

Erickson discussed each of the eight principles that Fuller had identified as principles of strategy. He did not mention that the principles were borrowed from Fuller's article, but in the revision of the lecture a year later, he stated that a complaint concerning the lack of a list of principles of war was made "in an article published in an English service journal during the early part of the World War."[50] Erickson went beyond Fuller's discussion by attempting to identify the origin of some of the principles. He suggested that the "Principle of the objective" had been, if not originated by Clausewitz, at least expostulated upon by Clausewitz. He also claimed that the "Principle of security" had been handed down by Foch and that the "Principle of co-operation" had been thoroughly demonstrated during the world war. His discussion was truly eclectic.

Erickson was not alone in his call for the incorporation of a list of principles of war in U.S. doctrine in the early 1920s. In addition to Naylor's comments from the Leavenworth school, the belief that "there should be a uniform and simple presentation of the principles of war, developed into a part of the officer's mental background" seemed to pervade the military educational system of the army.[51] Because of his position and because of the relationship that existed between the Army General Staff and the General Staff College, Erickson became the key figure in the incorporation of the concept and content of Fuller's principles into U.S. doctrine.

Since Erickson taught the training course, which was closely involved with the work of the War Plans Division of the General Staff, it was not surprising that a training regulation published in December 1921 by the War Plans Division contained a definitive list of nine "principles of war" (see appendix 43). The only addition to the eight principles that Erickson had borrowed from Fuller was "the principle of simplicity." In this regulation,

Training Regulation 10-5, *Doctrines, Principles and Methods,* the principles appeared as titles without further explanation of their individual meaning, but the paragraph that followed the list gave insights into their collective characteristics and applicability. The ideas in this paragraph were unoriginal; they were borrowed from Fuller and from the 1920 British *Field Service Regulations.* The paragraph read:

> These principles are immutable. Their application varies with the situation, the fundamentals of which are time, space or distance, terrain, weather, relative strength, including the physical and disciplinary factors, such as numbers, morale, communication, supply, and armament. Their proper application constitutes the true measure of military art, and it is the duty of all officers to acquire their true meaning by study, particularly the study of history, by reflection, and by practice, not only in purely military work, but in administration and business operation. All practical military problems, whether on the map or in the field, will be examined, and critiques thereof will mention the manner of the application of the fixed principles of war. All active military operations will be planned and executed in accordance with these principles.[52]

The "principles" were to be applicable to an extremely broad range of topics, and students at the General Staff College tested their applicability by examining the value of each principle as it had applied during different campaigns of World War I. The "principles" seemed to be confirmed, and military history seemed to have a greater utility than ever. At the General Service School, Fort Leavenworth, Colonel Naylor, whose acceptance of the efficacy of "principles" was apparent in his enunciation of two principles of strategy in 1921, began lecturing in 1922 on "the Marne miracle illustrating the principles of war."[53] He was quick to adopt the War Department's "official principles" for these lectures. He also defined a principle by distinguishing it from a rule. A rule was more definite; a principle was "a profession of faith [with] the spirit and sense of law, leaving to the judgment of the individual the application."[54] Naylor also attempted to clarify the difference between a "principle of war" and principles of branches of war, such as strategy, tactics, and logistics. To Naylor, the principles of the branches were "based on the broad general principles of war."

Eight of the nine "principles of war" presented in December 1921 by the U.S. War Department in Training Regulation 10-5 were identical in title to the eight principles of strategy that appeared in Fuller's 1916 journal article. Apparently the authors of the training regulation were more inclined to favor the titles Fuller used rather than the titles used in the 1920 British *Field Service Regulations*. Four of the titles were identical in all three lists: economy of force, surprise, security, and cooperation. Fuller and the U.S. War Department used the titles *objective, offensive, mass,* and *movement* where the British *FSR* opted for *maintenance of the objective, offensive action, concentration,* and *maneuver*. The titles in the U.S. list and Fuller's also appeared in the same order, with the exception of "simplicity," which was an addition to the U.S. list that was inserted before the final principle, "cooperation." Naylor's discussion of "simplicity" suggested that this "principle," which lacks the background in military theory that is characteristic of other principles, was possibly added to the American list in reaction to the "French way of doing things in World War I." Naylor wrote:

> Before the World War, our General Service Schools taught that orders and instructions should be brief and straight from the shoulder. When we got to France we began to receive orders, metaphorically speaking, "a mile long" and the idea became quite general that in order to "get by" with an order, it has to be long anyway.[55]

Naylor further confirmed the idea that "simplicty" was a true principle of war by stating that Napoleon preferred simple maneuvers. In citing the origins of each of the other principles, Naylor claimed that they were illustrated throughout history but that it was necessary to "go no further than the days of Napoleon for the enunciated word."[56] No mention was made of Fuller or of the British *Field Service Regulations* with regard to the "enunciated word." When discussing the origins and meaning of each "principle," Naylor cited the theory and practices of Foch, von Moltke, Napoleon, and even Epaminondas, the Theban warrior who defeated the Spartans in 371 B.C.

Shortly after the appearance of the official U.S. list, both acceptance and criticism of the concept of a definitive list of principles of war were evident in military literature. The debate over "principles" that raged in Great Britain and France extended. Charles Howland, an instructor at Leavenworth, and Robert Albion, a civilian history professor, each published books, *A Military History of the World War* and *Introduction to Military History,* respectively, that used the War Department's nine "principles of war" as pedagogical tools. A cavalry officer accepted them as "good old fashioned horse sense" in a 1926 article, and in 1930 a young lieutenant concluded that Joshua "carried out to the letter those nine principles of war which have since so often been broken by leaders considered by many to be greater than Joshua."[57]

Criticism of the principles was also heard. Lieutenant Colonel Oliver Robinson commented from Fort Leavenworth, "I have preferred to use the *idea* as the framework around which to build, rather than the *principle,* as there is ample ground for doubt as to whether some of them are true principles."[58] In 1934 at the Infantry School at Fort Benning, Georgia, *Infantry in Battle* was published under the direction of Colonel George C. Marshall. The purpose of the book was to emphasize the lessons of the world war for leaders of small units, and its opening sentence read, "The art of war has no traffic with rules, for the infinitely varied circumstances and conditions of combat never produce exactly the same situation twice."[59] As in Great Britain, criticism led first to a change in the "immutable principles"— "Fire and Movement" replaced "Movement" as the fifth principle and "Simplicity" moved ahead of "Security" (see appendix 46)—and in August 1928 to the abandoning of the list altogether.[60]

No definitive list of "principles of war" in the format of title and terse explanation appeared in official U.S. Army doctrine between 1928 and 1949, but the concept reappeared during the 1930s both in service journals and in service school publications. In 1931, for example, a list of ten "principles of offensive combat" appeared in the army's *Tactics and Technique of Infantry in Offensive Combat* (see appendix 48). Each of the ten principles was listed with title and explanation, and six of the titles were identical with titles of "principles of war" enumerated in the training regulations of the 1920s. In 1934, an instructor at the Command and General Staff School at Fort Leavenworth, wrote, "No set of principles is the last word, because human beings are not infallible. But each set, honestly built up and dispassionately tested by practical work, will undoubtedly push us farther along in the knowledge of war, the science, and therefore in the practice of war, the art."[61] He proposed that combat power, control, objective, mass, movement, and security were among the most important concepts to be considered, and in an article published under the pseudonym, "Signifer," in 1935, he offered a new list and format for the "principles of war" that recalled some of the metaphysical trappings Fuller used in *The Foundations of the Science of War.*

Perhaps Signifer's contorted list drove more ordered thinkers to return to a simple enumeration of principles, for in 1936 the staff school published a list of seven "principles of strategy for an independent corps or army in a theater of operations" (see appendix 50). Each of the seven concepts was identical with one of the nine former "principles of war." This publication was used in the curriculum at the Fort Leavenworth staff school, and hence, the list concept returned to the mainstream of U.S. Army military education. The general discussion of the application of the "principles," however, contrasted markedly with the discussion that had appeared in Training Regulation 10-5 in 1921, for a caveat concerning the "principles' " applicability was now strongly voiced:

In war we deal with concrete cases. For this reason, the principles of strategy can serve only as a sort of general guide. Each campaign must be thought out and analyzed in all its parts. Out of this analysis should come the decision which can never be deduced from preconceived abstract principles.[62]

Ironically, the "1921 nine" were republished in 1936 in the inaugural volume of the *Military Digest* where it was stated, "These principles are immutable and unchanging. They are not subject to exception or variation. They are basic and as old as warfare itself. . . . The proper application of these principles of war constitutes the true measure of military genius."[63] The credit line of the article indicated that it was taken from Command and General Staff School publications.

The nine certainly were not universally accepted, for in the next few years, articles appeared that proposed a variety of guiding principles for the conduct of war. One source listed singleness of purpose, simplicity of procedure, and spirit of initiative, and another proposed the principle of preparation, the principle of offensive action, and the principle of commitment.[64] The latter author, Captain Theodore Kalakuka, began by stating that "our military instruction is based on nine tenets of war," but he added that the nine and other lists "overlooked the lessons of history" and confused principles with requirements. To confuse further the entire matter of principles of war, the Leavenworth staff school published yet another list of "principles of war" in 1939. This list was introduced with the statement, "There are certain *principles of war* whose observance is vital in war" (see appendix 52).[65] The titles of the "principles" in this list were nearly identical with those from the 1921 list, and the concepts behind the titles were certainly in agreement with six of the concepts behind the 1921 titles.

The official U.S. Army conceptions concerning the form, content, and existence of principles of war was further complicated throughout the 1920s and 1930s by the references, content, and form of principles stated in the U.S. Army *Field Service Regulations* (*FSR*). Pre-World War I editions of the *FSR* had addressed principles in an increasingly definitive manner, and the first postwar revision of the *FSR*, published in 1923, contained nine terse enumerated subsections in a section entitled, "Combat. General Principles" (see appendix 45). No titles were used with the subsections, but eight of them accurately, though apparently incidentally, explained eight of the nine titles used in the 1921 Training Regulation 10-5. For example, the first sentence in the "Combat,

General Principles" section, "The ultimate objective of all military operations is the destruction of the enemy's armed forces by battle," would have explained the training regulation's "Principle of the Objective." The "Principle of Surprise" corresponded to the subsection of the *FSR* that began, "All combat action must be based upon the effect of surprise." No subsection in the *FSR* explained the "Principle of Unity of Command." Many sections other than the combat section of the 1923 *FSR* began with general principles, and the term *principle of war* was not used. However, the ideas that corresponded to the "principles" in the training regulations were clearly stated.

In 1939, *FSR* was revised, and the resulting manual was known as FM 100-5, *Field Service Regulations.* It was the first time that the "FM" abbreviation and a number was assigned to a U.S. Army field manual. This manual continued to reflect the trend toward the definitive statement of a list of "principles of war." Its section "General Principles" in the chapter entitled, "The Conduct of War," like the 1923 edition, also had nine enumerated subsections. Seminal words were highlighted by italics: the *ultimate objective,* concentration of *superior forces, offensive* action, *unity of effort, surprise, security,* and *simple* and *direct* plans (see appendix 53). Two of the subsections were descriptive, but only one concept related to principles from the 1921 list was lacking (maneuver) because two other "principles" were addressed in a single subsection.

The 1941 edition of the *Field Service Regulations* paralleled the 1939 edition, but the chapter, "The Conduct of War," was renamed "The Exercise of Command," and "General Principles" became "Doctrines of Combat." The enumerated sections were reduced from nine to seven (see appendix 54). The 1941 edition also warned, "Set rules and methods must be avoided. They limit imagination and initiative which are so important in the successful prosecution of war."[66]

The concepts often referred to as "principles," however, prevailed. Although often claimed to be intrinsically eternal, the "principles of war" experienced an era of extreme uncertainty from the early 1920s through World War II. Different views on the efficacy of a list of "principles" were apparent within the armies of the major powers, and even after a position was accepted as doctrine, its detractors could always hope that the next revision of a capstone manual would bring military thought closer to the "reality" as they perceived it.

The first official list of "principles of war" appeared in Great Britain in 1920, and a kindred list followed in the United Stated in 1921. In most other countries, notably France and Germany, however, the formality of an official list was rejected throughout the 1920s and 1930s in spite of individuals in both countries who offered terse aphorisms as a basis for doctrine. The debate over the existence, benefit, and format of principles of war continued into the 1930s, but as the decade wore on, military minds turned increasingly from the ethereal concepts of principles to more practical theories manifested in Blitzkrieg and the Maginot mentality. In the early 1940s, theory was subordinated to events—Dunkirk, Pearl Harbor, and Stalingrad. Reactions to such events were specific and event oriented; little effort was expended in the formulation and promulgation of general rules and guiding principles.

## NOTES

1. J. F. C. Fuller, *Memoirs of an Unconventional Soldier*, p. 388.
2. Ibid.
3. Ibid.
4. Great Britain, War Office, *Field Service Regulations, Vol. II, Operations* (provisional), 1920, p. 14.
5. Ibid., p. 15.
6. Fuller, *Memoirs*, p. 389.
7. J. F. C. Fuller, "The Foundations of the Science of War," *Army Quarterly* 1 (October 1920):90.
8. A. H. Burne, "The Battle of Kadesh and the Principles of War," *Army Quarterly* 4 (April 1922):123.
9. J. F. C. Fuller, *The Foundations of the Sceince of War*, p. 221.
10. From the *Civil and Military Gazette* quoted in "The Value and Originality of 'The Foundations of the Science of War,' " *Army Quarterly* 12 (July 1926):358, and *Quarterly Review of Literature* (April 1926): 165. See also Anthony J. Trythall, *"Boney" Fuller*, pp. 122-27, for other opinions of *The Foundations of the Science of War*.
11. C. V. Usborne, "The Principles of War—A Dialogue," *Journal of the Royal United Service Institution* 74 (August 1929):475-76.

12. 'Phormio,' "Economy of Forces: A Plea for the Older Meaning," *Journal of the Royal United Service Institution* 75 (August 1930):492.

13. Frederick Maurice, *British Strategy: A Study of the Application of the Principles of War,* p. 47.

14. F. E. Whitton, "Economy of Forces," Letter to the Editor, *Journal of the Royal United Service Institution* 75 (November 1930):835.

15. John Keegan, "The Inter-war Years," *A Guide to the Sources of British Military History,* ed. Robin Higham, p. 461.

16. Basil H. Liddell Hart, "The 'Ten Commandments' of the Combat Unit, Suggestions on Its Theory and Training," *Journal of the Royal United Service Institution* 64 (May 1919):292.

17. As translated and quoted in Maurice, *British Strategy,* p. 3.

18. Eugène Cholet, *A propos de doctrine: les leçons du passé confirmées par celles de la grande guerre,* p. 40, my translation.

19. "The Value and Originality of 'The Foundations of the Science of War,' " p. 357.

20. France, Minister of War, Army Staff, *Instruction provisoire du octobre 1921 sur l'emploi tactique des grandes unités,* p. 14, my translation.

21. Henri Michel, "Pour l'enseignement de l'organization à l'École supérieure de guerre," *Revue militaire française* 3 (1922):210.

22. H. François, "Des Principes de guerre," *Revue militaire française* 3 (April 1922):104, my translation.

23. Ibid., p. 109.

24. L. Merat, "Un Principe—un procédé: Economie des forces, concentration sur le théâtre principal," *Revue militaire générale* 11 (March 1922):197

25. Bernard Serrigny, *Réflexions sur l'art de la guerre,* 2d ed., p. 201, my translation.

26. F. Culmann, *Stratégie, La Manoeuvre stratégique offensive dans la guerre de mouvements,* p. 21, my translation.

27. H. Lecomte, "Hérésies stratégiques," *Revue militaire suisse* 9 (September 1923):386, my translation.

28. Pascal Marie Lucas, *L'Evolution des idées tactique en France et en Allemagne pendant la guerre de 1914-1918,* pp. 316-17, my translation.

29. Ibid., p. 318.

30. Charles de Gaulle, "Doctrine a priori ou doctrine des circonstances?" *Revue militaire française* 15 (1925):306, my translation.

31. France, Minister of War, Army Staff, *Instruction sur l'emploi tactique des grandes unités,* 1936, p. 21, my translation.

32. Ibid., p. 32.

33. See Eugene Carrias, *La Pensée militaire française,* p. 332.

34. Friedrich von Bernhardi, *The War of the Future in the Light of the Lessons of the World War,* trans. F. A. Holt, 2d ed., p. 19.

35. Friedrich von Cochenhausen, *Die Truppenführung: Ein Handbuch für den Truppenführer und seine Gehilfen,* 1923, foreword, my translation.

36. Gerhard Ritter, *Frederick the Great, A Historical Profile,* trans. and ed. Peter Paret, p. 131.

37. Von Cochenhausen, *Die Truppenführung,* 11th ed., 1935, pp. 176-77, my translation.

38. Hermann Foertsch, *The Art of Modern Warfare,* trans. Theodore W. Knauth, p. 31.

39. Leon Trotsky, *Voennaia Mysl'i Revoliutsiia,* vol. II, 1921, p. 209 quoted in Raymond L. Garthoff, *Soviet Military Doctrine,* p. 33.

40. Robin Higham, *The Military Intellectuals in Britain, 1918-1939,* p. 72.

41. J.F.C. Fuller, *Lectures on F.S.R. III,* p. 10.

42. U.S.S.R., People's Commissariat of Defense, *Field Service Regulations,* trans. Charles Berman, p. i.

43. Ibid., pp. 1-2.

44. Jennings C. Wise, "The Battle of Elah," *Infantry Journal* 16 (March 1920):748.

45. William K. Naylor, *Principles of Strategy with Historical Illustrations,* pp. 49, 53.

46. Ibid., p. 1.

47. The discussion of Hjalmar Erickson's career is based on information contained in the *Army Register,* in the Army War College cross-reference file, Carlisle Barracks, Pennsylvania, and in an obituary, *Nevada State Journal,* 3 March 1949.

48. Hjalmar Erickson, "The Doctrine of War and of Training," lecture delivered at the U.S. Army General Staff College, 17 April 1920, p. 3.

49. Ibid.

50. Hjalmar Erickson, "Remarks on Doctrines of War and of Training," lecture delivered at the U.S. Army General Staff College, 20 April 1921, p. 3.

51. J. M. Scammel, "Military Education and Indoctrination," *Infantry Journal* 18 (March 1921):257.

52. U.S. Army, TR 10-5, *Doctrines, Principles, and Methods,* 23 December 1921, p. 2.

53. These lectures were published as *The Marne Miracle Illustrating the Principles of War.*

54. William K. Naylor, "The Principles of War," *Infantry Journal* 22 (February 1923):144.

55. Ibid., p. 146.

56. Ibid., p. 418. An instructor in the Department of Tactics at the

United States Military Academy issued the same complaint in a lecture to cadets on the "principles of war." His discussion was probably based on Naylor's journal article, but where Naylor complained of orders that were "metaphorically speaking 'a mile long,' " Captain Heraty complained of French orders "literally 'a mile long' containing many sheets of paper." The Heraty lecture was bound in a volume of lectures that has no title page or other bibliographical explanations. The cover of the volume reads, "Headquarters, U.S.C.C. [United States Corps of Cadets], Lectures, Office of the Commandant of Cadets."

57. W. F. Pride, "The Principles of War and Their Application to Small Cavalry Units," *Cavalry Journal* 35 (1926):54; Ralph E. Doty, "Joshua and the Principles of War," *Infantry Journal* 44 (August 1930):178.

58. Oliver P. Robinson, *The Fundamentals of Military Strategy,* p. v.

59. U.S. Army, *Infantry in Battle,* 2d ed., p. 1.

60. Thomas R. Phillips, "Word Magic of the Military Mystics," *Infantry Journal* 46 (September-October 1939):403, and U.S. Army, TR 10-5, *Doctrines, Principles, and Methods,* 15 August 1928.

61. Edward S. Johnson, "A Science of War," *Review of Military Literature: The Command and General Staff School Quarterly* 14 (June 1934):122.

62. U.S. Army Command and General Staff School, *The Principles of Strategy for an Independent Corps or Army in a Theater of Operations,* p. 14.

63. "A Brief Discussion of the Principles of War," *Military Digest* 1 (December 1936):16.

64. Frank Parker, "The Ever-changing Application of the Unchanging Principles of War," *Military Review* 19 (December 1939):6; Theodore Kalakuka, "Streamlined Principles of War, and the Greatest of These Is Preparation," *Military Digest* 4 (March 1939):53.

65. U.S. Army Command and General Staff School, *The Offensive* (Tentative), p. 8.

66. U.S. Army, FM 100-5, *Field Service Regulations—Operations,* May 1941, p. II.

# 7

# REFURBISHED PRINCIPLES AND DOCTRINAL DEBATE

THE MILITARY THEORY and doctrine of the 1930s were severely challenged by the reality of nearly six years of conflict in Europe and the Mediterranean and by nearly eight years of conflict in Asia and the Pacific. The numbers of men and the multimegatons of materiel to support them exceeded the magnitude of any previous war. War's destructiveness increased, too, and the fear of an atomic Armageddon followed the horror that fell on Hiroshima and Nagasaki. To those who tried to manage the violence of the century's second total war, it was a topsy-turvy world—a world gone mad. For military professionals, however, it was a world in which order and control had to be established.

The "principles of war" were well established in theory on the eve of the war, but doctrinal sources, like field-service regulations, had generally abandoned their definitive expression in the form of a list of titles and aphorisms. Individual principles were often spoken of in articles, books, and instructions published during the war, and the 1920 British titles were given new definitions and published as training memorandums in Canada and New Zealand in 1943. But no definitive list seemed destined to appear as either doctrine or as the panacea for victory. In the midst of operational planning and execution, it seemed unlikely that anyone would take the time to think of war in an abstract and philosophical sense. Even J. F. C. Fuller devoted his attentions during the war toward political and operational criticism rather than toward the presentation of what many still viewed as pedantic formulas.

Ironically though, one British officer placed great importance on the benefit of a list of "principles of war." Unlike Fuller's list, which had appeared anonymously in a military journal during World War I, the new list appeared in a pamphlet that was disseminated directly to the highest ranking officers in the Twenty-first Army Group and throughout the British Army. Its author had no desire to remain anonymous, for Field Marshal Bernard L. Montgomery rarely recoiled from any opportunity that publicized his views and opinions. His pamphlet encouraged the acceptance of the definitive list of "principles of war" throughout the British Commonwealth. The pamphlet was also indicative of the trend that resulted in the almost universal acceptance of the idea suggested by Jomini a century earlier: that the principles of war are few in number and are capable of being simply expressed.

Bernard Montgomery issued four pamphlets to his forces in the course of the war. The first three dealt with the infantry division in battle, the armored division in battle, and air power in support of land operations, and Montgomery concluded that the fourth, "High Command in War," was necessary to complete the series.[1] In the introduction to this pamphlet, he wrote:

> The first part of this pamphlet deals with the principles of war as I consider them to be. These are:—

(a)    Air power.

(b)    Administration.

(c)    The initiative.

(d)    Morale.

(e)    Surprise.

(f)    Concentration.

(g)    Co-operation.

(h)    Simplicity.

I have written at some length on the first four as their great importance has come to the fore in this war.

The last four are old stagers and can speak for themselves.

Montgomery continued by stating that his pamphlets had no official significance and that he recognized that not all senior officers would agree with his views, but he hoped that they might provide assistance "to one or two commanders in the stress and strain of modern battle."

Montgomery was the only senior commander to present a list of "principles of war." In fact, it is unusual to find a modern senior commander who has written extensively on the theory of war. Hence, Montgomery's reasons for enunciating his theory are particularly revealing. He wrote in "High Command in War":

1.   A war is won by victories in battle. No victories will be gained unless commanders will sort out clearly in their own minds those essentials which are vital for success, and will ensure that those things form the framework on which all action is based.

2.   There are certain points which are fundamental; they are important always and to neglect any of them will probably lead to failure; they will apply, in a greater or lesser degree, to all commanders at all times.

3.   I give below those points which, in my opinion, are fundamental and are vital for success. Close attention to these points has paid me a good dividend, and I commend them to all commanders. I consider that these points form the principles of modern war.

He made no claim to infallibility or to immutability. His views were balanced and his intentions sincere.

Upon Montgomery's appointment as chief of the Imperial General Staff after the war, he called together the senior service commanders and chiefs of staff of the Dominion armies to tackle "essential and urgent" matters. He wrote in his memoirs: "The first thing was obviously to get inter-Service agreement to the fundamental principles of war, and I drafted out these principles as I saw them, and got them agreed to by the First Sea Lord and the Chief of the Air Staff."[2] Montgomery's new list included ten principles. The principles of Administration and the Maintenance of Morale were the significant additions to the 1920 British list. "Selection and Maintenance of the Aim" replaced "Maintenance of the Objective"; "Flexibility" replaced "Mobility"; "Economy of Effort" replaced "Economy of Force"; "Concentration of Force" replaced "Concentration"; "Offensive Action," "Surprise," "Security," and "Co-operation" remained unchanged from the earlier British list. The ten principles have remained part of British doctrine to the present day. Canada, New Zealand, and Australia followed Montgomery's and the British lead.

French doctrine slowly evolved toward the presentation of a definitive list of "principles of war," but the French have been less fastidious than the British or Americans in their identification of a single list of fundamentals. French sources continued to speak of rules, laws, and principles without clearly defining the relationship of such terms. Hence, the "fundamentals" in French doctrine since World War II have appeared in various guises. In lectures at the École supérieure de guerre in the mid-1950s, for example, six "fundamental laws of war and of strategy" were presented:

The law of movement.
The law of force.
The law of the offensive.
The law of protection.
The law of friction.
The law of the unforeseen.[3]

Six "fundamental laws of war and of tactics" also appeared. These were identical to the laws of war and strategy except that "Shock" and "Fire" replaced the laws of the offensive and of force.

A decade later, the school published *Notes relative à la tactique* (Tactical notes) in which the principles of concentration of effort and of freedom of action were discussed in detail. The discussion concluded that the art of war consisted of establishing the proper balance, referred to as "economy of forces" between these two opposing principles. In *Instruction générale sur les forces terrestres* (General directive on land forces), published in 1973, three principles and five rules that "have a permanent character" were presented. The introduction to them stated, "The principles constitute the fundamental laws of tactics; the rules which are derived from them define the proper behavior or attitudes to guarantee success."[4] The "principles" were entitled, "Concentration of efforts," "Freedom of action," and "Economy of forces," and the rules were called, "the Initiative," "Surprise," "Aggressiveness," "Continuity of action," and "Simplicity and flexibility."

These two brief lists, the most definitive expression of principles and rules that have appeared in French doctrine to date, bore striking resemblances to Jomini's, Bonnal's, and Foch's thoughts on the theory of war. Jomini had written in 1806 that a few fundamental principles govern the conduct of war and that the first of these was "to operate with the greatest part of one's forces in a combined effort on the decisive point," or in the shortened form characteristic of the twentieth century, "Concentration of efforts." From the fundamental principle, Jomini derived supporting maxims. Most of the ideas contained in the five rules of the *Instruction générale* had appeared in these enumerations. In 1849, Jomimi wrote that possibly only three or four principles existed. He never definitively enumerated them, but half a century later, Foch listed four. A century and a half later, an official French publication listed three. The principles recalled the teachings of Bonnal and Foch that maintained that the commander's mental attitudes and behavior were the critical components of success in war. Two of the 1973 principles, "Freedom of action" and "Economy of forces," were identical to principles that Foch had spoken of in the 1890s. Little evidence exists to support the claim that the French enunciation of principles of war resulted from either the British list or from the influence of British writers. Rather the first definitive list of principles announced in French doctrine appeared to be derived largely from earlier and peculiarly French institutions.

In the post-World War II era, the German Army continued to reject the elucidation of a single brief list of principles of war.

"Principles," however, which might guide the commander and which claimed to be neither definitive nor immutable, were discussed in official publications. For example, in a section entitled, "Basic Operational Principles" (*Führungsgrundsätze*) in the *Truppenführung* of 1962, the first paragraph stated that since the leading of troops is an art, its doctrines can never be completely described and that there are no formulas for the battlefield. The paragraph continued by stating, "Every commander, however, must be guided by clear principles."⁵ The next twenty-two contained the "principles" that were applicable in both nuclear and non-nuclear wars, and thirteen further paragraphs addressed the "principles" applicable either exclusively to nuclear or exclusively to non-nuclear war. Key words were emphasized in these pithy paragraphs so that each paragraph or "principle" could be referred to by a title or name. The "principle," "Great success is based on bold *risks,*" therefore could become the "principle of risk." Many of the emphasized words were identical to the titles of principles identified in the doctrine of other nations—freedom of action, mobility, speed, and simplicity—but significantly, the German doctrine neither referred to the principles by title alone nor attempted to summarize the most important principles in a brief list.

The 1973 edition of the *Truppenführung* was more explicit in its discussion and definition of principles of war. This German regulation talked of tactical principles, but since tactics was defined as encompassing all areas of command, its "tactical principles" were like the "principles of war" in Great Britain and the United States. In spite of the acceptance of some "tactical rules and principles," the German regulation maintained the German preference for the Moltkean idea that war is a series of unique events that cannot be subjected to rigid formulas. The regulations stated, "Success is ensured only by the free action of the commanders within the framework of their missions. Creative, exacting, and critical thinking during maneuvers of all kinds will prepare military commanders of all ranks in peacetime for their combat assignments." However, the regulations continued in an un-Moltkean way: "This gives rise to uniform tactical concepts which constitute a decisive prerequisite for the necessary cooperation of all forces."[6] A series of enumerated paragraphs contained advice and counsel similar to that found in some lists of principles of war.

> 1007. Freedom of action must be preserved or gained and must be the constant concern of all commanders. . . .
>
> 1008. He who would be successful, must dare. . . .
>
> 1009. Simple, logical action is the most reliable. . . .
>
> 1010. The speed, mobility, and firepower of a unit can be fully brought to bear only through the skill of the commander. . . .
>
> 1011. Success in battle depends on the performance of each and every individual, but especially on the coordinated cooperation of all participating commanders, units and equipment. . . .
>
> 1012. Success can be achieved with less effort through surprise.[7]

The enumerations continued for pages, and the resulting list was far longer than the comparable American and British lists. The concepts were present in German doctrine, but their form continued to reflect German traditions more strongly than non-German traditions.

Military theory in the Soviet Union began to identify concepts that closely resembled the British and American principles during World War II. It is doubtful that the Western lists had any impact on Soviet theory, for there was relatively little exchange of ideas even after Lend-Lease and the entry of the United States into the war. In the early 1940s Soviet military doctrine emphasized a number of "permanently operating factors," which were said to "decide the course and outcome of wars."[8] In contrast to the permanently operating factors, transitory or temporary factors were fundamentals that might be significant at any given stage of a war. The most important of the transitory factors was surprise. The "permanently operating factors" were codified by Joseph Stalin in order number 55 of 23 February 1942, but the ideas had been dominant in Soviet doctrine long before the Stalin order. In the words of Stalin, the permanently operating factors were:

1. The stability of the rear.
2. The morale of the army.
3. The quantity and quality of divisions.
4. The armament of the army.
5. The organizing ability of the command personnel.[9]

As long as Stalin remained in power, the permanently operating factors formed the basis of Soviet doctrine. They were widely repeated in military writings and by such high-ranking leaders as Marshals Zhukov, Malinovsky, Konev, Vasilevsky, and Sokolovsky. When Nikita Khruschev began his denunciation of Stalin and the Stalin cult, the use of the term *permanently operating factors* virtually ceased, but the concepts remained. In 1957, fundamental factors attributed to Lenin were presented:

the economic and moral basis of the rear

the morale of the armed forces

the quantity and quality of combat technology

the ability of military men.[10]

Stalin had been dead for four years, but "permanently operating factors" survived in a slightly modified guise. In the late 1960s and 1970s, a more elaborate basis of doctrine, which included "the principles of the military art," ultimately supplanted the permanently operating factors.

According to Colonel Vasili Ye. Savkin, a member of the faculty of the Frunze Military Academy, the principles of the military art are based upon an understanding of the laws of war and the laws of armed conflict. Savkin equated the principles of the military art to the concept of principles of war as stated in postwar editions of the U.S. Army's FM 100-5, *Field Service Regulations,* with the exception that the "principles of war" were not deduced from the objective laws of war and of armed conflict. Savkin explained that this failure resulted from the fear of bourgeois military theorists "to admit the presence of objective laws of social life, the action of which in the final account determines the inevitable fate of capitalism and the victory of socialism."[11] Savkin stated and discussed at length the four laws of war (see appendix 66) and the two laws of armed conflict (see appendix 67), from which he claimed that the principles of the military art were deduced. The principles were defined as the "basic ideas and most important recommendations for the organization and conduct of battles, operations, and war as a whole."[12] By definition these principles included the principles of tactics, strategy, and operational art, which in Soviet terminology is the connecting branch between strategy (political decisions) and tactics (the activities of the battle-field). Savkin's principles were:

a.   Mobility and high rates of combat operations;

b.   Concentration of main efforts and creation of superiority in forces and means over the enemy at the decisive place and at the decisive time;

c.   Surprise;

d.   Combat activeness;

e.   Preservation of the combat effectiveness of friendly forces;

f.   Conformity of the goal and plan of the operation (battle) to the conditions of the actual situation;

g.   Coordination.[13]

He claimed that these principles were "the most important ones" and that as the means of war develop, other principles can be form-ulated. Furthermore, Savkin claimed that the list he compiled was "according to views of 1953-1959," but his views are undoubtedly widely held contemporary ones in the Soviet Union as well. The Savkin book, *The Principles of Operational Art and Tactics,* in which he expostulated his theory, is not a doctrinal source, but the fact of its publication demonstrates a high degree of official sanction. Official or unofficial, it demonstrated the proclivity of a leading Soviet military scholar toward the enumeration of a few fundamental principles. A free translation of the titles reveals long-established bourgeois ideas:

The Principle of Mobility.

The Principle of Concentration.

The Principle of Surprise.

The Principle of the Offensive.

The Principle of Security.

The Principle of the Objective.

The Principle of Cooperation.

Stripped of their ideological base, Soviet principles closely resembled many Western "principles of war."

The tendency evident in the Soviet Union to attribute its fundamentals of war to a national hero such as Stalin or Lenin was also evident in the doctrine of the Red Chinese Army, whose principal tenets were attributed to Mao Tse-tung. In lectures delivered at the Red Army College in 1936, Mao discussed the laws of revolutionary war and enumerated six problems of strategy, each of which pointed out considerations that commanders should be cognizant of (see appendix 51). They bore little resemblance to the concepts included in Western lists. Mao claimed that the problems of strategy could be elevated to the "higher plane of principle," but he warned:

> In studying the laws for directing wars that occur at different historical stages, that differ in nature and that are waged in different places and by different nations, we must fix our attention on the characteristics and development of each, and must oppose a mechanical approach to the problem of war.
>
> We need directors of war who can play a significant role. All the laws for directing war developed as history develops and as war develops; nothing is changeless.[14]

Mao also warned of the hazards of using principles to solve problems of war:

> All military laws and military theorists which are in the nature of principles are the experience of past wars summed up by people in former days or in our own times. We should seriously study these lessons, paid for in blood, which are a heritage of

past wars. That is one point. But there is another. We should put these conclusions to the test of our own experience, assimilating what is useful, rejecting what is useless, and adding what is specifically our own. The latter is very important, for otherwise we cannot direct a war.[15]

In spite of his warnings and of similar warnings by many serious students who have reflected upon the question of the existence of principles of war, Mao developed ten basic principles of war. They were revised through the decades of the communist Chinese struggle against Japan and nationalist China; after the Korean War, they were:

The principle of aims.

The principle of mobile concentration.

The principle of annihilation.

The principle of fighting on the move.

The principle of the offensive.

The principle of surprise attack.

The principle of continuous action.

The principle of autonomy.

The principle of unity.

The principle of military spirit.[16]

(See appendix 61 for an explanation of each principle.) The concepts are similar to those presented in Western lists, but to claim that Mao was influenced by such lists is not possible.

The relationship that exists between the content and form of the various officially sanctioned principles suggests the objective value of one "principle" or another; the genesis of the lists reveals often subtle relationships that exist within the respective societies. For example, the attribution of the Soviet permanently operating factors to Stalin and later to Lenin suggests the influence and importance of national heros in the Soviet Union. Montgomery's role in the reintroduction of the "principles of war" to British doctrine is indicative of the influence he possessed throughout the armed forces of Great Britain and the Commonwealth. In the United States, however, the principles seemed to have an anonymous corps of supporters rather than a single benefactor. In fact the trend toward the increasingly definitive expression of principles that is apparent from the "Combat Principles" of the 1914 *FSR* (see appendix 26) through the "Combat, General Principles" of the 1923 *FSR* (see appendix 45), through the "Conduct of War, General Principles" of the 1939 *FSR* (Tentative) (see appendix 53) through the "Doctrines of Combat" of the 1941 *FSR* (see appendix 54) to the "Principles of War" of the 1949 *FSR* (see appendix 56) is so progressive that the list seemed to be the logical and preordained result of labors of generations of military writers.

A close examination of the descriptive paragraphs in the various *FSR* discussions reveals long phrases and entire sentences that can be followed from edition to edition until the thought is finally established as a descriptive element of one of the listed "principles." For example, the 1914 *FSR* stated, "Simple and direct plans are productive of the best results in warfare." The 1923 edition and the 1939 edition stated, "Simple and direct plans and methods are alone practicable in war." The 1941 edition read, "Simple and direct plans and methods with prompt and thorough execution are often decisive in the attainment of success." And in 1949, the same thought was found in the opening sentence of the paragraph entitled "Simplicity": "Plans should be as simple and direct as the attainment of the objective will permit."

The ideas associated with each of the "principles" can be traced through all or some of the succession of twentieth-century *FSR*s, and the same ideas in other forms can be found in the predecessors of the *FSR*s: for example, in the *Regulations for the Army of the United States: Troops in Command* (1892) and the earlier *Revised U.S. Army Regulations, 1863*.[17] And earlier writers on the theory of war from Jomini back to Sun Tzu discussed all or some of the concepts that became "principles." Ideas behind the titles of principles are often as old as the art of war itself, but the titles and the acceptance of the definitive list of relatively few principles are modern inventions. The exclusive use of titles dates to the late nineteenth century, and the definitive list was a product of J. F. C. Fuller's critical and ordered mind. The return of the definitive list of nine "principles of war" to U.S. Army doctrine occurred with the publication of the 1949 *FSR*. The list undoubtedly was influenced by the persistence of the concepts and titles associated with the lists published in the U.S. Army training regulations of the 1920s, by the succession of thoughts in the twentieth-century *FSR*s, and to a lesser extent by the list that Montgomery had brought to British doctrine at the end of World War II. The list from the 1949 *FSR,* however, was unique even though there was much similarity with both the British twentieth-century lists and the U.S. training regulation list of 1921. The 1949 list appeared as just nine numbered paragraphs, each center-headed by a boldfaced capitalized title: "the objective," "simplicity," "unity of command," "the offensive," "maneuver," "mass," "economy of forces," "surprise," and "security."[18] (See appendix 56 for the explanations that accompanied the titles.)

The extent to which the format and content of these principles was influenced by one or more key individuals is difficult to determine, but the contribution of one person can be clarified. General J. Lawton Collins was the army chief of staff when the 1949 *FSR* was published, and he had given several lectures at the Army War College between 1938 and 1940 that suggested that he might have been an ardent supporter of either the list concept of principles or of concepts that formerly had been or might be established as principles. When asked about the principles, however, he could not "recall what the lectures were even about, let alone fix them in the context of the principles of war."[19]

When the list of "principles" was published in the British *Field Service Regulations* of 1920, an intense debate concerning the existence, format, and content of "principles of war" began in military journals and books on war. The debate, if it could be called that, that followed the reintroduction of the "principles of war" to British doctrine after World War II was mild by comparison—in large part, undoubtedly, because of Montgomery's association with and support of the new list. Some attention to the list was evident in British journals long after the war, and significantly,

the commentators included an admiral, a major from the Pakistani
Army, and a major from the Royal Australian Army. The admiral
proposed that three "principles" should be added to the list of ten:

1. Constantly attack the armed forces of the enemy.
2. Time.
3. Justice, or more accurately, justification.[20]

The Pakistani major proposed separate lists for grand strategy,
strategy, and tactics and claimed that "administration . . . slipped
in under false pretenses," and the Australian major offered a plea
for the inclusion of "intelligence" as a "principle of war."[21]

The establishment of the lists in the Commonwealth nations
generated a mild debate in Australian and, especially, Canadian
journals. An Australian captain proposed a list different from the
sanctioned one:

  (i)   Brilliant, inspiring leadership at all levels.
  (ii)  Correct selection and maintenance of the aim.
  (iii) Full, accurate information; none but deceptive information for
  the enemy.
  (iv)  Carefully planned, adequate organization.
  (v)   Sound, forward planning of operations.
  (vi)  Speedy, vigorous execution of plans.[22]

The possibilities of a nuclear war inspired an Australian ordnance
captain to write in 1961 that the "principles of war" were not
unchangeable and that a need existed for a revised list in light of
nuclear considerations.[23] More recently, an Australian engineer
proposed a new list of seven "immutable and fundamental principles of war": deception, security, concentration and dispersion,
the offensive, selection and maintenance of the aim, the ability to
move, and cooperation.[24] "Dispersion" was added as a result of
the mass casualties that can result from the detonation of a single
nuclear warhead in the vicinity of concentrated troops.

Articles in Canadian journals covered a variety of responses
and opinions concerning the list of "principles" accepted by the

Canadian chiefs of staff. Among the first to appear was an editorial stressing that military history confirmed that the official list was not "a set of iron-clad rules from which there must be no jot of deviation."[25] A cavalry captain took up the semantic question of principles; he concluded that the object, surprise, flexibility, concentration, command, and offensive action were true principles. The others, he claimed, were a "bewildering assortment of concepts."[26]

In 1960, students at the Canadian Staff College were called upon to write an essay on the Canadian "principles of war." Three of these essays were published, and each expressed a different view of the principles. The first to be published expressed the view that the principles stated in Canadian doctrine were "inadequate and confusing to the student of war." The author, Captain D. G. Loomis, had published an earlier article on communist concepts of principles of war in which he admitted the difficulty of eliciting a brief Soviet list of principles (he presented such a list, however), and hence, his solution to the Canadian principles of war was to present two lists: one of principles of war and the other of rules of war.[27] Loomis's principles and rules attempted to relate the nature of war with societal values as Soviet theory did. The second student essay accepted the official list and offered a thoughtful discussion of each of the principles.[28] The third essay found the list to be acceptable for conventional war but lacking for nuclear war. A list and discussion of principles for nuclear war was proposed: selection and maintenance of the aim, offensive action, surprise, administration, command and leadership, flexibility, and the economical use of time and space.[29]

Doctrinal debate in the Commonwealth nations had little impact on the doctrine itself, but in the U.S. Army doctrinal responses to criticism and comment on the form and, to a lesser extent, on the content of the official principles had a significant impact on U.S. doctrine. Several reasons exist for this difference. First, the list concept of principles of war had never been closely identified with any American who might claim to be a national hero. Second, the U.S. Constitution guarantees freedom of speech, and speaking out was encouraged by the Army's chief of staff in 1977.[30] Third, civilian scholars in America have been especially critical of the concept of a list of "principles of war." For example, historian Peter Paret referred to the official principles of war as "a catalogue of commonplaces that . . . has served generations of soldiers as an excuse not to think things through for themselves."[31] The late Bernard Brodie's criticism of the "principles" was also evident. His *War and Politics* was particularly acerbic in this regard:

> It may be well that the consideration of a catalog of numbered principles (usually fewer than a dozen) with the barest definition of the meaning of each may be necessary to communicate to second-order minds (or minds too busy with the execution of plans to worry much about the specific validity of the ideas behind them) some conception of what the business is all about.[32]

A final factor that might explain the often intense doctrinal debate concerning "principles of war" in the United States since World War II is that some of the individuals involved in the debate were influential general officers. Debate that occurred outside the United States involved a great many captains and a few officers of higher and lower rank, but nothing was heard from generals, who set the tone for doctrine and policy. The rank of U.S. officers who wrote on the "principles of war" tended to be higher than that of officers writing in other countries as soon as the "principles of war" were reaffirmed in 1949, and as the debate continued in the 1970s, it involved some of the nation's highest-ranking generals.

The debate over "principles" involved many of the same topics involved in other countries and in other times. Definitions remained a problem to some writers; content and applicability bothered others. An engineer colonel proposed in 1953 that "democracy" be added to the list.[33] In 1954, "conservation" was suggested as a new principle.[34] In 1956, "bold imagination" was proposed as the "underlying principle that illuminates [all] the principles of war"; the same author argued that the "catechism" of principles had become obsolete, in part because of the advent of airborne and atomic warfare.[35] A brigadier general wrote in 1956 that the "principle of command" was in jeopardy—in spite of its absence from every official list of principles.[36] A signal corps major used a little imagination in fitting the official titles to definitions that involved psychological war requirements in a 1957 article.[37] Colonel Virgil Ney in *Notes on Guerrilla War; Principles and Practices* proposed a list of ten principles of guerrilla war: the environment, community security, community support, propaganda, proximity, deliberate delay, personal security, part-time function, modus operandi, and organization.[38] The form was familiar, the content cryptic. The impact of guerrilla war in general and the Vietnam war in particular prompted an infantry colonel, who believed that since 1921 the "principles" had proved to be impervious to change though subjected to "minor semantic revision," to call for a tenth principle: public support.[39] In 1966, a lieutenant colonel concluded that the official nine were quite adequate in counterinsurgency operations.[40] The form of the principles was also shown support by the proposing of a list of principles of logistics in 1977.[41] In the journals, the schools, and a variety of books on military theory, the "principles of war" stimulated rhetoric and original thinking.

Doctrinally, definitive lists of principles were officially adopted and generally accepted by the air force, navy, and marine corps, but in the army in the mid-1970s, the principles became a subject of debate and disagreement among the army's generals charged with the promulgation of doctrine.

In January 1973, a reorganization of major U.S. Army commands occurred. The Continental Army Command (CONARC), which had been responsible for training and forces within the continental United States, was supplanted in part by the Forces Command (FORSCOM), responsible primarily for units and unit training, and the Training and Doctrine Command (TRADOC), responsible primarily for individual training, army schools (except the United States Military Academy and the Army War College), and the formulation of doctrine. The rewriting of army doctrine to incorporate the lessons of the Arab-Israeli wars, especially the Yom Kippur war of 1973, and to disestablish some of the policies, methods, and practices that resulted from the army's long involvement in Vietnam, was one of the difficult tasks facing General William E. DePuy as the commander of TRADOC. In 1974,

Major General John H. Cushman, the commander of the Combined Arms Center and the commandant of the staff college at Fort Leavenworth, was directed by General DePuy to revise FM 100-5. Since 1949, FM 100-5 had been revised in 1954, 1962, and 1968, when the title was changed from FM 100-5 *Field Service Regulations* to FM 100-5 *Operations of Army Forces in the Field.* In each of these editions, the nine "principles of war" were presented and explained (see appendixes 62, 63, and 65). The titles of the principles were unchanged from the 1949 edition except that "economy of forces" became "economy of force" in the 1954 and subsequent lists. The order in which the principles appeared changed generally from edition to edition except that the 1968 and 1962 lists were identical. "Simplicity," for example, was second mentioned in 1949, third in 1954, and ninth in 1962 and 1968. "Security" was ninth in 1949 and 1954 and fourth in 1962 and 1968. "The Objective" has been first on every list. No mention was ever made that the order suggested a priority in applying the principles, but the changes in order certainly indicated a shift in priorities. The explanations of the principles generally changed, too, from edition to edition, but the general concepts, like the titles, have been largely unchanged. Perhaps therein lies the fundamental characteristic and merit of the "principles of war": their titles are general enough that a variety of explanations can apply to them. The argument can be made that the titles are symbol as well as description of a concept that can be only imperfectly explained with terms that are necessarily temporal.

One of the questions that faced General Cushman concerned the future of the "principles of war." Well aware of pedantry and the criticism directed against the official lists, he also recognized that a great deal of wisdom and history were included in the concepts behind the titles and their explanations.[42] When the content and format of the newly drafted FM 100-5 was discussed at a TRADOC commanders conference held in December 1974, the place of the "principles of war" was an item of considerable debate. Several papers dealing with the principles were examined, but the prevailing opinion was that the "principles of war" would not be enumerated in the next FM 100-5 as they had been since 1949. The concepts could not be ignored, but the terms, like the "principles of war" or the "principle of unity of command," appeared neither with a definitive list nor in the narrative of the manual when it was published in 1976. Entitled simply FM 100-5 *Operations,* the manual was new from its looseleaf black and green camouflage pattern cover to the organization and content. Only vestiges of the former "principles" could be found. In boldface lettering and boxed in the chapter entitled, "How to Fight" were the words "Decisive results require skillful concentration of combat power."[43] In the same chapter, "cover, concealment, suppression and teamwork" were identified as the "rules by which the battle is fought."[44] Elsewhere in the chapter, the following appeared:

To win a battle, four prerequisites must be met:

1.  Adequate forces and weapons must be *concentrated* at the critical times and places. The combination is combat power.

2.  The battle must be *controlled and directed* so that the maximum effect of fire and maneuver is concentrated at decisive locations.

3.  The battle must be fought using *cover, concealment, suppression, and combined arms teamwork* to maximize the effectiveness of our weapons and to minimize the effectiveness of enemy weapons.

4.  Our teams and crews must be *trained to use the maximum capabilities of their weapons.*[45]

The principles were refurbished in a guise that to many disguised their identity. Archer Jones, a professor of military history, recommended in his review of the new manual that "subsequent editions of the manual should clarify the fundamental principles."[46] He did not specifically call for a return to the former titles and format, but others did. The catalog of nine was destined to return.

FM 100-5 had been the most general manual in the army's library of hundreds of manuals since 1939 when manuals were first designated as "FM" and number. Through six editions (1939, 1941, 1944, 1949, 1954, and 1962), FM 100-5 had been the *Field*

*Service Regulations*, and before the numbering system, *Field Service Regulations* had been the army's principal manual. The predecessors of the *FSRs* carried the tradition of the capstone manual to the early nineteenth century. In this succession of manuals and regulations, the principles, whether in the modern definitive sense or the earlier general sense, for the leading of armies had been presented in this capstone manual. But in September 1978, the lineage of the *FSRs* and 100-5 as the capstone manual was broken by FM 100-1 *The Army*. Its purpose was to express "the fundamental roles, principles, and precepts governing the employment of United States Army forces in support of United States national security objectives." The manual was prepared at the Pentagon in the Office of the Deputy Chief of Staff for Operations, and its third chapter, "The Operational Dimension," began with a section on the "traditional" principles of war (see appendix 68). The titles and the order in which the principles were listed were identical with the 1962 and 1968 editions of FM 100-5. The explanations of the principles and the short introductory paragraph were very nearly identical with the explanations found in the 1968 FM 100-5. The principles had returned to army doctrine with the blessings of the army's senior general, General Bernard W. Rogers, the chief of staff of the army. For the time being, General Rogers had resolved the doctrinal debate.

Less than a year after the publication of FM 100-1, General Donn A. Starry, who succeeded General DePuy as the commander of TRADOC, half-jokingly referred to himself "as one of the ancient sages who had a hand in [the 1976 FM 100-5]." He continued:

> I guess we failed when we didn't put a list of the principles on the first page. It wasn't our intent, I assure you, to ignore those principles or the history from which they have been repeatedly distilled. But instead of giving a bland, dry listing of the principles, we tried to apply them appropriately in modern terms to the battlefield.[47]

The failure was not in the omission of the list from the manual but in failing to understand the strength and mystique that has become associated with the catalog of nine, or ten, or however many a given army has come to accept.

After World War II, neither French nor German thought embraced a single definitive list of "principles of war," but both nations moved closer to a definitive identification of principles intended to facilitate the study and conduct of war. France, having accepted three principles and five rules in a regulation for ground forces, continued to place a high regard on the moral and behavioral aspects of principles—a tradition that dates from Ardant du Picq's *Etudes sur le combat* (Battle studies) and the "lessons" of the French collapse in their war with Prussia in 1870 and 1871. German doctrine maintained a strong link with the thought that prevailed among its military leaders at the conclusion of the Franco-Prussian War by continuing to reflect the Moltkean and Clausewitzian thought that the individual situation and not unchanging rules determine correct actions in war. In other nations, however, many Jominian ideas survived, and even in communistic societies a blend of Jominian and Marxian ideas was used to fashion a theory predicated on the existence of a few fundamental principles of war.

The debate over principles and "the principles" was particularly intense in the United States. As in the post-World War I assessments of doctrine, the United States followed the lead of Great Britain in the post-World War II years; the definitive list format of the "principles of war" returned to the capstone manuals of both nations. The "principles" were altered little in the 1950s and 1960s, but as the United States turned its attention from the humiliating lessons learned in Southeast Asia, it briefly dropped the "principles" from official doctrinal sources. But the "principles" hastily returned to U.S. doctrine in 1978 after just two years in limbo.

That the principles of war exist, that they can be easily expressed, that their number is relatively small, and that they can be stated by a title are all tenets widely accepted among those who concern themselves with the conduct of war in the modern world. In spite of their rejection from doctrine, in spite of scathing criticism from both within and outside the military community, and in spite of the different numbers and titles and concepts embodied in the various lists, the "principles of war" exist, and they have since their codification in the early 1920s.

## NOTES

1. All references to the pamphlet are from Bernard L. Montgomery, "High Command in War" (June 1945). The cover of the pamphlet read in part, "This pamphlet must NOT fall into enemy hands. Officers in possession of a copy will be responsible for its safe custody." It was reprinted in Canada in November 1946 by Edward Cloutier, King's Printer and Controller of Stationery by permission of the Controller of His Majesty's Stationery Office.

2. Bernard Montgomery, *The Memoirs of Field-Marshal the Viscount Montgomery of Alamein, K.G.,* p. 374.

3. France, War College, *Recueil des conférences, Problèmes opérationnels et logistiques,* p. 10, my translation.

4. France, Army Ministry, *Instruction générale sur les forces terrestres,* 27 September 1973, p. 12, my translation.

5. Germany, Federal Defense Minister, *Truppenführung,* 25 October 1962, p. 31, my translation.

6. Germany, Federal Defense Minister, Army Service Regulation 100/100, *Command in Battle,* trans. German Army Main Liaison Staff, U.S. Army Training and Doctrine Command, p. 62.

7. Ibid., p. 63.

8. Raymond L. Garthoff, "Soviet Doctrine on the Decisive Factors in Modern War," *Military Review* 39 (July 1959):3.

9. Ibid., p. 4.

10. Colonel Baz, "V. I. Lenin on the Fundamental Factors Which Decide the Course and Outcome of Wars," (March 1957) as cited by ibid., p. 13.

11. Vasili Ye. Savkin, *The Basic Principles of Operational Art and Tactics (A Soviet View),* trans. and published under the auspices of the United States Air Force, p. 123.

12. Ibid., p. 1.

13. Ibid., p. 165.

14. Mao Tse-tung, *Selected Military Writings,* trans. Foreign Languages Press, p. 80.

15. Ibid., p. 87.

16. Kenmin Ho, "Mao's 10 Principles of War," *Military Review* 47 (July 1967):96-98.

17. See Virgil Ney, *Evolution of the United States Army Field Manual Valley Forge to Vietnam,* pp. 43-67.

18. U.S. Army, FM 100-5, *Field Service Regulations—Operations,* August 1949, pp. 21-23.

19. J. Lawton Collins to the author, 12 February 1974.

20. Reginald A. R. P. Ernle-Erle-Drax, "Principles of War," *Journal of the Royal United Service Institution* 107 (February 1962):65-66.

21. F. B. Ali, "The Principles of War," *Journal of the Royal United Service Institute* 108 (May 1963):165, and J. Fletcher, "Intelligence: A Principle of War," *Military Review* 50 (August 1970):52 (originally published in the *Army Journal* (Australia) in December 1969.

22. P. Coakley, "Economy of Principles," *Australian Army Journal* 84 (May 1956):44.

23. D. B. Gruzman, "Some Thoughts on the Principles of War," *Australian Army Journal* 148 (September 1961):41.

24. D. J. MacBride, "Fundamental Principles of War," *Army Journal* (Australia) 272 (January 1972):33.

25. "Military History and the Principles of War," *Canadian Army Journal* 4 (December 1950):1.

26. K. C. Kennedy, "The Principles of War," *Canadian Army Journal* 5 (November 1951):69-74. This article also appeared in the *Australian Army Journal* in August 1952.

27. D. G. Loomis, "Principles of War and the Canadian Army," *Canadian Army Journal* 15 (Winter 1961):33; and D. G. Loomis, "Communist Concepts of the Principles of War," *Canadian Army Journal* 12 (October 1958):4-22.

28. J. C. C. Richards, "The Principles of War," *Canadian Army Journal* 15 (Spring 1961):2-7.

29. R. M. Stevenson, "Principles of War and the Canadian Army," *Canadian Army Journal* 15 (Spring 1961):7-12.

30. See General Bernard W. Rogers, "Speaking Up/Speaking Out," paper distributed to officers army-wide, 15 June 1977.

31. Peter Paret, *Innovation and Reform in Warfare,* p. 11.

32. Bernard Brodie, *War and Politics,* p. 448.

33. George C. Reinhardt, "The Tenth Principle of War," *Military Review* 33 (July 1953):22-26.

34. John E. Greenwood, "New Principle," *Marine Corps Gazette* 38 (July 1954):12-15.

35. James A. Huston, "Re-examine the Principles of War," *Military Review* 35 (February 1956):30, 36.

36. V. H. Krulak, "A Principle in Jeopardy," *Marine Corps Gazette* 40 (November 1956):26.

37. R. D. Connolly, "The Principles of War and Psywar," *Military Review* 36 (March 1957):37-46.

38. Virgil Ney, *Notes on Guerrilla War: Principles and Practices,* p. 1.

39. Herbert E. Wolff, "9 + 1 = 10," *Infantry* 55 (March-April 1965):30.

40. Josiah A. Wallace, "The Principles of War in Counterinsurgency," *Military Review* 46 (December 1966):72.

41. Richard L. Kelley, "Applying Logistics Principles," *Military Review* 57 (September 1977):57.

42. The discussion of the place of the "principles of war" in U.S. Army doctrine since 1973 is based on my personal involvement and interest in the "principles" and on discussions with individuals involved in the writing of the recent revisions of FM 100-5, among them General Cushman and General Starry, who succeeded General DePuy as commander of TRADOC. While a student at the Command and General Staff College in the fall of 1974, I was asked to write a paper on the "principles of war" for inclusion in the post-Vietnam revision of 100-5. It was my understanding that General Cushman wanted the "principles" included in an appendix to the manual, but at the TRADOC commanders conference in December 1974, the "principles" were stricken from the draft. In September 1981 the nine "principles" that had appeared in the 1949 through 1968 versions of 100-5 and in the 1978 version of FM 100-1 were returned, as an appendix, in the revision of 100-5 approved by Army Chief of Staff, General E.C. Meyer.

43. U.S. Army, FM 100-5, *Operations,* July 1976, p. 3-6.

44. Ibid., p. 3-11.

45. Ibid., p. 3-3.

46. Archer Jones, "The New FM 100-5: A View from the Ivory Tower," *Military Review* 58 (February 1978):36.

47. Donn A. Starry, "History, the Principles of War, and Military History," keynote address to the Army Historians Conference, 2 May 1979, p. 7.

# 8

## LOOKING BACK TO FUTURE WAR

THE MODERN BATTLEFIELD is a confused chorus of cacophony. Filthy sweat, painful exhaustion, utter misery, sickness, and death generally characterize the experiences upon that field. For the individual participant, survival is often goal enough, but for the professional leader and the directors of war, the goal must be victory over the trials of the operations, the confusion of the battle, and ultimately over the enemy forces. The task is formidable, and throughout the written history of war, hardly a leader exists who has not known the bitterness of defeat. But in spite of the mercurial nature of the fortunes of war and of the knowledge that for every victor there must be vanquished, writers and teachers, military and civilian, have sought to identify the elements of victory and to ensure ordered thinking where physical confusion abounds. Their efforts often resulted in the charge of pedantry, a scathing criticism of the profession of practical men of action; but the cost of defeat is too great to rebuke any effort that might contribute to success in battle. Extensive educational programs for officers were established; the reason was extolled above the main entrance to the famous military academy at Saint Cyr: "They teach themselves to be victorious."[1] The concepts embodied in the modern "principles of war" have played an important role in battles fought in the past. In the present the concepts facilitate the study and understanding of war.

To forsake the knowledge of past wars would be foolish; to try to fight the next war as the last war was fought is also foolish. History confirms both observations. The one great lesson from history is not that we cannot learn from history but that judgment derived from intelligence and reflection must constantly guide our thoughts and decisions. The "principles of war" "are simply tools. They must remain our servants. They must never become the master of our thoughts. They are not, as some think, ingredients which will, if compounded in the right proportions, produce a species of victory cake."[2] Few serious students of war have addressed the topic of the principles of war without warning of their potential danger. Jomini himself warned:

> Of all the theories on the art of war the only reasonable one is that which, based on the study of military history, lays down a certain number of regulating principles but leaves the greater part of the general conduct of war to natural genius, without binding it with dogmatic rules. On the contrary, nothing is more likely to kill this natural genius and allow error to triumph than those pedantic theories, based on the false notion that war is a positive science and that all its operations can be reduced to infallible calculations.[3]

Specious knowledge has no place in war, and although the anonymous authors of the modern lists that have appeared in official publications never intended to stifle thought and reflection upon the conduct of war, "One wishes at least that they had the modesty of the writers of the Holy Gospel, who did not state that theirs was THE Gospel, but only the Gospel according to the writer."[4] Like rules and regulations, principles do not have the force of law. The violation of rules and regulations and principles involves risks, but there are situations where violations can lead to success. Judgment is the one true guide.

August Comte, the leading exponent of the positivist school stated, "To know science well, its history must be known."[5] To understand the "principles of war," their history must be known. The forces that ordained and inspired their development and the acceptance of their content and format are perhaps more significant than their metamorphic chronology, but these forces are far more difficult to identify. Individual authors were instrumental in the development, but often they were either synthesizers of broader intellectual currents or merely articulators of widely held beliefs. As a rule their ideas were more eclectic than original. Nevertheless, without their dedication to the profession they served, reflection upon the role of principles in the proper conduct of war would have occurred less frequently, and the development of military theory would have occurred more slowly. The principles of war represent one strand in the evolution of military thought; they reflect general intellectual currents and the relationship of these currents to military doctrine and practice.

Within the context of environmental constraints and requirements for survival, people have consistently attempted to improve upon methods and practices known to others. Competition is a human attribute, and the desire for success is natural. From the earliest known writings on war, man sought to organize his forces and his thoughts, for organization itself was recognized as an asset to societies in general and to military commanders in particular. Organization is essential in writing and hence in any theory of war. Brevity is an asset, too, especially when brevity contributes to clarity. The earliest military theorists tended to write with organization, clarity, and brevity. The result of such goals was often a compendium of principles, or fundamentals, intended to benefit their contemporaries and progeny.

The Renaissance was accompanied by new motivational goals. Writers were learned men who were aware of the discipline of science as a method of revealing and confirming truth rather than of science as a body of accepted statements of truth. The quest to observe and test permeated all branches of knowledge, and war was no exception. The testing of battle techniques, however, was limited, and military history became a surrogate laboratory for military science. Principles, scientifically established, could serve as guides for action rather than simply as descriptive truths. Until the Napoleonic period, the most significant contribution to the development of the modern concept of principles of war was the widespread acceptance of the belief that principles existed within the realm of war. To many war was a science.

The second phase in the development of modern concepts of principles of war was the acceptance of the idea that not only did the principles exist but that the most important ones were few in number and could be simply expressed. Jomini was instrumental in this phase of the development, but he did not himself believe that war is a science based on a few fixed principles. It was not at all uncommon to speak of a science of war when Jomini published his *Précis de l'art de la guerre* in 1838, but significantly, Jomini spoke of the "art of war" rather than the science of war in his title. "Science of war" would have suggested a more dominant role of principles, and indeed some authors of the Napoleonic period wrote treatises either on the science of war or on the science of various branches of war. Guibert, for one, wrote that grand tactics was the science of the general in chief.[6] Archduke Charles of Austria wrote that strategy was the science of war and based his works largely on the existence of principles in war. The treatise on war by the French theorist Gay de Vernon was translated into English as *A Treatise on the Science of War*. Obviously Jomini was aware of the close association of science with war and with branches of war, but he was not so overwhelmed by a belief in science that he would entitle his compendium on war, a science of war. In fact, he defined strategy, the realm in which he spoke of principles, as the "art of making war on the map" and not as the science. Agreement was widespread, however, in the learned world in the early nineteenth century that neither the arts nor the sciences could be cultivated in isolation. A contemporary suggested that "the word 'science' should be abolished altogether and a new term expressing the intimate union of science with the arts be substituted."[7] He proposed the term "*connaissances humaines*" (human knowledge). In light of this trend, Jomini understandably believed that principles existed within the art of war. His subsequent influence upon generations of military men who grew up in a world increasingly dominated by science and technology was also facilitated by this pervasive theme.

Jomini's theories and their subsequent influence on the conduct of war in the post-Napoleonic period was central to the development of the modern forms of principles of war. Spenser Wilkinson, a leading British military intellectual at the start of the present century and later professor of the history of war at Oxford, remarked:

> Jomini's analysis and classification of operations, in spite of its artificial terminology, was correct and useful. It was the first scientific exposition of strategy as a system of principles, and it has been used by all the subsequent strategical thinkers. Willisen in Germany and Hamley in England are Jomini's disciples, and the appreciation of Napoleon's campaigns has been for the most part little more than the application to them of Jomini's categories. The formal lore of strategy has been advanced but little since Jomini published his *Précis.* . . . Accordingly the military literature of the nineteenth century is hardly intelligible without a study of Jomini's chapter on strategy.[8]

Jomini's chapter outlined the fundamental principle of war and the maxims derived from it and became an important source of the belief that the conduct of war was regulated by a few unchanging principles. The belief in the existence of principles in warfare came to be widely accepted in the nineteenth century, but the forces that shaped the belief differed from nation to nation.

French military thought, for example, was profoundly influenced by the French defeat in the Franco-Prussian War. The defeat also altered French views of principles of war, for the conclusion was drawn that organizational and technological failures were not as responsible as attitudinal and behavioral failures. This lesson led Henri Bonnal and Ferdinand Foch to conclude that the enduring principles in warfare should be concerned more with spirit, morale, and attitudes than with purely physical considerations. Thus in France the principle of freedom of action, which applied to the commander's mental set concerning the employment of his forces, was accepted, and an operational principle, such as the enemy army should be the ultimate objective of every campaign, had little appeal.

In Germany, the Jominian belief in the existence of a few immutable principles governing the conduct of war was eclipsed by the idea advanced by Clausewitz, the elder von Moltke, and other officers that war could not be subjected to general rules. Some senior German soldiers, however, did write of principles regulating the conduct of war. These men, Colmar von der Goltz and Rudolf von Caemmerer among them, were not representative of a Jominian school in regard to their expostulation of principles but were led in that direction by trends in late nineteenth-century German philosophy, which sought principles that encompassed not only narrow segments of experience like the conduct of war but "experiences of the whole personality."⁹

In a similar vein, Alfred Thayer Mahan believed that "principles" should encompass broad areas of human activity. For example, he held that the principle of concentration applied not only to the military units on the battlefield but to ships at sea, to the necessity for maintaining the fleet in one ocean, and to the massing of facts to insure accurate historical conclusions. Intellectually, these views contrasted sharply with the applicatory methods used in nearly all Western military schools, but able instructors often reduced the esoteric ideas of philosophy to concepts acceptable to students with highly practical inclinations. Both G. F. R. Henderson at the British Staff College and Matthew Steele at the U.S. staff college displayed this characteristic near the turn of the century, and both recognized the efficacy of identifying comprehensive "principles" to serve this end. An intellectual basis for the acceptance of principles was established, and in the early years of the twentieth century, principles for sundry activities of war were common.

By the end of World War I, the existence of principles in warfare led to the belief—at least in Anglo-American nations—that a brief list of the fundamental principles could and should be articulated in army doctrine. Such positive statements were quickly adopted in Great Britain and the United States, but in France and in Germany, the authors of revised doctrine saw more danger than benefit in a brief list of positive rules. Yet the trend toward the more definitive statement of principles of war was apparent throughout the first half of the twentieth century. The trend was present in the Soviet Union, too, but there bourgeois ideas had to be masked in Marxian rhetoric.

In addition to synthesizing broader intellectual currents, individual authors involved in the presentation of principles of war often articulated commonly held views. Throughout the military services and especially in military schools and other doctrine-producing agencies, such as the war departments and special study groups, concepts like the principles of war were subjected to extensive review, comment, and possible rejection by a multitude of superior and collateral agencies before they could appear and become institutionalized. Thus, writers who reflected broader intellectual trends also frequently presented views shared by many of their contemporaries.

Original ideas appeared in some of the theoretical literature, but most theories either borrowed from other fields or from other nations. They also frequently expressed ideas that were popular in their own right and void of controversy. The military schools served as the focal point of development, for a prime opportunity for thought and reflection leading to a better understanding of war existed within the service schools. Furthermore, the need for comprehensive texts and other written references stimulated some instructors to write, and many others published their lectures either after they retired from teaching or after their views became well accepted. Books on the theory of war proliferated like the schools that spawned them, but the books sometimes generated more criticism than learning. To some observers, the books that tried to reduce complex topics to enumerable considerations were pedantic. To practical men, the same books were often thought to be valueless abstractions because, though they could be useful in preparing for required examinations of one sort or another, they discouraged thinking and hardened a prevalent attitude that generals are born and not made. "Traditionally military machines have always rejected intellectual grit."[10] In spite of these values, however, other forces placed enumerable concepts of principles in a favorable light.

Scientific methods and attitudes influenced military education, and throughout the nineteenth century, the gap between science and its military applications consistently narrowed. Scientific and technological developments demanded that specialized military schools be founded, and science dominated the early curricula, thus strongly influencing military thought. A science based on a few immutable principles could be readily learned, and by the late nineteenth century, courses addressing the study of war focused on the identification of such principles. In addition to being scientific, the principles furnished "what the military side of this busy world so much needs, a short-cut to general knowledge of a vast subject."[11] The "scientific shorthand" seemed to please the pedagogues as well as the profession at large.

Two other forces interacted closely with the development of the modern principles of war: the adoption of new methods of military instruction inspired largely by the recognition of Prussia as the model of all things military and the influence of the rapid technological developments on the conduct of war. Prussia's victories in wars against Denmark in 1864, Austria in 1866, and France in 1870-1871 placed Prussia at the zenith of the military powers of the world. The Prussian general staff was envied and emulated by great and lesser services alike. Prussian educational systems impressed foreign military observers, and the applicatory method, which relied on practical and participatory instruction, was heralded throughout the world as the best method of instruction. Learning by doing was the key. But although Prussian officers like von Peucker, Verdy du Vernois, and von Moltke maintained that each military situation required its own evaluation and solution, English and American officers seemed able to combine a belief in principles of universal validity with the applicatory method and pragmatism.

In the advanced military schools of Great Britain and the United States, the purpose of studying individual cases was to determine the general principles illustrated by the case. The case method was often indistinguishable from the applicatory method, but important differences existed between the two. The former called for the study of specific cases, usually drawn from history, from which enduring lessons were to be learned. The latter method also used specific cases, usually drawn from history, but it required the student to make periodical decisions and to take prescribed actions that allowed him to apply an appropriate solution to a set of former circumstances. Schools of war attempted to use the best of both methods, for each had limitations when violence and man as antagonist were involved. The case method failed to give military students the flavor of the dynamics of war, and the applicatory method could but imitate the battlefield since the major ingredients of battle, the enemy and the friction of war, could only be simulated. In both methods, however, military history was called upon to be the surrogate laboratory for the study of war. From historical examples and reconstructions, students were encouraged to seek the principles that had led to the great victories of the past. Eben Swift, an instructor and later commandant of the U.S. staff college, observed in 1904:

> The old idea of teaching the art of war as a doctrine is changed. Now the higher theory as taught by the books is put aside and we study the campaigns first, and pick out the strategy afterwards, thus reversing the former method. Here then we have a brilliant example of the study of principles by their application. It was [Napoleon's] own practice as we now know, but the added importance of the study of military history in the curriculum of the war college is a recent idea.[12]

Thus out of the Prussian experience came not only increased attention to the study of military history but also the search of history for principles of war.

The second factor that at the least paralleled the development of the principles of war was the influence of the technological advances that occurred during the formative period of the modern principles. The rapidity of change in the conduct of war brought about by technological advances in the late nineteenth century created an atmosphere in which the "unchanging" was held in high regard. Many instructors expressed the view that principles served as a firm foundation for both the theory of war and the study of military history.

While the rapidity of technological change suggested the necessity for the identification of clear principles to some, the nature of the changes suggested the need to others. The replacement of sail by steam brought a certainty to the navies of the world. Railroads provided general staffs with the capability of planning mobilization schedules that allowed troop concentrations at the critical areas to be calculated to the minute. Breech-loading weapons facilitated the tasks of the rifleman and artilleryman; better cartridges and explosives improved accuracy and reliability. The telegraph and later radio provided faster and more reliable communications than had been previously known. The tank and aircraft brought accurate determinations of movement rates to and on the battlefield. The impact of each of these technological advances and other lesser discoveries upon the statement of principles is difficult to assess, but the progressive trend was toward greater predictability upon the battlefield. That greater predictability should be possible within the metaphysical aspects of war seems to have been assumed. Many twentieth-century teachers believed that the definitive expression of principles served this end.

A further characteristic of the modern battlefield made the definitive expression of principles of war appear efficacious and desirable. Great wars in the past had always required the transition of large numbers of men from sundry callings to the profession of arms. When neither equipment nor methods were too sophisticated, the transition was accomplished with comparatively little difficulty. Among the officers the transition from aristocrat to commander seemed so natural that the duke of Wellington, for one, feared that the education of officers would disrupt this proven system. Proponents of military education overcame such opposition, but during the mass mobilizations of World Wars I and II, military education programs were abbreviated to the point that they became little more than orientations on rudiments and on the immediate situation at the front. Staff schools were closed, military history was abandoned, and philosophical topics were supplanted by highly utilitarian ones. A few people continued to think about the metaphysics of war, and throughout each of the world wars, the need for leaders at all echelons to understand certain basic truths common to an extreme range of situations was widely recognized. This recognition contributed to the acceptance of the definitive lists of principles of war in Great Britain and the United States in the early 1920s and the late 1940s.

A final factor that may have influenced the widespread acceptance of the modern concept of principles of war is the proclivity of modern societies for slogans and aphorisms. Since the days of *Poor Richard's Almanac,* Americans especially have been raised in the midst of philosophy by simple analogy. Soldiers have tended to encapsulate weeks and months of experience into pithy phrases. An infantry major wrote about his experiences in World War II: "As the war went on we adopted more and more of these hard and fast rules. There are hundreds of them and they're all very familiar by now. . . . 'stay out of the woods,' 'tanks before infantry,' 'perimeter defense,' 'attach the mortars.' "[13] In Vietnam familiar advice included: "Keep your head down," "The night belongs to the Viet Cong," "Firepower is cheaper than manpower." The phrases became the fundamental unwritten doctrine of the respective wars. They were not an excuse not to think but something to think about. And in the midst of the uncertainty of war, these pithy sayings might spur a moment's reflection that could mean life or death. Although slogans may be a primitive form of education, they can serve a useful function. The modern "principles of war" are not slogans, but their pithy advice derived from centuries of experience—often by men of great intellect—exists in a familiar format. Concepts that are familiar, concise, and clearly stated are readily remembered and accepted, especially by those who have experienced the confusion of battle.

Myths concerning the origins of the "principles of war" have been nearly as numerous and pervasive as the interpretations of the principles themselves. The two most widely held inventions concerning the "principles" are that the "principles" always existed in the same form and that the modern lists of principles are directly, and according to some commentators, solely attributable to either Clausewitz or to J. F. C. Fuller. The first myth possibly developed from the nature of principles. If a given list or a single principle is accepted, then from the definition of principle, it follows that it must have been valid for all times. That the "principles" must have been known for all times and accorded similar importance in all times has been too quickly concluded. For example, an American officer commented in 1961: "Principles of war have long been accepted by the world's armies as the basis for tactical doctrine, in spite of major changes in the weapons of war. Even the development of nuclear weapons has failed to dislodge them from their esteemed position."[14] If this author was speaking of the nine "principles of war," first adopted by the United States in the *Field Service Regulations* of 1949, which he undoubtedly was, then he failed to recognize that this enumeration of "principles of war" succeeded rather than preceded the nuclear age. An Indian officer, schooled in British instruction, also wrote in 1961:

> [The principles of war] are accepted as the basis of teaching which provides a solution for success in battle. Eminent military thinkers and commanders have endorsed them and have fully quoted them in their writings. Their truth has not yet been seriously questioned. Like the Ten Commandments, the principles are now hallowed and enshrined on the altars of our military schools.[15]

Such emphasis and suggested agelessness of the "principles" included in the modern official lists places undue importance on modern interpretations of war and, concomitantly, deemphasizes perceptions of war that existed in other times. The use of the "principles of war" as a pedagogic tool contributes greatly to this aberration. Although Frederick the Great undoubtedly knew the value of surprise, security, and the offensive, he began his instructions for his commanders with a discussion of desertion, which must certainly have held an extremely high position in his perception of important considerations in war. When a modern list is used as the basis to critique Frederick's campaigns, his own perceptions tend to be overlooked in favor of modern perceptions. Even though the "principles" may possess timeless characteristics, they were not known for all times and in all places. An anonymous Prussian general officer perspicaciously observed in 1806:

The art of war certainly, will never become simply a science. The fundamental principles of it may, indeed, hereafter be demonstrated in a more simple manner than has hitherto been done . . . but, be the existing system what it may, those principles must ever, and necessarily, be modified in the application of them, by political, moral, and physical causes; and men of genius will always find room, in the profession of arms, to display and exert the talents they may have received from nature or acquired by study.[16]

The military student may gain great benefit from the "principles," but "he should not come to regard them as 'immutable,' much less should he derive the impression that wars should be conducted on pedantic lines."[17] Even Jomini, though searching for principles evidenced by Frederick's campaigns of a half century earlier, understood that the principles that he identified should not be used to judge commanders of times other than his own:

There are in my historical chapters, observations on operational plans that are based on the system of magazines, and on all the dispositions that can result from the system; but it should be agreed that if my conclusions are contrary to the maxims established in those days by experience, it is also true that the methods of the generals cannot help but be in accord with the principles recognized at the time when they were operating. Their methods, which I shall try to present objectively, should not then be the scale on which my conclusions should be weighed. It is only in the chapters containing my personal observations that the true principles that guide me can be found; all the rest is relative to time and to place.[18]

Jomini studied the past to derive the principles of his own day, and he recognized the fallacy of judging the past with principles of a different time and place. This belief contradicted the immutable characteristic of principles that Jomini set forth. He did not resolve the paradox, and it remains unresolved to the present day. In Jomini's later writings, he emphasized the immutable characteristic, and today the paradox is generally ignored because acceptance of the immutable characteristic of the "principles" far outweighs consideration of their timebound quality.

The second myth concerning the modern "principles of war" involves the role that Clausewitz and Fuller played in their formulation. It is neither surprising nor unusual that Clausewitz has been misinterpreted with regard to principles of war. Early translations of his works into English were poor and led to frequent misunderstandings of his thought. He has often been misquoted, and due to his untimely death, many of his early ideas appeared without the advantage of reexamination by their matured creator. Since the adoption of the first British list of "principles of war" in 1920, numerous authors have claimed to find in Clausewitz's instructions to the crown prince, an intentionally didactic work written for a sixteen year old, an enumeration of principles that were similar to "principles" in the British list. Little else that Clausewitz wrote, especially in his more analytic writings, was drawn upon when labeling Clausewitz the father of the modern principles of war. For example, his thought concerning the principles was presented in a most misleading fashion in the pamphlet published by the Department of Military Art and Engineering at West Point that read:

Clausewitz's principles of war (in addition to that of *Unity of Command,* mentioned earlier) include the following:

a.  The Objective: . . .
b.  Mass: . . .
c.  Economy of Force: . . .
d.  Surprise: . . .
e.  Mobility: . . .
f.  Simplicity: . . .[19]

Clausewitz never presented such a list of "principles" and repeatedly warned against the adoption of absolute conclusions and rules. For example, in *On War* he wrote, "[Theory] must also take the human factor into account, and find room for courage, boldness, even foolhardiness. The art of war deals with living and with moral forces. Consequently, it cannot attain the absolute and certain."[20] Such statements deny the definitive characteristic claimed by the authors of the modern lists.

Fuller's contribution to current concepts of "principles of war" is far greater than Clausewitz's, but it is similarly often misinterpreted. No other person did as much to shape the form and content of the modern "principles," and Fuller pointed out these contributions with exaggeration and some pride in his published memoirs. Fuller, however, did not present a single, definitive list of "principles of war" prior to the publication of the first official British list. The official list must also be credited with the publicity and prestige afforded the "principles." Soon after the official list appeared, Fuller used the principles in an attempt to establish a philosophy of war or as the title of his book stated, *Foundations of the Science of War*, but this attempt to broaden the knowledge of war with the "principles" as the framework had little positive impact on either the official "principles" or on the theory of war in general. A contemporary remarked of the work, "Its evil outweighs its good because it has become the chief source of inspiration for those who create images of a science of war at which to worship."[21]

When Fuller published his memoirs a decade and a half after the appearance of the official list in the *FSR,* he admitted that his enthusiasm for the "principles" had waned, "for their purpose has been completely misunderstood, mainly because the military and naval literature which has arisen out of them (in the U.S.A. as well as here) has most successfully obscured their aim, use and value."[22] Fuller did not elaborate on the aim, use, and value that he intended for the "principles," but his writings gave frequent clues. In his memoirs, for example, he wrote, "True education consists in training the mind how to think, in place of cramming it with what to think."[23] In his journalistic writings during World War II, he complained in a similar vein, "Why do so few soldiers think? Because so many have never been taught to do so."[24] He foresaw the danger of dogmatic interpretations of the official list, for he was never one to discourage cogitation and reflection. Fuller certainly influenced the form and the content of the modern "principles," but he was not the author of the first modern list of "principles of war" nor one to insist upon their dogmatic application.

The "principles of war" in their modern guise as a list of titles and brief explanations have existed for well over a half-century. Staff officers and service school instructors have been primarily responsible for their inclusion in the doctrine of the United States and Great Britain, but both Field Marshal Montgomery in the mid-1940s and General Rogers in the late 1970s were extremely influential in returning lists of "principles" to doctrinal sources after designed absences.

Prior to the Napoleonic age of warfare, the most significant theories of war and treatises on principles were written by senior officers, almost all from the aristocracy. After the Napoleonic age, the aristocratic influence in war declined, and officers with intellectual tendencies, and generally with talent as well, began to write most of the popular books on war. By the end of the nineteenth century, the officer-writers were nearly all associated with the faculty of their particular service's staff college. Nearly all who contributed to the development of the modern concept of "principles of war" had either an avid interest in or at least a profound respect for the discipline of history. Also many of those who significantly contributed to the enunciation of "principles of war" have been individuals in whose lives religion has played an important role. Dennis Hart Mahan and his son, Alfred Thayer Mahan, were devout. Ferdinand Foch's early education was in Jesuit schools. J. F. C. Fuller was descended from Roundheads and from Huguenots. His father was an Anglican clergyman. Bernard Montgomery's father was an Irish bishop. The conclusion might be drawn that if life has its moral principles, then surely war has principles too. Those who enunciated principles were the sheepskins who sought justice in war and principles in war's practice. To conclude that war is more civilized because it has known principles, however, would carry the association with religion too far.

The individual authors, teachers, and theorists who contributed to the development of modern concepts of principles of war shared a desire to further their understanding of war and to identify the significant aspects of war. But in spite of this basic common interest, they had different ideas as to what constituted the basis of the theory of war. To many, "principles" lay at the root, but "principles" conveyed different meanings. To some a principle was a law that demanded certain actions. To some it was a prevailing condition that always led to success in war. To others it was a general truth, an element, or a fundamental inherent in the nature of war, and to still others, a principle was a guide that could sometimes be violated but always had to be considered. Even though the definitions varied, most of those who contributed to the enunciation of principles in warfare were reasonable and practical men; they would have agreed that there was a difference between the causal power of the principle of concentration and principles, like those of oxidation or planetary motion, that could be confirmed by mathematical models or through the rigorous cycle of hypothesis, test and control that comprised the scientific method. But in their writings, lectures, and theories, they tended to state their ideas boldly and convincingly. This characteristic of their statements existed for several reasons. No one, for example, who spoke of war in a diffident manner could hope to appeal to the professional soldier. No one who ignored the pedagogic need for concise theories could expect his ideas to be espoused in the schools of war, and no one who was incapable of reducing the complex to the essential could provide the expertise needed in a profession whose technical aspects and expectations were increasing constantly. Principles of war, few in number and simply stated, seemed to satisfy both pedagogical and professional requirements.

Some generalizations about the principles themselves can be made. Four of the concepts from among those that have been identified as one of the few basic "principles of war" emerge as being regarded in a manner that sets them in a class above the other "principles." The first of these is "concentration" or "mass," titles that are both linked to Jomini's great fundamental principle, which in simplified language states, "Be superior at the decisive point." Simply to concentrate troops or to mass troops carries risks, however, for firepower, both conventional and nuclear, can quickly alter the balance of power at any given point. "Concentration" or "mass" has been popular, too, because both connote that moral as well as physical force must be considered. The second of the leading "principles" is "surprise." Its connotations include that surprise is achieved through deception as well as through activities unsuspected by the enemy. The third popular principle is the "objective," for it connotes that political and military goals must be in consonance and that these goals must be clearly defined. The objective increased in importance when the control of land and enemy armies ceased to be the major military objectives and the control of societies and ideas became major military objectives. The last of the most dominant "principles" of the past is "economy of force," connoting a balance between what is available and what is needed. It also connotes an understanding among commanders, between commanders and troops, and between the military and the society that the minimum essential force will be employed. It suggests rationality the use of force and the understanding of the value of human life.

The "principles of war" are firmly rooted in the military traditions of the United States and Great Britain. Neither the titles nor the explanations of the concepts behind the titles are immutable. Neither the titles nor their explanations are universally accepted. Neither the titles nor the explanations will guarantee success to anyone in future war. The question that must be asked is whether the "principles" are benefit or detriment to those who prepare to fight a future war should it occur.

The search for principles in other disciplines may foretell the value of the principles of war.

> After Newton's great discoveries, which had revealed the laws ruling the physical universe, interest focused on finding those which would determine social life. Thus even the power struggle among states was considered to have its laws. The attempt to discover these laws, though condemned to futility because of an erroneous belief in the rationality of human society, resulted in a clear insight into the nature of diplomacy and in a sharper definition of its tasks.[25]

Perhaps continuing quests to understand the "principles of war" will yield clearer insights and sharper definitions to our understanding of war, and the study and conduct of war will build on a stronger base than has been possible thus far. But to whatever form or content the "principles of war" may lead, the proper role of theory in war must remain paramount in the minds of teachers and students alike:

Theory must take into account the infinite diversity of actual war and avoid the restrictive character that pertains to any synthesis. Its task is not to produce a guide for action, but to help educate judgment and to provide ideal standards with which to measure and evaluate the forms that war assumes in reality.[26]

Theory and its principles alone are insufficient protection should future war break upon us. To ignore their role in battle, however, would be to ignore the wisdom of the past. Sheepskins are needed to keep the lessons of the past fresh in the corporate mind of the modern armies of the world and to refine our understanding of war, but goatskins, physically strong warriors, are needed too. Today the attributes of Ares are furnished by physically vigorous individuals and by complex weapon systems. But Pallas Athene, the goddess with whom most military men identify and with whom the sheepskin tradition is identified, was given a goatskin shield by Zeus. In spite of her gifts of wisdom and beauty and her ability to see justice done, she needed a goatskin to survive in the face of battle. The sheepskin and goatskin fought together—and prevailed.

## NOTES

1. From A. G. Salisbury-Jones, "The Sandhurst of France: Some Impressions of the École Spéciale Militaire de Saint-Cyr," *Army Quarterly* 6 (April 1923):85, my translation.
2. C. R. Brown, "The Principles of War," *United States Naval Institute Proceedings* 75 (June 1949):633.
3. Antoine-Henri Jomini, *Précis de l'art de la guerre*, I, p. 12, translated in Michael Howard, *Studies in War and Peace*, p. 27.
4. M. J. W. Wright, "The Principles of War—An Analysis," *Army Quarterly* 80 (July 1960):200.
5. From Jean Mordacq, *La Stratégie, Historique évolution*, p. 23, my translation.
6. Ibid., pp. 14-15.
7. Roger Hahn, *The Anatomy of a Scientific Institution: The Paris Academy of Sciences, 1666-1803*, p. 270.

8. Spenser Wilkinson, *The French Army before Napoleon,* p. 14.

9. W. Stark, "Editor's Introduction," in Friedrich Meinecke, *Machiavellism, The Doctrine of Raison d'état and Its Place in Modern History,* trans. Douglas Scott, p. xi.

10. K. Booth, "History or Logic as Approaches to Strategy," *Journal of the Royal United Service Institute for Defence Studies* 117 (September 1972):34.

11. George F. MacMann, Foreword to R. A. E. Voysey, *An Outline of the Principles of War,* p. v.

12. Eben Swift, "Remarks Introductory to the Course in Military Art, at the Infantry and Cavalry School and Staff College, Fort Leavenworth, Kansas," Lectures Delivered at the Infantry and Cavalry School by Instructors and Student Officers of the Staff College during November and December 1904, pp. 14-15.

13. David E. Milotta, "One Eye on the Last War," *Infantry Journal* 61 (August 1947):13.

14. Emil Edmond, "The First Principle of War," *Military Review* 41 (February 1961):12.

15. J. Nazareth and M.J.W. Wright, "Two Views on the Principles of War," *Military Review* 41 (February 1961):26.

16. A Prussian general officer, *The Spirit of the Modern System of War,* p. v.

17. H. G. de Watteville, "The Principles of War," *Journal of the Royal United Service Institution* 75 (May 1930):274.

18. Antoine-Henri Jomini, *Traité de grandes opérations militaires,* III, pp. 6-7.

19. United States Military Academy, *Jomini, Clausewitz, and Schlieffen,* p. 25.

20. Carl von Clausewitz, *On War,* trans. Michael Howard and Peter Paret, p. 15.

21. Edward Atlas, "The Shape of War as It Is," *Infantry Journal* 50 (February 1942):71.

22. J. F. C. Fuller, *Memoirs of an Unconventional Soldier,* p. 389.

23. Ibid., p. 458.

24. J. F. C. Fuller, *Watchwords,* p. 61.

25. Felix Gilbert, *To the Farewell Address: Ideas of Early American Foreign Policy,* p. 92.

26. Peter Paret, "Clausewitz and the Nineteenth Century," in Michael Howard, ed., *The Theory and Practice of War: Essays Presented to Captain B. H. Liddell Hart on His Seventieth Birthday,* p. 29.

# APPENDIXES

# THE ESSENCE OF VICTORY: A CHRONOLOGICAL COMPENDIUM

The following appendixes provide the lengthy substantive matter contained in lists of guides intended to facilitate either the conduct or the study of war. The lists that follow are typical of a given era or author and are indicative of the forms and content that contributed to the development of the modern definitive lists of "principles of war." They appear in chronological order.

# APPENDIX 1

## SUN TZU, "CONSIDERATIONS BY WHICH VICTORY OR DEFEAT CAN BE FORECASTED," C. 500 B.C.

(1) Which of the two sovereigns is imbued with the moral law?

(2) Which of the two generals has most ability?

(3) With whom lie the advantages derived from Heaven and Earth?

(4) On which side is discipline most regularly enforced?

(5) Which army is stronger?

(6) On which side are officers and men most highly trained?

(7) In which army is there the greater constancy both in reward and punishment?

—From Thomas R. Phillips, ed., *Roots of Strategy*, p. 22.

# APPENDIX 2

## NICCOLÒ MACHIAVELLI, "GENERAL RULES IN MILITARY DISCIPLINE," 1521

You must know, then, that whatsoever is of service to the enemy, must be prejudicial to you, and contrarywise. He that is most careful to observe the motions and designs of the enemy, and takes most pains in exercising and disciplining his army, will be least exposed to danger, and has most reason to expect success in his undertakings. Never come to an engagement till you have inspired your men with courage, and see them in good order and eager to fight; nor hazard a battle till they seem confident of victory. It is better, if you can, to subdue an enemy by famine than the sword; for in battle, fortune has often a much greater share than either prudence or valour. No enterprize is more likely to succeed, than one which is concealed from the enemy till it is ripe for execution. Nothing is of greater importance in time of war, than to know how to make the best use of a fair opportunity when it is offered. Few men are brave by nature; but good discipline and experience make them so. Good order and discipline in an army are more to be depended upon than courage alone. If any of the enemy's troops desert them, and come over to you, it is a great acquisition, provided they prove faithful; for the loss of them will be more felt than that of those who are killed in battle; though deserters, indeed, will always be suspected by their new friends, and odious to their old ones. In drawing up an army in order of battle, it is better to keep a sufficient reserve to support your front line, upon occasion, than to extend it in such a manner as to make but one rank, as it were, of your army. If a general perfectly knows his own strength and that of the enemy, he can hardly miscarry. The goodness of your soldiers is of more consequence than the number of them; and sometimes the situation of the place is of greater advantage and security than the goodness of your soldiers. Sudden and unexpected accidents often throw an army into confusion; but things that are familiar, and have come on by slow degrees, are little regarded; it is the best way, therefore, when you have a new enemy to deal with, to accustom your men to the sight of them as often as you can by slight skirmishes, before you come to a general engagement with them. He whose troops are in disorder themselves, whilst they are pursuing a routed enemy, will most probably lose the advantage he gained before and be routed in his turn. Whoever has not taken proper care, to furnish himself with a sufficient stock of provisions and ammunition, bids fair to be vanquished without striking a stroke. He that is either stronger in infantry than cavalry, or in cavalry than infantry, must chuse his ground accordingly. If you would know whether you have any spies in your camp, in the day time, you have nothing more to do than to order every man to his tent. When you are aware that the enemy is acquainted with your designs, you must change them. After you have consulted many about what you ought to do, confer with very few concerning what you are actually resolved to do. Whilst your men are in quarters, you must keep them in good order by fear and punishment; but when they are in the field, by hopes and rewards. Wise generals never come to an engagement but when they are either compelled by downright necessity, or can do it with great advantage. Take great care that the enemy may not be apprized of the order in which you design to draw up your army for battle: And, above all things, make such a disposition that your first line may fall back with ease and convenience into the second, and both of them into the third upon occasion. In time of action, be sure not to call off any of your battalions to a different service from what they were destined to at first, lest you should occasion disorder and confusion in your army. Unexpected accidents cannot well be prevented; but those that are foreseen may easily be obviated or remedied. Men, arms, money and provisions, are the sinews of war; but of these four, the two first are most necessary; for men and arms will always find money and provisions; but money and provisions cannot always raise men and arms. A rich man without arms, must be a prey to a poor soldier well armed. Accustom your men to abhor a soft and effeminate way of life, and to despise all manner of luxury, extravagance and delicacy, either in their diet or dress.

—Nicholas Machiavel [Niccolò Machiavelli], *The Art of War,* [trans. Ellis Farneworth], pp. 270-72.

## APPENDIX 3

## HENRY, DUKE OF ROHAN, "GUIDES FOR THE GENERAL WHO WISHES TO ENGAGE IN WAR," C. 1644

1. Never allow yourself to be forced to combat against your will.

2. Choose a field of battle according to the number of your troops, their quality, and the type of engagement you wish to undertake.

3. Arrange your army in battle in a manner that enables you to renew the fighting several times with ordered troops.

4. Have good leaders at the head of each principal corps.

5. Place the different lines in such a manner that they can sustain each other; without it the overthrow of one leads to the overthrow of the others.

6. Put the best troops on the wings and attack with the wing that is strongest.

7. Do not allow pillage, but pursue until the enemy is completely beaten.

—From Jules Vial, *Cours d'art et d'histoire militaires,* II, pp. 379-80, my translation.

## APPENDIX 4

### Marquis de Silva, "Principles of Maneuver," 1778

First principle: All maneuvers must be simple, prompt, easy, and sure. If they do not have these characteristics as completely as possible, they are bad.

Second principle: Nearly all maneuvers must be made by direct movements, and wheeling movements and oblique marches must be made only by small fronts and under special circumstances.

Third principle: Different means must never be used for a single purpose nor different maneuvers for a single objective. Synonymous maneuvers must be consequently rejected.

Fourth principle: All maneuvers must be covered, that is to say, that the troops that are maneuvering must always be covered by those who are no longer maneuvering.

Fifth principle: All maneuvers must be made by the center, this center being the head of the maneuvering corps is very nearly impossible to oppose because the central maneuvers are always the shortest by half, the simplest, the easiest, and the best covered.

Sixth principle: In all maneuvers, the different maneuvering elements must be in the same order and arranged among themselves in the same manner, and these arrangements must be changed only when absolutely necessary or when very useful for the moment.

Seventh principle: All maneuvers that seek to advance must be made entirely at the front, and all those that seek to withdraw must be made at the rear.

Eighth principle: All changes of front must be made with the greatest rapidity and in a manner that promptly removes the flanks from the enemy and protects the flanks from any insult.

Ninth principle: The movements of troops must be combined in such a way to facilitate the employment of the different arms, their mutual support, without confusion, and with the greatest simplicity.

Tenth principle: As it is always necessary to draw the enemy into error, one must reveal his dispositions only when it is impossible to oppose them.

—Marquis de Silva, *Pensées sur la tactique et la stratégique ou, Vrais principes de la science militaire*, pp. 83-84, my translation.

## APPENDIX 5

## Henry Lloyd, "Rules Concerning Firepower," 1781

1. Since the greatest silence is necessary, the battalion commander alone should be allowed to speak.

2. A regiment or a battalion marching toward the enemy must never break its line unless they are forced by the nature of the terrain.

3. The first rank must never kneel to give the third ease of firing because it is dangerous before the enemy; moreover, repetition of this movement tires the soldiers and makes them useless.

—Henry Lloyd, *Mémoires militaires et politiques du général Lloyd*, p. xliv, my translation.

## APPENDIX 6

## Henry Lloyd, "Axioms on the Line of Operations," 1781

1. When the nature of the frontier that you wish to attack and the position of your depots affords you the freedom, it is necessary to choose the shortest and least difficult line of operations.

2. Your direction must be such that the enemy is not able to act on your flanks and consequently on your line of operations. That would happen if the enemy were the master of the provinces that are found on the right and left of your march because then, the more you advance into the country, the more you assure your defeat; soon you would no longer have communications with your depots; your line would be destroyed; you would be entirely enveloped and defeated.

3. It is necessary that this line of operation lead you to some essential objective, otherwise ten campaigns, although extremely successful, would produce nothing useful.

—Henry Lloyd, *Mémoires militaires et politiques du général Lloyd,* pp. 163-64, my translation.

## APPENDIX 7

### ANTOINE-HENRI JOMINI, "MAXIMS ON LINES OF OPERATIONS," 1805

1. Between two equally maneuverable armies, an extended flank (*crochet*) can be used with success against an attack on a flank.

2. To assure the success of this movement, it is not necessary to restrain oneself in the forming of the extended flank, which would serve only against the danger of the moment; but the army must change its front to the same direction in order to present its entire line to the enemy and repulse them.

3. Finally, if the attacked army believes itself strong enough, it should act offensively against its adversary instead of changing the direction of its front, which is only a defensive movement; after it has rapidly extended its flank to check the front of the enemy and has protected its menaced flank, the rest of the line must simply place itself in column at the flank by platoons or divisions and extend itself from the same position that it occupied so that it strikes in turn the flank of the enemy that had sought to make its own attack.

4. A flank extended to the front of the line . . . does not cover the flank of an army as well as a flank extended to the rear.

5. It is concluded from the preceding maxims that by remaining immobile in one position, regardless of the strength of the force, an army will always be taken by the flank or turned, and that the only way to oppose such an attempt is to maneuver in the same way as the enemy, that is, offensively and by menacing his main line.

—Antoine-Henri Jomini, *Traité de grande tactique,* I, pp. 240-43, my translation.

## APPENDIX 8

### ANTOINE-HENRI JOMINI, "DIDACTIC RÉSUMÉ ON LINES OF OPERATIONS," 1805

1. . . . a double line can be good when the enemy has a similar line; but in this case the parts of the enemy line must be exterior and yours interior. . . .

2. An army whose lines are closer together than those of the enemy, can, by a strategic movement, successively crush the enemy's lines by alternatively uniting the mass of your forces against them.

3. To assure every advantage for the success of this movement, it is necessary to leave a small division before that part of the enemy that you wish to hold in check. . . .

4. It follows that a double line of operations, placed exteriorly to the parts of a line of operations drawn closely together, will always be fatal if the enemy knows how to profit from the advantages of his position and from the rapidity of reinforcement afforded to the interior of his line.

5. A double line of operations will always be much more dangerous than a single line of operations when the parts of the double line are more than a few days march apart.

6. Inversely to the two preceding maxims, simple and interior lines of operations are always the surest. They offer no advantage to the enemy, and on the contrary allow massed action against his isolated divisions if he is imprudent enough to separate them.

7. First, two interior lines can support each other, and they must be able to face the two exterior lines at a certain distance; they must avoid being confined by the enemy to a space that is too small where its divisions can act simultaneously.

Second, the interior lines must avoid the danger of the opposite mistake, that of pushing their operations too far, because the enemy would have the time to crush the division that had been weakened in order to allow a mass on the other point, and he would be able to make progress and conquest that would be irreparable.

—Antoine-Henri Jomini, *Traité de grande tactique*, I, pp. 396-98, my translation.

## APPENDIX 9

# ANTOINE-HENRI JOMINI, "MAXIMS ON LINES OF OPERATIONS," 1805

1. Simple maneuver lines on a single frontier are the most advantageous. . . .

2. Double lines against single lines have never succeeded in the two

wars; the reason is very natural and relates to the general principles of all operations.

3. The lines on two frontiers that have an interior direction have always triumphed over two exterior lines.

4. The most advantageous direction for a maneuver line is that which places it on the rear and on the extremity of the line of defense of the enemy. The operations of 1805 have proved this truth in a brilliant manner.

5. The configuration of the frontiers can be of great importance in the direction of these lines. Central positions that form a salient angle toward the enemy . . . are the most advantageous and additionally those that lead to the rear or to one of the extremities of the line of defense. The flanks of this angle are so important that one must use all the resources of the art and of nature to make them incapable of being attacked.

6. In the absence of central positions, one can correct the deficiency by the relative direction of the maneuver lines. . . .

—Antoine-Henri Jomini, *Traité de grande tactique*, II, pp. 208-11, my translation.

# APPENDIX 10

## ANTOINE-HENRI JOMINI, "GENERAL PRINCIPLES UPON WHICH THE ART OF WAR RESTS," 1816

The fundamental principle upon which every military combination rests, is to operate with the greatest mass of forces, a combined effort, upon a decisive point. . . .

The methods of applying this maxim are not numerous; let us endeavor to point them out.

I.   The first measure is to take the initiative of the movements. The general who secures this advantage, is enabled to employ his own forces wherever he sees it best to direct them; that one, on the other hand, who waits for his enemy, may be incapable of originating a single combination, since he has to subordinate his movements to those of his adversary, and there may be no longer time to arrest these when they are in full course of execution. The general who takes the initiative, knows what he is to do; he conceals his march, surprises and overwhelms one extremity or a feeble part of his adversary's lines. He who awaits the attack is beaten upon one of his points even before he may be informed of the attack.

II.   The second measure is to direct our movements against the most advantageous feeble part. The choice of that feeble part depends upon the position of the enemy. The most important point will always be that one, the occupation of which will ensure us the most favorable chances and procure us the most favorable results. For example, such will be those positions that tend to give us control of the enemy's communications with his base of operations, and to throw him back upon an insurmountable obstacle; such as a sea; a great river, without a bridge; or the territory of a strong neutral power. . . .

III.   The result of the preceding truths proves, that as it is preferable to attack the extremity of a line, we should be careful about attacking both at the same time, lest our forces should not prove very superior. . . .

IV.   In order to operate a combined effort with a strong mass upon a single point, it is important in the strategic movements to hold our forces concentrated upon a space nearly square, that they may be more disposable. Large fronts are as contrary to good principles as parceled lines, great detachments, and isolated divisions, out of sustaining distance.

V.   One of the most efficacious means of applying the general principles just laid down is to induce the enemy to commit faults contrary to this principle. By means of a few bodies of light troops we may disquiet our adversary on several important points of his communications. It is probable that, not knowing their force, he will oppose to them numerous divisions, and will scatter out his masses; these light troops, besides, will contribute perfectly to give information to the army.

VI.   It is most important, when we take the initiative of a decisive movement, that we should be careful to perfectly inform ourselves of the positions of the enemy and of the movements which he can make. . . .

VII.   It is not sufficient to bring about a good operation in war, to bring our masses skillfully to bear upon the most important point, it is necessary to know how to engage them there. Whenever we become established upon the desired points, and rest in inaction, the true principle is lost sight of. The enemy may then make counter-manoeuvres, and in order to deprive him of the power of doing this, whenever we gain his communications, or one of his extremities, we must march upon and combat him. It is then, above all, of the greatest importance that the combined attack of all our forces be simultaneous. It is not the masses present which decide the battle, but those which are brought into action. . . .

VIII.   All the combinations of a battle may be reduced to three systems. The first, which is purely defensive, consists in awaiting the enemy in a strong position, without any other aim than maintaining ourselves there; such were the dispositions of Daun at Torgau, of Marsin at the lines of Turin. Those two occasions demonstrate the erroneous nature of such dispostions.

The second system, on the other hand, is entirely offensive. It consists in attacking the enemy wherever we can encounter him, as Frederick did at Leuthen and Torgau, Napoleon at Jena and Ratisbon, and the allies at Leipsic.

Finally, the third system is a mean between these two. It consists in the choice of a field of battle embracing all the strategic conditions and the proper advantages of ground, with the intention of awaiting the enemy in this position, and on the day of battle, at a convenient moment, to take the initiative and fall upon our adversary with every chance of success.

It is difficult to lay down fixed rules to determine when the last two systems should be employed when the other can not be resorted to. We must take into consideration the morale of the troops on the part of each, also the national character, more or less phlegmatic or impetuous, and lastly, the difficulties of the ground. These circumstances alone ought to guide the genius of a general, and they may be reduced to the three following:

1st. With troops which are hardy and accustomed to war, the absolutely offensive, or initiative of the attack, will always be the best.

2d. That in ground of difficult access, from natural or other causes, and with disciplined and subordinate troops, it would probably be better to let the enemy arrive at some appointed position, in order to take the initiative against him when his troops shall have become exhausted by their first efforts.

3d. It frequently happens from the strategical position of the two parties, that an attack by the main force has to be made upon the enemy in his position, without any reference whatever to local considerations. Such, for instance, would be the case when we desired to prevent the junction of two armies of the enemy, to fall upon a detachment or an isolated corps beyond a river, etc., etc.

IX.   Orders of battle, or the most suitable dispositions for conducting troops to combat, should have for their object to secure at the same time mobility and solidity. . . .

X.   In ground difficult of access, such as vineyards, enclosures, gardens, and bristling heights, the defensive order of battle should be composed of troops deployed in two ranks, and covered by numerous companies of riflemen. But troops intended for the attack, as well as the reserve, should be arranged in columns of attack on the center, as we have indicated in the preceding article; for the reserve having to fall upon the enemy at the decisive moment, it should be done with force and rapidity, that is to say, in columns. A part of this reserve can be kept deployed until the moment of falling on the enemy, for the purpose of imposing upon him by an appearance of numbers.

XI.  If the art of war consists in concerting a superior effort, with a mass against weak portions, it is most indispensably necessary to follow up closely a beaten army.

The strength of an army consists in its organization, in the unity resulting from the connection of all the several parts with the head or the central power. After a defeat this unity or oneness no longer exists; all harmony between the head which combines, and the several corps which execute, is destroyed; their relations are suspended, and nearly always broken. The entire army becomes weak; an attack upon it is almost certain triumph. . . .

XII.  To render the superior shock of a mass decisive, it is equally necessary for a general to bestow the same care upon the *morale* of his army. Of what use is it to bring into action fifty thousand men against twenty thousand, if they lack the impulsion necessary to rush upon and overthrow the enemy? It is not the soldier alone who is to act, it is more particularly those who are to conduct him. All troops are brave when their leader sets the example by a noble emulation and a true, heroic devotion. It is not well that a soldier should remain under fire from fear of discipline alone, but from pride and self-esteem, not yielding to being outdone by his officers in honor and bravery; and, above all, from that confidence which should exist in his mind in the sagacity of his leaders and the courage of his companions in arms.

A general should be able to rely upon the devotion of his lieutenants for the honor of the national arms. He ought to feel that a vigorous shock will be given wherever he orders one to be made. The first means of securing this end is to make himself loved, respected, and feared; the second is to place in the hands of this general the choice and fate of his lieutenants. If they attain that grade by seniority alone, it may be concluded in advance that they will rarely possess the qualities required to fulfil their important functions, that circumstance alone may cause the miscarriage of the best conceived enterprises.

—Antoine-Henri Jomini, *Treatise on Grand Military Operations: or a Critical and Military History of the Wars of Frederick the Great, as*

*Contrasted with the Modern System. Together with a Few of the Most Important Principles of the Art of War,* trans. S. B. Holabird, vol. 2, pp. 448-459.

## APPENDIX 11

## ANTOINE-HENRI JOMINI, "COMPENDIOUS SUMMARY OF THE GRAND PRINCIPLES OF THE SCIENCE OF WAR," 1817

The fundamental principle is, *to operate a combined effort with the greatest possible mass of force upon the decisive point.* . . . The means of applying this maxim, are not very numerous; we will endeavour to indicate them.

I.    The first means is, to assume the initiative of movements.

II.    The second means is, to direct our movements against the weak and most advantageous point.

III.    . . . if we must in preference attack the extremity of a line, we must also carefully avoid attacking both extremities at the same time, unless our forces are very superior.

IV.    To make a combined effort with a great mass against a single point, it is necessary in our strategic movements to keep our forces together on a space nearly square, in order that they may be more disposable.

V.    One of the most effectual means of applying the general principles that we have laid down, is to induce the enemy to commit faults that violate this principle.

VI.    It is of the greatest importance when we assume the initiative of a decisive moment, to neglect no means of learning the positions of the enemy, and the movements that they may make.

VII.    To operate with success in war, it is not sufficient to skillfully carry our forces against the most important points; we must also know how to there engage them. . . . *It is not the forces present, but those engaged, that decide the fate of battles.*

VIII.    All the combinations for battle, may be reduced to three systems. The first is purely defensive. . . . The second system is, on the contrary, entirely offensive. . . . The third system is a kind of medium between the other two. . . .

IX. The orders of battle or most suitable dispostions for bringing troops into action, should possess both solidity and mobility; for the troops must neither be too extended, nor too crowded together.

X. In grounds of difficult access, such as vineyards, enclosures and *fenced* countries, gardens, *woods,* and steep heights, the defensive order of battle should be composed of displayed battalions, covered by numerous platoons of sharpshooters.

XI. In a defensive battle upon open ground, we may also substitute for these columns, squares of battalions, by doubling the lines of the two ranks, so as to form four deep.

XII. If the science of war consists in combining a superior effort of a mass against weak points, it is indisputably necessary to vigorously pursue a beaten army.

XIII. To render decisive the superior shock of a mass, the General must pay the utmost attention to the morale of his army.

—From Simon Gay de Vernon, *A Treatise on the Science of War,* trans. John M. O'Connor, pp. 483-90.

# APPENDIX 12

# Jean T. Rocquancourt, "Aphorisms on Strategy," 1826

I. A campaign plan must foresee all that the enemy is able to do and possess the means to overcome it. . . .

II. All war must be methodical and undertaken with means proportionate to the obstacles that can be foreseen. . . .

III. It would be absurd to outline in advance the actions that a general must pursue in the course of a campaign; because, in addition to the fact that success often depends on circumstances that cannot be foreseen, the inspirations of genius are stifled by leading an army in accordance with an unknown will.

IV. Once war is decided upon, said Montecuculli, doubts, scruples and all the bad that may come must be put aside forever. . . . Success in war is assured by giving command to the leader alone, because when authority is divided, sentiments are often different and operations lack cohesiveness. . . .

It is a principle to hold together or in some measure of unity all parts of an army. . . .

V.   In general an army should have but a single principal line of operations. . . .

VI.   Do nothing that the enemy wishes, for the reason that he wishes it. This maxim, drawn from the nature of war itself, requires:

1.   That one constantly strive to seize the enemy's line of operation.

2.   That the field of battle must be avoided when the enemy is entrenched or when the enemy alone knows and has studied it.

3.   That care must be taken not to attack the front of a position that is capable of being turned.

4.   That it is generally advantageous to pursue a defeated enemy to the extreme.

VII.   It is proof of great skill, in strategy as well as in tactics, to operate by interior lines, doing so forces the enemy to divide himself.

VIII.   In a methodical way, it is necessary to have a strong place or an entrenched position on the line of operations at every five or six days march. . . .

IX.   It is a principle never to assign a point that the enemy occupies or can occupy before you as the meeting place for different parts of the army. . . .

X.   The art of mountain warfare consists principally in occupying camps on the flanks or in the rear of the enemy so that he has no alternative but to evacuate his positions without combat. . . .

—Jean T. Rocquancourt, *Cours élémentaire d'art et d'histoire militaires à l'usage des éléves de l'École royale spéciale militaire,* pp. 422-24, my translation.

# APPENDIX 13

# Antoine-Henri Jomini, "Principal Maxims," 1830

1.   If the art of war consists of putting the greatest possible number of forces into action at the decisive point in the theater of operations, the choice of the line of operations, being the first way to arrive at this

condition, can be considered as the fundamental basis of a good campaign plan. . . .

2. The direction to give to this line is dependent not only on the geographic situation in the theater of operations, but also on the emplacement of the enemy forces on the strategical checkerboard. Still the line is placed only on the center or on one of the extremities; in the single case where one has infinitely superior forces, it may be possible to act on the front and the extremities at the same time; in all other cases, it would be a gross error. . . .

3. By following the principle that we here announce, it is an established fact that with equal forces, a simple line of operations on a common frontier would have the advantage over a double line of operations.

4. Nevertheless, it may happen that a double line becomes necessary, first because of the configuration of the theater of war, and further because the enemy may use a double line himself, it will be necessary to oppose a part of the army against each of the two or three masses that he forms. In this case the interior line or central line will be preferable to the exterior line since the army that has the interior lines would be able to have each of its parts act in cooperation in a combined plan, and they would also be able to assemble the greatest parts of their forces in the promptest manner to decide the success of the campaign.

5. For the same reason, two concentric lines are more valuable than two divergent lines; the former, conforming more to the principles of strategy, also have the advantage of covering the lines of communications and supplies; but, in order to be out of danger, one must combine them in such a manner that the two armies that use them cannot be encountered separately by the united forces of the enemy before they themselves can effect their own junction.

6. Divergent lines can be attempted only after a victory, or a strategical operation by which one would reunite to divide the enemy forces. Then it becomes natural to use divergent directions to achieve the dispersion of the defeated forces.

7. It often happens that an army sees itself forced to change the line of operations in the middle of a campaign (what we have called accidental lines). It is a most delicate and important maneuver, which can yield great results, but can also lead to great defeats when it is not used with wisdom because one helps himself but little when he pulls his army from an embarrassing situation.

—Antoine-Henri Jomini, *Tableau analytique des principales combinaisons de la guerre,* pp. 84-87, my translation.

## APPENDIX 14

### G. F. FRANÇAIS,
### "THE MEANS OF APPLYING THE FUNDAMENTAL PRINCIPLE OF WAR," 1832

1. The first way is to take the initiative of movement. . . .

2. The second way is to direct your movements on the most advantageous weak point of the enemy. The choice of this point depends on the position of the enemy. The most important point will always be that whose occupation yields the most favorable chances and the greatest results. For example, positions that allow the gaining of the enemy's communication with his base of operation, or that hurl him against an insurmountable obstacle like a sea, a large river, a neutral country. . . .

3. If it is convenient to attack the extremity of a line, it is necessary to take care not to attack the two extremities at the same time. Even if one has highly superior forces, it is necessary to put them into action at the same time and on the same point. . . .

4. One of the most effective ways of applying the general principle is to make the enemy commit errors contrary to the principle, by harassing him at important points along his communications with small bodies of light troops.

5. It is not sufficient for the proper conduct of war to skillfully bring masses to the most important points; it is necessary to know how to engage them there. . . .

6. If the art of war consists of concentrating the effort of a superior mass against weak points, it is incontestably necessary to actively pursue a beaten army. . . .

7. To make the shock of a superior mass decisive, it is necessary for the general to give great attention to the morale of his army.

—G. F. Français, "Cours d'art militaire, à l'usage des élèves de l'École d'application de l'artillerie et du génie," pp. 6-8, my translation.

# APPENDIX 15

## DENNIS HART MAHAN, "PRINCIPLES REGULATING THE PLAN AND PROFILE OF INTRENCHMENTS," 1836

I.  A flanked position should be the basis of the plan of all intrenchments.

II.  Every angle of defence should be 90°.

III.  A line of defence should not exceed 160 yards.

IV.  A salient angle should not be less than 60°.

V.  A strong profile is essential to a vigorous defence.

VI.  The bayonet should be chiefly relied on to repel the enemy.

VII.  Intrenchments should be arranged to facilitate sorties.

VIII.  Intrenchments should contain a reserve proportioned to their importance.

IX.  Intrenchments should be defended to the last extremity.

—Dennis H. Mahan, *Field Fortifications,* pp. 9-14.

# APPENDIX 16

## ANTOINE-HENRI JOMINI, "MAXIMS THAT SUPPORT THE APPLICATION OF THE FUNDAMENTAL PRINCIPLE OF WAR," 1838

From the different articles that compose it, we may conclude that the manner of applying the general principle of war to all possible theaters of operations is found in what follows:—

1.  In knowing how to make the best use of the advantages that the reciprocal directions of the two bases of operations may afford. . . .

2.  In choosing, from the three zones ordinarily found in the strategic field, that one upon which the greatest injury can be done to the enemy with the least risk to one's self.

3.   In establishing well, and giving a good direction to, the lines of operations; adopting for defense the concentric system of the Archduke Charles in 1796 and of Napoleon in 1814; or that of Soult in 1814, for retreats parallel to the frontiers. . . .

4.   In selecting judicious eventual lines of maneuver, by giving them such directions as always to be able to act with the greater mass of the forces, and to prevent the parts of the enemy from concentrating or from affording each other mutual support.

5.   In combining, in the same spirit of centralization, all strategic positions, and all large detachments made to cover the most important strategic points of a theater of war.

6.   In imparting to the troops the greatest possible mobility and activity, so as, by their successive employment upon points where it may be important to act, to bring superior force to bear upon fractions of the hostile army. . . .

—Antoine-Henri Jomini, *The Art of War,* trans. G. H. Mendell and W. P. Craighill, pp. 175-76.

## APPENDIX 17

## NIKOLAI OKUNEV, "MAXIMS CONCERNING THE THREE ARMS," 1841

1.   Actions by infantry must be based on the preparatory action of skirmishers and artillery.

2.   Offensive action of infantry must be based on the use of this arm with artillery.

3.   Engagements that the infantry decides will be completed by the cavalry.

4.   Infantry retreats must occur under the protection of artillery and cavalry.

5.   Infantry deployment must occur under the protection of artillery and cavalry.

6.   Cavalry actions and the undertaking of offensive movements must be based on the preparatory action of infantry and artillery.

7.   Cavalry retreats must take place under the protection of infantry.

8. Cavalry deployment must take place under the protection of light cavalry and horse artillery.

9. Artillery must act only under the protection of infantry or cavalry.

10. Whenever circumstances and terrain permit, never separate the artillery from the infantry and cavalry.

—Nikolai Okunev, *Considérations sur les grandes opérations* . . . , p. 295.

## APPENDIX 18

## PATRICK L. MACDOUGALL, "MAXIMS," 1856

*Maxim* 1.—Never abandon your line of communications from over-confidence. (Napoleon.)

*Maxim* 2.—Although it is a maxim never to abandon your line of communications, yet to change that line is one of the most skillful ma-noeuvres of the art of war, where circumstances authorise it.

*Maxim* 3.—If you march to the conquest of a country with two or three armies, which have each its line of operation, towards a fixed point where they are to unite, it is a maxim that the union of these different *corps d'armée* must never take place near the enemy, because not only may the enemy, by concentrating his forces, prevent their junction, but he may moreover beat them in detail.

*Maxim* 4.—An army ought to have but one line of operation, which it must carefully guard, and never abandon except from an overruling necessity.

*Maxim* 5.—When two armies are ranged in battle, and one of them has but one point to retreat upon, while the other can retreat on all the points of the compass, all the advantage is with the last. It is in such a case that a commander should be bold to strike great blows, and manoeuvre on his enemy's flank; Victory is in his hands. (Napoleon.)

*Maxim* 6.—It is one of the most important principles of war to unite the scattered bodies of an army at the point which is the most distant and the best protected from the attempts of an enemy. (Napoleon.)

*Maxim* 7.—To operate by lines distant from each other and without intercommunication, is a fault which generally leads to another. The advancing columns of an army must be in constant communication with each other, so that an enemy cannot penetrate between them. (Napoleon.)

*Maxim* 8.—The communication between the different fractions of an army, whether in position or in movement, must always be perfectly open and easy.

*Maxim* 9.—To besiege a fortified place whose possession would be useless to yourself, and which gives the enemy no power of annoyance, is to waste time and means.

*Maxim* 10.—The excellence of a position is always relative,
1st. To that occupied by the enemy.
2nd. To the number of troops intended to line it.
3rd. To the composition of those troops.

*Maxim* 11.—A position must not be commanded by heights in the direction of the enemy within artillery range.

*Maxim* 12.—Every position must cover the line of communications of the army with its base.

*Maxim* 13.—The lines by which the army must retreat from its position, if defeated, must be as numerous and easy as possible.

*Maxim* 14.—The part or parts of a line of battle which are in front of any line or lines of retreat must be made the strongest (if not so already from natural causes), either by entrenchments, or by posting the greatest force at such parts of your line.

*Maxim* 15.—Every position must afford easy communication, in rear of the line, between the different parts of your line of battle.

*Maxim* 16.—The ground in front of your position should be such as to impede the movements of an enemy advancing to attack you, and should be so completely commanded by your position as to insure its being swept by your artillery to the full extent of its range.

*Maxim* 17.—Every position must afford secure protection to the flanks of your army.

*Maxim* 18.—A position cannot be too strong; lose no opportunity of strengthening it by means of field works.

*Maxim* 19.—Occupy your position in such a manner that you can defend a part of it with a smaller force than that which the enemy can bring against it, so that the greater part of your force may be available to assail the weaker of the enemy.

*Maxim* 20.—When on the eve of a battle recall all your detachments, do not neglect one however small, one battalion the more sometimes decides the day. (Napoleon.)

*Maxim* 21.—Never detach a force either on the eve or on the day of a battle for the purpose of co-operating with your main body in attacking the enemy, unless your communications with the detachment can be easily maintained.

*Maxim* 22.—Never leave intervals between the different divisions of your line of battle, where the enemy might penetrate, unless to draw him into a snare. (Napoleon.)

*Maxim* 23.—Never attack with a fraction of your force, when a short delay will enable you to attack with masses.

*Maxim* 24.—Nothing can be more rash or contrary to the principles of war than to make a flank march before an enemy in position. (Napoleon.)

*Maxim* 25.—There are two ways of obliging an enemy to abandon a position, viz, by attacking and driving him from it; and by manoeuvring so as to make it impossible for him to hold it.

*Maxim* 26.—An attack on the enemy's centre, if successful, is in general the most decisive. That on a flank is the most secure.

*Maxim* 27.—If your enemy is entrenching and it is your intention to attack his position, do not delay a moment. Every hour's delay may cost the loss of 1000 men in the assault.

*Maxim* 28.—An army on the march and an army in position in an enemy's country, should never be for one moment without its advanced guard and its advanced posts.

*Maxim* 29.—To defend a defile, never take a post in front, but always in rear, of the defile.

*Maxim* 30.—Every disadvantage may be removed by skill or fortune, except *Time*. If a general has Time against him he must fail. And conversely, *Time* is the best ally.

—Patrick L. MacDougall, *The Theory of War Illustrated by Numerous Examples from Military History,* 2d ed., pp. 98-108, 146-69.

# APPENDIX 19

## Kraft zu Hohenlohe-Ingelfingen, "Strategical Axioms," 1887

I.   National policy must be closely allied at every point with strategy.

II.   At the onset the destruction of the enemy's army must form the objective. Everything else, the occupation of cities or territories, is only of secondary importance.

III.  It is impossible to be too strong for a decisive battle. The whole efforts of strategy must be directed to this end, not diverting more forces for secondary objects than are absolutely necessary.

IV.  No rigid system must be adhered to, the object should be to choose by sound judgment the shortest path to the desired goal.

V.  Changes in the plan of operation lead to incalculable losses of strength and time. Unless therefore the enemy or the elements enforce such alternations they are to be avoided. Sudden changes of intention in the leader have often produced the greatest misfortunes.

—Kraft zu Hohenlohe-Ingelfingen, *Letters on Strategy,* trans. Walter James, I, pp. 9-10.

# APPENDIX 20

## JAMES MERCUR, "PRINCIPLES OF MOUNTED TACTICS OF CAVALRY," 1889

1.  Never attack over unknown ground.

2.  Always attack at speed.

3.  Never receive an attack at a halt; but charge to meet it, or maneuver to avoid it.

4.  Always endeavor to strike your enemy's flank.

5.  Never charge without a support, under cover of whose action you may rally.

6.  Always endeavor to have a reserve force, even if small, which is only brought into action after the hostile troops are all engaged.

7.  So handle your consecutive supports and reserves as to fall upon the flanks of those of the enemy, as they are successively brought into action; using your last reserve to strike him in the flank.

8.  Charge in such formations as will give you the desired density on contact, but always avoid unnecessary depth.

—James Mercur, *Elements of the Art of War,* 2d ed., pp. 47-48.

# APPENDIX 21

## G. A. LEYER,
## "BASIC PRINCIPLES OF THE ART OF WAR," 1894

1.  Principle of extreme exertion of force at the beginning of a war—to begin each war (campaign, operation) not only with sufficient forces, but also with an extreme exertion of these forces, without the fear of assigning too many forces, but on the contrary, with the fear of assigning too few.

2.  Principle of simultaneity of actions—the simultaneous deployment of forces in a theater of war.

3.  Principle of economy of forces—grouping them in time and space in accordance with the relative importance of different sectors.

4.  Principle of concentration of forces on the decisive point—concentrating the main body on the most important sector, sacrificing for this purpose all accessory, secondary ones.

5.  To hit the enemy at his most sensitive point, having the enemy army as the chief objective—not to be diverted by geographic objects of action, but to have the enemy army as the immediate target, as the chief representative and bearer of the will and force of the enemy; the goal of a march must be the enemy camp, and the goal of battle—destruction of his army.

6.  Principle of surprise—to concentrate superior forces on the battlefield unexpectedly (secretly and swiftly) for the enemy and place them before the battle in as favorable a position as possible.

7.  Internal integrity and unity in actions as the high ideal in strategy and tactics—to conduct the operation or battle in a spirit of their inner integrity and unity of actions.

8.  Importance of preparing the attack—a decisive attack in battle is preceded by its preparation (in all forms), brought to the degree of maturity permitted by the circumstances of a particular occasion.

9.  The importance of victory in its energetic exploitation—not to limit oneself to winning the battlefield, but to develop aftereffects of the victory through energetic pursuit, following immediately after the victorious battle.

10.  Principle of security of the operation—have secured rear and

flanks in all positions of the army, i.e., an operational line secure in all senses.

11. Principle of initiative and dominance over the enemy's will and mind—from the very beginning of an operation enlist the support of benefits of the initiative and of dominance over the enemy's will and mind and retain it to the end.

12. Strive to be strong where the enemy is weak—present the strong side and shun the weak side.

—G. Leyer, *Metod voyennykh nauk,* pp. 53-54, quoted in Vasili Ye. Savkin, *The Basic Principles of Operational Art and Tactics (A Soviet View),* trans. and published under the auspices of the United States Air Force, p. 31.

# APPENDIX 22

# JOHN DONALDSON, "LESSONS IN TACTICS," 1905

(i)   Councils of war are invariably fraught with danger in military operations. In most cases they merely lead to nothing decisive being accomplished; successful war is not waged by a congress but by one single military leader.

(ii)   Concentration of force at the decisive point is essential.

(iii)   It is dangerous to base plans on conjecture, *i.e.* to decide what the enemy will or will not do, and to base a course of action on that supposition, ignoring all other possible developments. . . .

(iv)   Before attempting to turn an enemy's flank, it is necessary to know with some degree of accuracy where that flank rests. . . .

(v)   Combination of action and good communications between frontal and flank attacks are essential.

(vi)   Careful reconnaissance is essential to success. . . .

(vii)   Every plan of attack should contemplate and provide against counterattack.

(viii)   A flank march within striking distance of the enemy is a dangerous manoeuvre. . . .

(ix)   The proper and timely use of the general reserve will often be the deciding factor in battle. . . .

(x)  A decisive counterattack requires great forethought and careful preparation. The flanks must be secure; it must be superior in numbers to that part of the enemy's line attacked; its delivery must be well timed, and its blow must be swift and heavy. . . .

(xi)  The best plans may be spoiled by faulty staff work. . . .

(xii)  Success at the decisive point brings success everywhere.

(xiii)  Difficult situations require decisive results.

—John Donaldson, *Military History Applied to Modern Warfare, A Guide to the Study of Military History Exemplified by Studies of the Campaigns of Austerlitz, Jena, Vimiero, Corunna, Salamanca, Waterloo, and the Shenandoah Valley,* 2d ed., pp. 53-55.

# APPENDIX 23

# G. J. FIEBEGER,
# "MILITARY PRINCIPLES," C. 1906

I.  In forming a plan of campaign, it is requisite to foresee everything the enemy may do, and to be prepared with the necessary means to prevent it.

II.  Nothing is so important in war as undivided command. Two independent armies should never be in the same theater of operations.

III.  At the commencement of a campaign, to advance or not to advance, is a matter for grave consideration, but when once the offensive is assumed it must be sustained to the last extremity. However skillful the maneuver, a retreat will always weaken the morale of an army.

IV.  An army should have but one line of operations; it is contrary to all true principles to make corps which have no communications act separately against a central force whose communications are open; an army should always keep its columns so united as to prevent an enemy passing between them with impunity.

V.  When the conquest of a country is undertaken by two or three armies, each of which has a separate line of operations until they arrive at a point fixed upon for their concentration, it should be laid down as a principle, that the junction should never take place near the enemy, because the enemy by uniting his forces, may not only prevent the union of the armies but may defeat them in detail.

VI.  The lines of operation should be preserved with care and never abandoned save in the last extremity; but it is one of the most skillful maneuvers in war to change it when circumstances authorize it, or render it necessary.

VII.  An army should be ready every day, every night, and at all times of the day and night, to oppose all the resistance of which it is capable.

VIII.  A commander-in-chief should ask himself frequently in the day, what should I do if the enemy's army should now appear in my front, on my right, or on my left? If he have any difficulty in answering these questions, he is badly posted, and should seek to correct his disposition.

IX.  The art of encamping in a position is the same as the art of deploying in order of battle in the position. To this end, the artillery should be advantageously placed. Ground should be selected which is not commanded nor liable to be turned, and, as far as possible, the guns should cover and command the surrounding country.

X.  Never lose sight of this maxim, that you should establish your cantonments at the most distant and best protected point from the enemy, especially where a surprise is possible. By this means you will have time to unite all your forces before he can attack you.

XI.  The first principle of war is that a battle should be fought only with all the troops that can be assembled on the field.

XII.  It is an approved maxim in war, never to do what the enemy wishes you to do, for this reason alone, that he desires it. A field of battle, therefore, which he has previously studied and reconnoitered, should be avoided, and double care should be taken where he has had time to fortify or intrench. One consequence deducible from this principle is, never attack a position in front which you can gain by turning.

XIII.  The strength of an army, like power in mechanics, is estimated by multiplying the mass by the rapidity; a rapid march augments the morale of an army, and increases all the chances of victory.

XIV.  In a war of march and maneuver, if you would avoid a battle with a superior army, it is necessary to intrench every night, and occupy a good defensive position. Those natural positions which are ordinarily met with, are not sufficient to protect an army against superior numbers without recourse to art.

XV.    A general of ordinary talent occupying a bad position and surprised by a general with a superior force, seeks safety in retreat; but a great captain supplies all deficiencies by his courage, and marches boldly to meet the attack. By this means he disconcerts his adversary, and if this last shows any irresolution in his movements, a skillful leader profiting by his indecision, may even hope for victory, or at least employ the day in maneuvering. At night he intrenches himself or falls back to a better position.

XVI.    Nothing is so rash or contrary to principle, as to make a flank march before an army especially when this army occupies heights at the foot of which you are forced to defile.

XVII.    When an army is driven from a first position, the retreating columns should always rally sufficiently in the rear, to prevent any interruption from the enemy. The greatest disaster that can happen, is the attack of the columns in detail before they are united.

XVIII.    Of all obstacles which cover the frontiers of empires, a desert is certainly the greatest, a chain of mountains like the Alps holds the second rank, rivers, the third.

XIX.    Throw by strategic movements, the mass of your army, successively, on the decisive points of a theater of war, and also upon the communications of the enemy as much as possible without compromising your own.

XX.    Maneuver to engage fractions of the hostile army with the bulk of your own forces.

XXI.    Simple maneuvers consistently carried out are the most certain to attain their end.

—Gustave J. Fiebeger, *Elements of Strategy,* pp. 74-102.

# APPENDIX 24

# J. BÜRDE,
## "CHIEF TACTICAL PRINCIPLES," 1908

(1)    Attacking infantry, when exposed to the fire of hostile infantry which cannot be located, must use widely extended formations. But as soon as the opponent's position is discovered, the firing line must be strengthened in proportion as it gets closer to the enemy.

(2)    The initiative for the assault must come from the firing line.

(3)    Attacking infantry must be distributed in depth within its unit. . . .

(4)    Troops engaged with the enemy must be made to do all the work they are capable of, before being replaced.

(5)    Troops engaged with the enemy cannot be withdrawn except under cover of night.

(6)    In a defensive position which is meant to be held, no undefended gaps must be left between trenches.

(7)    Troops cannot execute movements towards a flank under fire of the enemy. . . .

(8)    Troops detailed to hold advanced positions temporarily (advanced posts), or to act temporarily on the offensive (local counter attack) must be made so weak that they possess no inherent fighting power.

—J. Bürde, *Tactical Principles,* pp. 23-24.

# APPENDIX 25

## MATTHEW F. STEELE, "A FEW OF JACKSON'S MAXIMS," 1909

(1)    Always mystify, mislead, and surprise the enemy if possible.

(2)    When you strike him and overcome him never give up the pursuit as long as your men have strength to follow; for an enemy routed, if hotly pursued, becomes panic-stricken, and can be destroyed by half their number.

(3)    Never fight against heavy odds if by any possible maneuvering you can hurl your whole force on only a part, and that the weakest part, of your enemy, and crush it.

(4)    To move swiftly, strike vigorously, and secure all the fruits of victory is the secret of successful war.

(5)    A defensive campaign can only be made successful by taking the offensive at the proper time. Napoleon never waited for his adversary to become fully prepared, but struck him the first blow.

(6)    I had rather lose one man in marching than five in battle.

—Matthew F. Steele, *American Campaigns,* p. 115. Steele credited Imboden's *Battles and Leaders* for the first three maxims and G. F. R. Henderson for the last three.

## APPENDIX 26

## United States Army, "Summary of Combat Imperatives," 1911

1. Avoid combats that offer no chance of victory or other valuable results.

2. Make every effort for the success of the general plan and avoid spectacular plays that have no bearing on the general results.

3. Have a definite plan and carry it out vigorously. Do not vacillate.

4. Do not attempt complicated maneuvers.

5. Keep the command in hand; avoid undue extension and dispersion.

6. Study the ground and direct the advance in such a way as to take advantage of all available cover and thereby diminish losses.

7. Never deploy until the purpose and the proper direction are known.

8. Deploy enough men for the immediate task in hand; hold out the rest and avoid undue haste in committing them to the action.

9. Flanks must be protected either by reserves, fortifications, or the terrain.

10. In a decisive action, gain and keep fire superiority.

11. Keep up reconnaissance.

12. Use the reserve, but not until needed or a very favorable opportunity for its use presents itself. Keep some reserve as long as practicable.

13. Do not hesitate to sacrifice the command if the result is worth the cost.

14. Spare the command all unnecessary hardship and exertion.

—United States Army, *Infantry Drill Regulations*, p. 122.

## APPENDIX 27

## United States Army, "Combat Principles," 1914

The following principles apply to both offensive and defensive combat:
Fire superiority insures success.
Unity of command is essential to success. The regiment united in combat

has greater force and fighting power than have its three separate battalions. A battalion acting as a unit is stronger than are four companies acting independently. All the troops assigned to the execution of a distinct tactical task must be placed under one command.

The task assigned any unit must not involve a complicated maneuver. Simple and direct plans and methods are productive of the best results in warfare.

All the troops that are necessary to execute a definite task must be assigned to it from the beginning. Avoid putting troops into action in driblets.

Detachments during combat are justifiable only when the execution of the tasks assigned them contributes directly to success in the main battle or when they keep a force of the enemy larger than themselves out of the main battle. When combat is imminent all troops must be called to the probable field of battle. A force is never so strong that it can needlessly dispense with the support of any of its parts during combat.

Too many troops must not, however, be committed to the action in the early stages, no matter what be the nature of the deployment or the extent of line held. Some reserves must be kept in hand.

Use the reserve only when needed or when a favorable opportunity for its use presents itself. Keep some reserve as long as practicable, but every man that can be used to advantage must participate in the decisive stage of the combat.

Flanks must be protected either by reserves, fortifications, or the terrain.

Flank protection is the duty of the commanders of all flank units down to the lowest, whether specifically enjoined in orders or not. This applies to units on both sides of gaps that may exist in the combat lines.

Reconnaissance continues throughout the action.

—United States Army, *Field Service Regulations,* 1914, pp. 67-68.

# APPENDIX 28

# United States Army, "Employment of Cavalry, General Principles," 1914

1.   Mounted action is the principal method of fighting of cavalry. Animated by an aggressive spirit, it will seize every opportunity to attack

with the horse and saber. Success is achieved by simplicity in conception and vigor in the execution of plans.

2.   The rifle enables Cavalry on foot to engage in effective combat, offensive or defensive, against forces of all arms.

3.   In combining shock with fire action, the latter may be provided by the Horse Artillery, machine guns, or rifles, or by any combination of these arms.

4.   On account of the variety of its weapons and methods of action, Cavalry is capable of independent operations under practically all the conditions of war.

5.   The large size of modern armies and the great extension of their fronts have rendered it more difficult than ever to change disposition once made and have augmented the importance of celerity and endurance in marching.

6.   Cavalry reconnoiters the theater of operations and the enemy's dispositions; it protects the army against surprise and screens its movements.

7.   *Habitual reliance on dismounted action will weaken and eventually destroy initiative;* difficulties of terrain are likely to be overestimated. Cavalry imbued with the true spirit of the arm does not remain inactive, waiting for a more favorable opportunity for a mounted charge.

8.   When small bodies of Cavalry unaccompanied by horse artillery or machine guns meet similar bodies of the enemy's Cavalry, their best course of action will usually be to make an energetic mounted attack at once, should the ground be in any way suitable, without delaying or weakening the mounted attack by dismounting a part of the command.

9.   When opposing forces of Cavalry find themselves in contact, a decision as to the action to be adopted must be made and acted upon at once or disaster will result.

10.   During the operations preceding a general engagement, the first and most important antagonist is the enemy's Cavalry.

11.   In a battle of all arms even relatively small forces of Cavalry may achieve important results by seizing an opportune moment.

12.   The character of the enemy and the nature of the terrain exercise a controlling influence on the operations of Cavalry.

13.   Cavalry should be bold and enterprising.

14.   Cavalry must not only be strongly impressed with the power of its rifles, but must be ready to assault on foot and to capture positions held by the enemy with the same determination and resolution of Infantry.

15.  The most effective directions of attack are against the enemy's flank and rear. Enterprises against his communications may secure valuable results, but they should be so timed that the Cavalry will not be beyond reach for the use in a general engagement. *On the battlefield all bodies of troops must seek to contribute to the achievement of victory.*

16.  The mobility of Cavalry comes into full play in the pursuit, to reap the fruits of victory; and in a retreat, in the quick utilization of successive defensive positions, and in the rapid withdrawal therefrom after breaking off the engagement at the last moment.

—United States Army, *Cavalry Service Regulations,* pp. 220-22.

# APPENDIX 29

## GERMANY, "ESSENTIAL PRINCIPLES FOR THE DEFENSE," 1915

1.  The fundamental principle is that the *first line* must be held at all costs and that the enemy must be at once ejected, should he succeed in penetrating at some point.

2.  It is of the first importance that a hostile attack should be promptly recognized, in order that the fire trenches may be manned in time, and that the artillery may at once open barrage fire. . . .

3.  The best method of holding a position is by effective flanking fire, taking enfilade artillery fire for granted, machine guns are best adapted for the purpose. . . .

4.  The occupation and relief of positions must be so arranged that troops, in so far as possible, *always occupy the same trenches.* . . .

5.  In the case of hostile attack, the trenches must be occupied in sufficient strength. The garrison of the first line must never be drawn to provide units for support and reserve. . . .

6.  If the enemy succeeds in penetrating the first line, and if the garrison is unable to drive him out immediately, it is the duty of the garrisons of the neighbouring trenches to attack the enemy in flank, while at the same time the troops in the second and third line trenches, reinforced as required by their reserves, dash forward to retake the lost trench. . . .

7.  The second and third line must not only serve as a starting

point from which to retake ground lost, but must also be used for checking the assault of the enemy who has entered the first line. . . .

8. The second line should be organized on the principle that, if the enemy succeeds in capturing the first line, he should not be in a position to capture the second line without having to regroup his artillery. . . .

9. In accordance with the principle of only giving ground to the enemy foot by foot and when forced to do so, *intermediate positions* will be organized, whenever natural strongpoints and special conditions admit of this, as well as at points where there is a considerable distance between the first and second lines.

10. It is not advisable to construct artificial strongpoints, especially in the first line; they are easily located by aeroplanes and much exposed to the enemy's fire. . . .

—Germany, Army Headquarters, Second Army, "Essential Principles for the Defence of Positions as Laid down in Instructions Issued by G. H. Q.," trans. Great Britain, General Staff, Intelligence, pp. 1-2.

## APPENDIX 30

# Paul S. Bond and M. J. MacDonough, "General Observations on Combat — Attack and Defense," 1916

Decisive results are obtained only by the offense.

Fire superiority is the keynote of success.

Avoid too great dispersion of the front or separation of the troops in a decisive action.

All movements should be simple. Complicated maneuvers should never be attempted in battle.

Avoid half-hearted measures. If the decision is to attack, all available force should be thrown into the fight.

Do not uncover the line of retreat unless the force is small and the country friendly.

Put into the main fight all available force, calling in all detachments within reach.

A detachment operating as a containing force separated by some distance from the main body, should if practicable be relatively strong in cavalry and artillery.

Night attacks are usually dangerous, and ordinarily practicable only for small forces.

An attack order will be much more intelligently made when issued as a result of an examination of the ground rather than from the map alone.

Attacks which offer no chance of tactical success should generally be avoided. Combats which have no bearing on the general plan should also be avoided, as a rule, even though they offer the chance of easy victory.

Never neglect reconnaissance at any time.

Avoid splitting or mixing tactical units as far as possible.

Aggressiveness wins battles. If in doubt it is generally better to attack. But *make sure* that the advantage derived from victory will be well worth the cost.

—P. S. Bond and M. J. McDonough, *Technique of Modern Tactics*, 3d ed., pp. 204-205.

## APPENDIX 31

## LINCOLN C. ANDREWS, "TACTICAL RULES," 1916

On the march, distances in column must be kept closed up, to make quick, sure deployment possible, without long running up from the rear.

Covering detachments must always protect the main body from surprise attack. On the march and in camp, this is generally regarded. But at temporary halts, it is too often forgotten, and invites disaster.

Going into a fire fight, the men must not be winded, nor unduly excited by rushing pell mell into action.

Deploying from column for action, leading elements must hold back until all rear elements are properly on the line, as they would do at drill.

Never deploy, until by reconnaissance you are sure of the proper *direction,* and that you are as far advanced as practicable.

Deploy only the strength necessary for the immediate purpose. Always keep a reserve in hand, and use it only when the opportunity demands.

If suddenly confronted with an occasion for action, adopt a *simple, definite* plan; and then carry that plan out firmly.

Having undertaken any one engagement, concentrate *all* your resources on bringing it promptly to a successful issue. Forces detached for side issues are inexcusable, unless they keep larger forces out of the immediate opposition.

Small forces cannot safely undertake extended turning movement, etc. Concentration within supporting distance is necessary, unless part is strong enough to win by itself, is too small to fight anyway, or is extremely mobile, as mounted cavalry.

Always avoid fighting on ground of the enemy's own choosing, especially if he has had time to prepare it for you. By maneuvering, shift the scene if possible to your own advantage.

On the march, a position of the commander is with the advance guard, where he can get timely information at first hand; in action, it is where he can best see and control his forces. In both cases, he must avoid becoming involved too closely with the actual fighting, which makes clear perception of the whole situation quite impossible.

Going into a fight, each organization always has its scouts well out in front, and combat patrols well out on exposed flanks, and so far advanced as to prevent our line coming unexpectedly under enfilading fire.

Communications must be maintained at all times between the elements of a command. Thus a company going into action signals from one element to another and a man in each is detailed to be on the lookout for these signals.

A passive defense is deadly, and does not win battles. Aggressive action is safer, and more prolific of victory. Troops that have the initiative, hold the advantage. They force the others to play their game.

The position of your firing line should always be as nearly as possible perpendicular to the enemy's line of fire.

All the rules for fire discipline and control must be observed; but most disastrous of all is to open fire before it is ordered, or to allow excitement to start a fight with loss of fire control. It will hardly be regained again in that fight.

Never open fire on small forces of the enemy advancing upon you in position. They are trying to get you to do just that, so they may report back what your position is. Let them keep coming. They cannot hurt you, and will have to surrender, or be killed in trying to escape, if you let them get close enough.

It is impossible to shoot troops out of position; hence an attack involves a determination to assault.

Advancing under fire the greatest attention will have to be given by all the men to keeping a general alignment, and to avoiding the constant tendency to bunch into groups, which make such good targets for the enemy.

While actually under fire you can move only straight forward with any safety. To move toward a flank is very dangerous, to move toward the rear is deadly.

Even in small affairs, a few rifles delivering fire of position, will often be the most helpful thing for the attack.

In selecting defensive fire positions for delaying actions, a safe line of withdrawal, not exposed to the enemy's fire, is absolutely essential. Unless the situation demands the sacrifice of your men, this is the determining consideration in your selection of position.

In withdrawing from these positions, keep a few rifles busy in the line while the others get back to the next position, or otherwise make ready for a safe getaway.

If ordered to any military undertaking, never start on your mission until you are absolutely sure you have a clear understanding of each of the points you should know for its proper performance.

And finally, the least appreciated and the most important! In handling your men in the presence of actual conditions, you absolutely must use the same commands and the same movements that they have been taught on the drillfield. The men are going to be sensitive to disturbance, and to anything unusual. If they think that you cannot control them by the usual methods, that their training has failed, they are likely to believe that everything has gone to the bad, and their morale will go with it.

—Lincoln C. Andrews, *Fundamentals of Military Service,* pp. 212-15.

# APPENDIX 32

# J.F.C. FULLER,
## "STRATEGICAL PRINCIPLES," 1916

These fundamental principles are:—

1.   The principle of the objective.

2.   The principle of the offensive.

3.   The principle of mass.

4.   The principle of economy of force.

5.   The principle of movement.

6.   The principle of surprise.

7. The principle of security.
8. The principle of co-operation.

—[J. F. C. Fuller], "The Principles of War, with Reference to the Campaigns of 1914-1915," *Journal of the Royal United Service Institution* 61 (February 1916):3.

## APPENDIX 33

# J.F.C. FULLER, "TACTICAL PRINCIPLES," 1916

These principles are:—

1. The principle of demoralization.
2. The principle of endurance.
3. The principle of shock.

—[J. F. C. Fuller], "The Principles of War, with Reference to the Campaigns of 1914-1915," *Journal of the Royal United Service Institution* 61 (February 1916): 18.

## APPENDIX 34

# GERMANY, "PRINCIPLES OF COMMAND," 1917

(a)   The defence should not be based on the employment of the largest possible number of men, but must rely principally on its armaments. . . .

(b)   The Higher Command should not make it a rigid and unconditional rule that ground cannot be abandoned. It should so conduct the defence that its own troops are on favourable ground, while the attacking force is only left ground unfavourable for its operations.

(c)   Distribution in depth forms the basis of all preparations. . . .

(d)   The commander of the defence must not abandon the initiative in the conduct of the fighting. . . .

—Germany, Army, Chief of the General Staff of the Field Army, *Manual of Position Warfare for All Arms*, part 8, "The Principles of Command in the Defensive Battle in Position Warfare," trans. Great Britain, General Staff, Intelligence, p. 4.

## APPENDIX 35

## FRANCE,
## "PRINCIPLES WHICH SHOULD BE KNOWN TO ALL," 1917

ENERGY—Energy is the most important of soldierly qualities. From it spring bravery, fortitude, self-sacrifice, discipline, and the devotion to duty. It is the energy of the leader and of his men which enables them to carry a fight to a finish and which brings forth the highest acts of heroism. When the leader is considering various courses of action he will be sure to be right if he decides upon the most energetic.

UNITY OF ACTION—In order to defeat the enemy we must strike hard, as hard as possible and all together. One can never be too strong, either in attack or in defense. A good chief of platoon gets all of his men into action and leaves none of them idle during critical moments. If he loses touch with adjoining troops and has no orders, he will go wherever fighting is going on and place his platoon at the disposition of the commander.

SURPRISE—An attacking force will attain the greater results in proportion as its action is unexpected by the enemy. The advantage of surprise should always be sought for. Surprise is obtained by a combination of two essential conditions—*secrecy* in preparation and *celerity* in execution.

SECURITY—On the other hand, we must avoid being surprised. It is a fundamental duty of the commander to provide for the security of his men in every direction in which the enemy may appear.

—France, Minister of War, *Manual for Commanders of Infantry Platoons*, trans. at the U.S. Army War College, pp. 157-58.

# APPENDIX 36

## GREAT BRITAIN, "PRINCIPLES OF TRAINING," 1917

1. CONCENTRATION—To teach the soldier to apply on the battlefield the lessons he has learned on the training ground is the essence and aim of all training. It is by continued concentration only that any form of training can be so impressed as to become second nature.

2. VITALITY—Vitality of mind and body is essential to prevent staleness and monotony. Without vitality training is of little value. All work should be done in short, sharp bursts and be as intense as possible.

3. THE OFFENSIVE SPIRIT—Every form of battle training must be founded on the offensive spirit.

4. BULLET AND BAYONET—The bullet and the bayonet belong to the same parent, the rifle, which is still the deciding factor on the battlefield. One must work with the other.

5. FIRE AND MOVEMENT—Fire and movement are inseparable in the attack. Ground is gained by a body of troops advancing while supported by the fire of another body of troops.

—Great Britain, *British Tactical Notes*, edited and prepared at the U.S. Army War College, pp. 9-10.

# APPENDIX 37

## JAMES A. MOSS, "GENERAL PRINCIPLES; APPLIED TACTICS," 1917

Don't fail to be on the alert, on the lookout, *all the time.*

Do not separate your force too much; if you do, you weaken yourself—you take the chance of being "defeated in detail"—that is, of one part being defeated after another.

While too much importance cannot be attached to the proper use of cover, you must not forget that sometimes there are other considerations that outweigh the advantages of cover.

What is it, after all, that gives victory, whether it be armies or only squads engaged? It's just simply inflicting on the enemy a loss which he will not stand *before he can do the same to you.*

To win you must gain and keep a fire superiority.

The firing line should be as heavy as practicable.

If it becomes necessary to hold a line too long for the force available, it is better to keep the men close together and leave gaps in the line.

—James A. Moss, *Applied Minor Tactics,* pp. 34-35.

## APPENDIX 38

## GERMANY, "GENERAL PRINCIPLES FOR THE ATTACK IN POSITION WARFARE," 1918

*Education of the troops* in that spirit of bold attack, with which we undertook the present war, is the first guarantee of success. . . .

*Command.* The attack no less than the defence, requires that the troops should be *really commanded and that careful and detailed instructions are given to insure the cooperation of all arms* in a particular sector, and with the troops of neighbouring sectors. . . .

*Liaison. The maintenance of close liaison between all arms and all commanders* from the front to the rear, from the rear to the front, and to the flanks, is indispensable. . . .

*Centre of gravity of attack.* Every attack must have a centre of gravity.

*Various kinds of offensives. The objective, purpose and conduct of an attack will vary according to its extent and depth.* . . .

*Surprise.* The greatest successes in war are to be looked for from measures for which the enemy is least prepared. *Therefore, in all offensive actions, surprise of the enemy is of decisive importance.* . . .

*Flanking action.* The great importance of flanking action, even with small forces, especially of artillery and machine guns, has been repeatedly shown in all offensive operations. . . .

*Study of the ground.* All commanders should be thoroughly instructed in the tactical exploitation *of positions and natural features of the ground.* . . .

—Germany; Chief of the General Staff of the Field Army, *Manual of Poisition Warfare for All Arms,* part 14 (provisional), "The Attack in Position Warfare," trans. Great Britain, General Staff, Intelligence, pp. 3-4.

## APPENDIX 39

# UNITED STATES ARMY,
# "THE FUNDAMENTALS OF OFFENSIVE COMBAT
# FOR SMALL UNITS," 1918

Formation in depth of all offensive means.

The closest possible contact of assaulting units with the creeping barrage; this principle also applies to the contact with tanks.

Concentration of individual effort within the group; mutual co-operation of neighboring units, aided by supports properly disposed, which make it possible to break local resistance and to repel counterattacks.

The combination of fire and movement; that is advance by rushes of a fraction covered by the fire of the remainder; engaging the enemy by fire in front while groups work around his flanks; direct advance by a portion under cover of artillery, machine guns or other troops.

Continued maintenance of liaison in every form, and especially with *artillery.*

Rapidity, *order* and continuity in infantry action.

Careful organization and accurate execution of the "cleaning up."

The fearful effect of artillery, the action of tanks, and the German methods of combat restore to the infantry, *once within the hostile positions,* the necessary conditions for open warfare.

Therefore, the flexibility and mobility of infantry must be developed to the highest degree.

—United States War Department, *Instructions for the Offensive Combat of Small Units,* trans. from a French document at General Headquarters, Allied Expeditionary Force, France, p. 10.

## APPENDIX 40

# BASIL H. LIDDELL HART,
# "THE 'TEN COMMANDMENTS' OF THE COMBAT
# UNIT," 1919

1.   The combat unit . . . should not be extended into open order, until they are needed to form part of the actual firing line.

2.   While advancing prior to forming part of the firing line the chief aim must be to take advantage of all possible cover.

3.   Every combat unit which is represented, normally by two of its sections, in the front line must have its objectives and the limits of frontage which will be allotted to it in the future firing line carefully defined beforehand.

4.   Protection always.

5.   The decision as to the moment and spot at which the units forming the rear lines shall reinforce the firing line rests with their immediate superior commanders.

6.   If the leading sections are held up, the supporting sections should not reinforce them direct . . . but should be sent to a flank.

7.   If you are held up, open the heaviest possible fire on the enemy's position.

8.   Send back reports.

9.   Close with the enemy at the earliest possible moment. . . . Use their initiative all the time in order to get forward.[1]

10.   The combat unit must never withdraw unless definitely receiving orders from above to do so.

[1]The most important of the ten.

—Basil H. Liddell Hart, "The 'Ten Commandments' of the Combat Unit. Suggestions on Its Theory and Training," *Journal of the Royal United Service Institution* 64 (May 1919):290-92.


# APPENDIX 41

## UNITED STATES ARMY, "OFFENSIVE COMBAT; GENERAL PRINCIPLES," 1919

1.   The infantry must take the offensive to gain decisive results. Both sides are therefore likely to attempt it, though not necessarily at the same time or in the same part of a long battle line.

2. An infantry that knows how to attack will know how to defend, because it is easier to defend than to attack. The basis of training will be the attack.

3. The infantry attack has as its basis the fighting spirit and aggressiveness of officers and noncommissioned officers with fearless, intelligent leading on their part, and the individual initiative of the private soldier himself.

4. The primary duties of infantry commanders in combat are to maintain direction on their objectives, establish and maintain contact with the units on their flanks, and keep the higher command informed as to the situation.

5. There is no situation which can justify a commander for remaining in ignorance of the situation on his front.

6. Infantry has two general methods of action: fire and movement.

7. The movement of units in the advance to the attack should be made by bounds, i.e., successive positions along the axis of movement are selected as intermediate objectives and reconnoitered prior to occupation.

8. Surprise is an essential element of a successful attack.

9. The effect of surprise must be reinforced and exploited by fire superiority.

10. The success of any operation undertaken by a unit depends in a large measure on the degree to which subordinate units lend each other mutual support. The principle of mutual support is of especial application to units in support and reserve which have not been committed to action.

11. The critical points of a hostile defensive system are in general those points which afford extensive observation, either over the defensive zone and its rear or the ground over which the attack must advance; and those points which control the communications of the defensive zone (road centers, villages). Such points are the especially important objectives of the attack.

12. When officers and men belonging to fighting troops leave their proper places to carry back, or care for, wounded during the progress of the action, they are guilty of skulking. This offense must be repressed with the utmost vigor.

—United States Army, *Infantry Drill Regulations* (Provisional), 1919, pp. 96-98.

# APPENDIX 42

## GREAT BRITAIN, "THE PRINCIPLES OF WAR," 1920

The principles of war may be summarized as follows:

1. Maintenance of the objective.—In every operation of war an objective is essential; without it there can be no definite plan or co-ordination of effort. The ultimate military objective in war is the destruction of the enemy's forces on the battlefield, and this objective must always be held in view.

2. Offensive action.—Victory can only be won as a result of offensive action.

3. Surprise.—Surprise is the most effective and powerful weapon in war. Whether in attack or defence the first thought of a commander must be to outwit his adversary. All measures should therefore be taken, and every means employed to attain this end.

4. Concentration.—Concentration of superior force, moral, and material, at the decisive time and place, and its ruthless employment in the battle are essential for the achievement of success.

5. Economy of force.—To economize strength while compelling a dissipation of that of the enemy must be the constant aim of every commander. This involves the correct distribution and employment of all resources in order to develop their striking power to the utmost.

6. Security.—The security of a force and of its communications is the first responsibility of a commander. To guard against surprise; to prevent the enemy from obtaining information; to dispose his covering troops so as to allow his main forces to move and rest undisturbed; these are the considerations which must govern his actions in obtaining security. A force adequately protected retains its liberty of action and preserves its fighting efficiency against the day of battle.

7. Mobility.—Mobility implies flexibility and the power to maneuver and act with rapidity, and is the chief means of inflicting surprise. Rapidity of movement for the battle should, therefore, be limited only by physical endurance and the means of transportation available.

8. Co-operation.—Only by effective co-operation can the component parts of the fighting forces of a nation develop fully their inherent power, and act efficiently towards success.

—Great Britain, War Office, *Field Service Regulations,* Vol. II, *Operations* (Provisional), 1920, pp. 14-15.

## APPENDIX 43

### UNITED STATES ARMY, "THE PRINCIPLES OF WAR," 1921

The following are fundamental principles of war:

a. The Principle of the Objective.

b. The Principle of the Offensive.

c. The Principle of Mass.

d. The Principle of Economy of Force.

e. The Principle of Movement.

f. The Principle of Surprise.

g. The Principle of Security.

h. The Principle of Simplicity.

i. The Principle of Cooperation.

—United States War Department, TR 10-5, *Doctrines, Principles, and Methods,* 1921, pp. 1-2.

## APPENDIX 44

### GREAT BRITAIN, "THE GENERAL PRINCIPLES OF WAR ORGANIZATION," 1923

1. The first principle of war organization is therefore mobility.

2. The second principle is to insure unity of effort by all parts of the forces in the field towards the attainment of the common object.

3. The third principle is that the number of subordinates with whom each authority is required to deal personally and directly must be limited.

4. The fourth principle is that central control must be combined with subdivision of labour and decentralization of responsibility, the duties

and responsibilities of each individual being clearly defined and limited to those which he can adequately undertake.

5. The fifth principle is to economize military force by utilizing to the greatest extent possible the ordinary machine of civil life to assist forces in the field.

—Great Britain, War Office, *Field Service Regulations,* Vol. I, *Administration,* 1923, pp. 4-6.

# APPENDIX 45

# UNITED STATES ARMY, "COMBAT, GENERAL PRINCIPLES," 1923

378. The ultimate objective of all military operations is the destruction of the enemy's armed forces by battle. Decisive defeat in battle breaks the enemy's will to war and forces him to sue for peace.

379. Concentration of superior forces, both on the ground and in the air, at the decisive place and time, creates the conditions most essential to decisive victory and constitutes the best evidence of superior leadership.

380. Decisive results are obtained only by the offensive. Only through offensive action can a commander exercise his initiative and impose his will on the enemy.

A defensive attitude is never deliberately adopted except as a temporary expedient or for the purpose of economizing forces on a front where a decision is not sought in order to concentrate superior forces at the point of decisive action.

381. Numerical inferiority does not necessarily commit a command to a defensive attitude. Superior hostile strength may be overcome through greater mobility, higher morale, and better leadership. Superior leadership often enables a numerically inferior force to be stronger at the point of decisive action.

A strategically defensive mission is frequently most effectively executed through offensive action. It is often necessary for an inferior force to strike at an early moment in order to secure initial advantages or to prevent itself from being overwhelmed by a growing superiority in the hostile forces.

382. All combat action must be based upon the effect of surprise.

Surprise takes the enemy in a state of moral and material unpreparedness, prevents him from taking effective countermeasures, and often compensates for numerical inferiority of force. Surprise is sought not only in the initial stage of action and by the larger units but also throughout the action and by units of every echelon of command. The principle of surprise applies to fire as well as to movement.

The effect of surprise is dependent upon rapidity of maneuver, the efficiency of counterinformation measures, and the effectiveness of the means employed to deceive the enemy as to our own dispositions and intentions.

By feint and demonstration, the attacker attempts to mislead the enemy as to the time and place at which the principal effort is to be made. Attacks designed merely to hold the enemy along a certain portion of the front are so made that they can not be distinguished from the principal effort and that the enemy is compelled to commit the largest possible proportion of his forces to meet them. Provision is made for exploiting success wherever attained.

The defense seeks to attain the effect of surprise through concealment of the location of its principal defensive works and its reserves so that the enemy will encounter resistance where he does not expect it, fall under the surprise fire of unlocated defensive elements, and expose himself to the action of the counterattack. Provision for counteroffensive action is the most effective defensive measure against surprise.

The effect of surprise is furthered by variation in the means and methods employed in attack and defense. Fixed methods of procedure enable the enemy to estimate the character and object of an operation.

383.   The necessity for guarding against surprise requires adequate provision for the security and readiness for action of all units.

Each unit takes the necessary measures for its own local security as soon as the next higher unit has developed for action.

Provision for the security of flanks is of especial importance in combat.

384.   The effect of surprise must be reinforced and exploited by fire superiority.

The attack can dispense with fire protection only when covered by darkness, fog, or smoke.

The defense can not ordinarily gain fire superiority through superiority in the means which it puts into action. It must rely for fire superiority on better observation for the conduct of fire, on the more methodical organization of its fire, especially its flankings, more accurate knowledge of ranges and the terrain, the concealment of its dispositions, and the disorganization, which movement and accessory defenses produce in the attacker's dispositions.

385. The necessity for concentrating the greatest possible force at the point of decisive action requires strict economy in the strength of forces assigned to secondary missions. Detachments during combat are justifiable only when the execution of tasks assigned them contributes directly to success in the main battle.

386. The task assigned to any unit must not involve a complicated maneuver. Simple and direct plans and methods are alone practicable in war.

—United States Army, *Field Service Regulations,* 1923, pp. 77-78.

## APPENDIX 46

## UNITED STATES ARMY, "THE PRINCIPLES OF WAR," 1927

1. The Principle of the Objective.

2. The Principle of the Offensive.

3. The Principle of the Mass.

4. The Principle of Economy of Force.

5. The Principle of Fire and Movement.

6. The Principle of Surprise.

7. The Principle of Simplicity.

8. The Principle of Security.

9. The Principle of Cooperation.

—From C. M. Bundel, "Principles, Methods and Doctrines of War," lecture delivered at the U.S. Army War College, 12 February 1927, p. 12.

## APPENDIX 47

## REAR ADMIRAL C. V. USBORNE, "THE PRINCIPLES OF WAR," 1929

*Principle No. I*—A war is won by so injuring the enemy nation that it will sue for peace for fear of further injury.

*Principle No. II*—Be stronger than your enemy. In every encounter the stronger force at the point of contact will prevail.

*Principle No. III*—Strength is a product of weapon value, skill, *morale* and numbers; and of these, weapon value is the greatest factor.

*Principle No. IV*—Just enough strength must be allocated to defence, to resist the enemy's attack.

*Principle No. V*—To injure the enemy it is necessary to take offensive action. Such action if taken first has the further effect of weakening the enemy's attack, thus liberating strength from the defence.

*Principle No. VI*—The belligerent must choose as his object the infliction of the greatest degree of injury within his power to encompass in a single operation. To this object he must adhere tenaciously until it is achieved, unless new circumstances render it no longer possible or no longer desirable.

*Principle No. VII*—Simultaneous operations may only be undertaken in co-operation for a definite object.

*Principle No. VIII*—Embody surprise in the plan of every operation.

*Principle No. IX*—To possess mobility superior to the enemy's gives power to deal with the unexpected and to inflict it.

—C. V. Usborne, "The Principles of War—A Dialogue," *Journal of the Royal United Service Institution* 74 (August 1929):475-76.

# APPENDIX 48

# UNITED STATES ARMY, "PRINCIPLES OF OFFENSIVE COMBAT," 1931

1. Reconnaissance.—Reconnaissance, by means of which a commander gains information of the terrain and of the enemy confronting his command, will begin prior to, and continue throughout, an attack. Every commander, no matter what his unit, makes personal reconnaissances. Reconnaissance patrols are employed in almost all situations, and each is given a mission.

2. Security.—Security is closely related to reconnaissance, since measures adopted to obtain information afford considerable protections. However, each commander is directly responsible, regardless of provisions made by higher commanders, that his own unit is made secure.

3.  The Offensive.—Infantry troops must be aggressive, and must usually take the offensive in order to obtain decisive results.

4.  Surprise.—The principle of surprise requires that every effort be made to catch the enemy unaware, both in launching an attack and in carrying it through to a successful completion.

5.  Fire and Movement.—In offensive combat, to reach the enemy and overcome him in close combat is the object of infantry. To reach him, it uses a combination of fire and movement.

6.  Mutual Support.—Mutual support, like other forms of cooperation between units, increases the chances of success. The application of this principle requires that an infantry unit, regardless of its size, assist others adjacent to it in getting forward.

7.  Holding Advantages Gained.—If an attack is a success, commanders of all infantry units must clinch the advantages gained by the enemy's discomfiture. One of the most important and valuable means to accomplish this is the reserve.

8.  Simplicity.—Simple plans are likely to succeed; and, conversely, complicated schemes are liable to fail.

9.  Unity of Command.—It is a well-established principle that there shall be only one commander for each unit, and one commander in each zone of action, who shall be responsible for everything within his unit or within his zone of action.

10.  Reserves.—That adequate reserves should be withheld during the initial stage of the attack, in order to provide a means of influencing the latter course of the action, is an important doctrine.

—United States Army Extension Courses, *Tactics and Technique of Infantry in Offensive Combat*, pp. 2-4.

## APPENDIX 49

# BASIL H. LIDDELL HART, "THE CONCENTRATED ESSENCE OF WAR," 1932

1.  *Adjust your ends to your means.*

2.  *Keep your object always in mind,* while adapting your plan to circumstances.

3.  *Choose the line (or course) of least expectation.*

4.  *Exploit the line of least resistance*—so long as it can lead you to

an objective which would contribute to your underlying object.

5.  *Take a line of operation which offers alternative objectives.*

6.  *Ensure that both plan and dispositions are elastic, or adaptable.*

7.  *Don't lunge whilst your opponent can parry.*

8.  *Don't renew an attack along the same line (or in the same form) after it has once failed.*

—Basil H. Liddell Hart, *The British Way in Warfare: Adaptability and Mobility*, pp. 219-20.

## APPENDIX 50

## UNITED STATES ARMY COMMAND AND GENERAL STAFF SCHOOL, "THE PRINCIPLES OF STRATEGY," 1936

1.  The importance of offensive action.

2.  The importance of concentration of combat power.

3.  The importance of economy of force.

4.  The importance of mobility.

5.  The importance of surprise.

6.  The importance of security.

7.  The importance of cooperation.

—United States Army Command and General Staff School, *The Principles of Strategy for an Independent Corps or Army in a Theater of Operations,* p. 9.

## APPENDIX 51

## MAO TSE-TUNG, "THE PROBLEMS OF STRATEGY," 1936

1.  Giving proper consideration to the relation between the enemy and ourselves.

2.  Giving proper consideration to the relation between various campaigns or between various operational stages.

3.  Giving proper consideration to those parts which have a bearing on (are decisive for) the situation as a whole.

4.  Giving proper consideration to the special features contained in the general situation.

5.  Giving proper consideration to the relation between the front and the rear.

6.  Giving proper consideration to the distinction as well as the connection between losses and replacements, between fighting and resting, between concentration and dispersion, between attack and defence, between advance and retreat, between concealment and exposure, between the main attack and supplementary attacks, between assault and containing action, between centralized command and decentralized command, between protracted war and war of quick decision, between positional war and mobile war, between our own forces and friendly forces, between one military arm and another, between higher and lower levels, between cadre and rank and file, between old and new soldiers, between senior and junior cades, between old and new cadres, between Red areas and White areas, between old Red areas and new ones, between the central district and the borders of a given base area, between the warm season and the cold season, between victory and defeat, between large and small troop formations, between the regular army and the guerrilla forces, between destroying the enemy and winning over the masses, between expanding the Red Army and consolidating it, between military work and political work, between past and present tasks, between present and future tasks, between tasks arising from one set of circumstances and tasks arising from another, between fixed fronts and fluid fronts, between civil war and national war, between one historical stage and another, etc., etc.

—Mao Tse-tung, *Selected Military Writings of Mao Tse-tung,* trans. Foreign Languages Press, pp. 83-84.

## APPENDIX 52

## United States Army Command and General Staff School, "Principles of War," 1939

1.  Principle of Security.—We must assure *national security* or we shall cease to exist as a nation. National security is obtained through the avoidance of war and preparedness to meet war. The security of a military force in the field lies in a correct estimate of all enemy capabilities with

the provisions made to meet them; in maintaining freedom of movement, as well as in guarding against surprise.

2. Principle of the Offensive.—Decisive results are obtained only by the *offensive*. . . .

3. Principle of Superiority.—This principle is applicable to both offensive and defensive warfare. *Superiority* is vitally necessary to success when the national attitude is offensive. This statement applies both to the nation and to the armies in the field. . . .

4. Principle of the Unity of Effort.—*Unity of effort* is necessary to apply effectively the full power of the available forces. Complete unity of the nation in war implies a single control for each effort and a uniting of all efforts under one head. In the armed forces it is attained through unity of command. Where this is impracticable, dependence must be placed on *co-operation*.

5. Principle of the Common Objective.—There must be a common *objective* for all efforts. This objective is defined by the political objective of the war which must be clearly understood. For the nation, the common objective is usually secured through destroying the enemy's will to continue the war. For an armed force the military objective is the destruction of the hostile armed force. This may be secured either by direct action or an indirect approach, such as the occupation of an area vital to the continued existence of the hostile armed force. In conducting military operations, definite points, lines, or areas must be designated for the coordination of effort.

6. Principle of Simplicity.—There must be *simple conceptions* and the use of simple methods in war. In the excitement and confusion of war, complicated actions greatly increase the chance of error. The strength of a plan of operations is no greater than that of one of its subordinate parts, and if any part gives way because of an error or misunderstanding the whole plan may fall.

—United States Army Command and General Staff School, *The Offensive* (Tentative), pp. 9-13.

# APPENDIX 53

## United States Army, "Conduct of War, General Principles," 1939

90. The *conduct of war* is the art of employing the armed forces of a nation in combination with measures of economic and political con-

straint for the purpose of effecting a satisfactory peace. It is based on the skillful adaptation and application of the technique of modern science. New means are always giving it a different form. These developments must be anticipated, and their influence must be correctly evaluated and promptly exploited.

91. The *ultimate objective* of all military operations is the destruction of the enemy's armed forces in battle. Decisive defeat in battle breaks the enemy's will to war and forces him to sue for peace which is the national aim. To attain this ultimate objective one or more *intermediate objectives* may have to be determined. These objectives must be well defined and must contribute toward the attainment of the ultimate objective.

92. The situations that arise in war are numerous. They are subject to sudden and frequent change. Frictions and mistakes are common occurrences. Since the enemy is also free to act, situations seldom develop as expected. Imponderable factors often exercise a decisive influence. While certain principles, deduced from experience, serve as a useful guide, their application varies according to circumstances.

93. Concentration of *superior forces,* both on the ground and in the air, at the decisive place and time, creates the conditions most essential to decisive victory and constitutes the best evidence of superior leadership.

The necessity for concentrating the greatest possible force at the point of decisive action requires strict *economy* in the strength of forces assigned to secondary missions. Detachments during combat are justifiable only when the execution of tasks assigned them contributes directly to success in the main battle.

94. Only through *offensive* action can a commander exercise his initiative, preserve his freedom of action, and impose his will on the enemy. A *defensive* attitude may, however, be deliberately adopted as a temporary expedient while awaiting on opportunity for counteroffensive action, or for the purpose of economizing forces on a front where a decision is not sought.

In the offensive, the commander must focus his attention on the objective; in the defensive, on the front of greatest danger. In campaign, offensive action is occasional and for a limited period of time. Success comes from the ability of the commander to select the right time and place for offensive action.

Numerical inferiority does not necessarily commit a command to a defensive attitude. Superior hostile numbers may be overcome through greater mobility, more effective fire, higher morale, and better leadership. Superior leadership often enables a numerically inferior force to be stronger at the point of decisive action.

A strategically defensive mission is frequently most effectively executed through offensive action. It is often necessary for an inferior force to strike at an early moment in order to secure initial advantages or to prevent itself from being overwhelmed by a growing superiority in the hostile forces.

95.   *Unity of effort* is necessary to apply effectively the full combat power of the available forces. It is obtained through *unity of command.* Where this is impracticable, dependence must be placed upon *cooperation.*

96.   Whenever practicable, combat action should be based upon the effect of *surprise.* Surprise finds the enemy in a state of moral and material unpreparedness, prevents him from taking effective countermeasures, and often compensates for numerical inferiority of force. Surprise is sought not only in the initial stage of action but also throughout the action and by every echelon of command. Surprise applies to fire as well as to movement.

The effect of surprise is dependent upon rapidity of maneuver, the efficiency of counterinformation measures, and the effectiveness of the means employed to deceive the enemy as to our own dispositions and intentions. It must be reinforced and exploited by fire superiority.

The effect of surprise is furthered by variation in the means and methods employed in combat. Fixed methods of procedure enable the enemy to estimate the character and object of an operation.

97.   The necessity for guarding against surprise requires adequate provision for the *security* and readiness for action of all units.

Each unit takes the necessary measures for its own local security as soon as the next higher unit has developed for action.

Provision for the security of flanks is of especial importance in combat.

98.   The task assigned to any unit must not involve a complicated maneuver. *Simple* and *direct* plans and methods are alone practicable in war. Simple action, promptly and thoroughly executed, is the best guarantee of success.

—United States Army, FM 100-5, *Field Service Regulations* (Tentative), 1939, pp. 27-29.

# APPENDIX 54

# UNITED STATES ARMY, "DOCTRINES OF COMBAT," 1941

112.   The *ultimate objective* of all military operations is the destruction of the enemy's armed forces in battle. The ability to select objectives whose

attainment contributes most decisively and quickly to the defeat of the hostile armed forces is one attribute of the able commander.

113.    Simple and direct plans and methods with prompt and thorough execution are often decisive in the attainment of success.

114.    Unity of command obtains that *unity of effort* which is essential to the decisive application of full combat power of the available forces. Unity of effort is furthered by full *cooperation* between elements of the command.

115.    Through offensive action a commander exercises his initiative, preserves his freedom of action, and imposes his will on the enemy. A defensive attitude may, however, be deliberately adopted as a temporary expedient while awaiting an opportunity for counteroffensive action, or for the purpose of economizing forces on a front where a decision is not sought. The selection by the commander of the right time and place for offensive action is a decisive factor in the success of the operation.

Numerical inferiority does not necessarily commit a command to a defensive attitude. Superior hostile numbers may be overcome through greater mobility, better armament and equipment, more effective fire, higher morale, and better leadership. Superior leadership often enables a numerically inferior force to be stronger at the point of decisive action.

A strategically defensive mission is frequently most effectively executed through offensive action. It is often necessary for an inferior force to strike at an early moment in order to secure initial advantages or to prevent itself from being overwhelmed by a growing superiority in the hostile forces.

116.    Concentration of superior forces, both on the ground and in the air, at the decisive place and time and their employment in a decisive direction, creates the conditions essential to victory. Such concentration requires strict economy in the strength of forces assigned to secondary missions. Detachments during combat are justifiable only when the execution of tasks assigned them contributes directly to success in the main battle.

117.    Surprise must be sought throughout the action by every means and by every echelon of command. It may be obtained by fire as well as by movement. Surprise is produced through measures which either deny information to the enemy, or positively deceive him, as to our dispositions, movements, and plans. Terrain which appears to impose great difficulties on operations may often be utilized to gain surprise. Surprise is furthered by variation in the means and methods employed in combat and by rapidity of execution.

Surprise often compensates for numerical inferiority of force.

Surprise finds the enemy in a state of mental, moral, or physical unpreparedness. Every effort should be made to deny him time to take effective countermeasures. The effect of surprise may be lost through dilatory methods of execution.

118. To guard against surprise requires a correct estimate of enemy capabilities, adequate security measures, effective reconnaissance, and readiness for action of all units. Every unit takes the necessary measures for its own local ground and air security. Provision for the security of flanks and rear is of especial importance.

—United States Army, FM 100-5, *Field Service Regulations—Operations,* 22 May 1941, pp. 22-23.

## APPENDIX 55

## BERNARD L. MONTGOMERY, "THE PRINCIPLES OF MODERN WAR," 1945

(a)  Air power.

(b)  Administration.

(c)  The initiative.

(d)  Morale.

(e)  Surprise.

(f)  Concentration.

(g)  Co-operation.

(h)  Simplicity.

—Bernard L. Montgomery, "High Command in War," June 1945.

## APPENDIX 56

## UNITED STATES ARMY, "PRINCIPLES OF WAR," 1949

### THE OBJECTIVE

97.   The ultimate objective of all military operations is the destruction of the enemy's armed forces and his will to fight. The selection of intermediate objectives whose attainment contributes most decisively and

quickly to the accomplishment of the ultimate objective at the least cost, human and material, must be based on as complete knowledge of the enemy and theater of operations as is possible for the commander to gain by the exploitation of all sources and means of information available to him.

## SIMPLICITY

98.    Plans should be as simple and direct as the attainment of the objective will permit. Simplicity of plans must be emphasized, for in operations even the most simple plan is usually difficult to execute. The final test of a plan is its execution; this must be borne constantly in mind during planning.

## UNITY OF COMMAND

99.    Unity of command obtains that unity of effort which is essential to the decisive application of the full combat power of the available forces. Unity of effort is furthered by full cooperation between elements of the command. Command of a force of joint or combined arms is vested in the senior officer present eligible to exercise command unless another is specifically designated to command.

## THE OFFENSIVE

100.    Through offensive action, a commander preserves his freedom of action and imposes his will on the enemy. The selection by the commander of the right time and place for offensive action is a decisive factor in the success of the operation. A defensive attitude may be forced on a commander by many situations; but a defensive attitude should be deliberately adopted only as a temporary expedient while awaiting an opportunity for counteroffensive action, or for the purpose of economizing forces on a front where a decision is not sought.

## MANEUVER

101.    Maneuver in itself can produce no decisive results, but if properly employed it makes decisive results possible through the application of the principles of the offensive, mass, economy of force, and surprise. Better armament and equipment, more effective fire, higher morale, and better leadership, coupled with skillful maneuver, will frequently overcome hostile superior numbers.

## MASS

102.    Mass or the concentration of superior forces, on the ground, at sea, and in the air, at the decisive place and time, and their employment

in a decisive direction, creates the conditions essential to victory. Such concentration requires strict economy in the strength of forces assigned to secondary missions. Detachments during combat are justifiable only when the execution of tasks assigned them contributes directly to success in the main battle.

## ECONOMY OF FORCES

103.  The principle of economy of force is a corollary to the principle of mass. In order to concentrate superior combat strength in one place, economy of force must be exercised in other places. The situation will frequently permit a strategically defensive mission to be effectively executed through offensive action.

## SURPRISE

104.  Surprise must be sought throughout the action by every means and by every echelon of command. Surprise may be produced by measures which deny information to the enemy or deceive him as to our dispositions, movements, and plans; by variation in the means and methods employed in combat; by rapidity and power of execution; and by the utilization of terrain which appears to impose great difficulties. Surprise may compensate for numerical inferiority.

## SECURITY

105.  Adequate security against surprise requires a correct estimate of enemy capabilities, resultant security measures, effective reconnaissance, and readiness for action. Every unit takes the necessary measures for its own local ground and air security. Provision for the security of flanks and rear is of special importance.

—United States Army, FM 100-5, *Field Service Regulations—Operations,* 1949, pp. 21-23.

## APPENDIX 57

# United States Air Force, "Basic Principles of War," 1949

1.  The will to win (rapidly). (Applicable only to the offensive side.)
2.  Singleness of purpose.
3.  Coordination of ends and means.

4.   The principle of indirect approach.

5.   Surprise—Alternate objectives.

6.   Intelligence.

7.   Air supremacy.

—United States Air Force, Air University, *Outlines of the Principles of Warfare from Clausewitz to the Present Time,* pp. 5-6.

## APPENDIX 58

## COLONEL VASILI YE. SAVKIN, "THE PRINCIPLES OF MILITARY ART," C. 1950

a.   Mobility and high rates of combat operations;

b.   Concentration of main efforts and creation of superiority in forces and means over the enemy at the decisive place and at the decisive time;

c.   Surprise;

d.   Combat activeness;

e.   Preservation of the combat effectiveness of friendly forces;

f.   Conformity of the goal and plan of the operation (battle) to the conditions of the actual situation;

g.   Coordination.

—Vasili Ye. Savkin, *The Basic Principles of Operational Art and Tactics (A Soviet View),* trans. and published under the auspices of the United States Air Force, p. 165.

## APPENDIX 59

## VICE ADMIRAL RICHARD L. CONOLLY, "THE PRINCIPLES OF WAR," 1953

The Objective (as the master principle)

Simplicity

Control (in place of cooperation or unity of command)

The Offensive

Exploitation

Mobility (in place of Maneuver or Movement)

Concentration (in place of Mass or Superiority)

Economy of Force

Surprise

Security

Readiness (to include both readiness of personnel and readiness of materiel)

—Richard L. Conolly, "The Principles of War," *United States Naval Institute Proceedings* 79 (January 1953):9.

## APPENDIX 60

## COLONEL VASILI YE. SAVKIN, "THE BASIC PRINCIPLES OF OPERATIONAL ART AND TACTICS," 1953-1959

*Mobility and High Tempos of Combat Operations*
Mobility and high tempos of combat operations bring success in a battle or operation.

*Concentration of Main Efforts and Creation of the Necessary Superiority in Men and Weapons over the Enemy at the Decisive Place at the Decisive Time (Concentration of Efforts)*
To attain victory over the enemy one must not dissipate his forces and means equally across the entire front, but the main efforts must be concentrated on the most important axis or sector and at the right time in order to form there the necessary superiority over the enemy in men and weapons.

*Surprise*
Use of surprise brings success in a battle or operation.

*Combat Activeness*
Success in a battle or operation is achieved by that side which, with all else equal, acts more actively and resolutely, takes the initiative, and holds it firmly.

*Preservation of Combat Effectiveness of Friendly Troops*

In the course of an operation or battle the combat effectiveness of troops must be constantly maintained at the level which ensures successful accomplishment of assigned combat missions.

*Conformity of the Goal of the Operation or Battle to Conditions of the Actual Situation*

The goal of the operation or battle must fully conform to the conditions of the actual operational (combat) situation and be commensurate with the forces and means in their correlation with the enemy's forces and means and with consideration of the factors of space and time.

*Interworking*

The success of contemporary combat operations may be achieved only through the joint efforts of all forces and means participating in an operation or battle on the basis of their close and continuous interworking and fullest use of combat capabilities.

—Vasili Ye. Savkin, *The Basic Principles of Operational Art and Tactics (A Soviet View),* trans. and published under the auspices of the United States Air Force, pp. 167, 201, 230, 240, 258, 266, 273.

# APPENDIX 61

## MAO TSE-TUNG, "TEN BASIC PRINCIPLES OF WAR," c. 1954

Principle of aims. The chief aim of warfare is to annihilate the enemy, not to attempt to capture or hold a city or a region. It is obvious that after the enemy has been annihilated, his possessions fall to the victor.

Principle of mobile concentration. The most effective type of warfare is that in which the forces are invincibly superior to the enemy's, so that a relatively small group may concentrate its power against the weakest part of an enemy's defense. In order to seize every opportunity that might present itself, the forces must remain entirely mobile and be able to shift to whatever area may be attacked profitably.

Principle of annihilation. It is better to destroy one opposing enemy than to harm ten; it is better strategically to annihilate one enemy division than to wound or even defeat two. Thus, a war of attrition is an inferior type of battle.

Principle of fighting on the move. Armies in the field must make sudden assaults and retreats in order to attack the opposing forces while they are in motion. An example would be the ambush of a column while passing along a road where an entire group may be strung out in single file. But after the enemy is able to regroup and begins to counterattack, a retreat is in order. Another battle may be joined on the following day or later, when the enemy is again on the move.

Principle of the offensive. The primary aim of the army is to attack, not to retreat. Thus, even in the midst of retreat, the posture of offense is assumed. As long as contact with the enemy is maintained, he must be allowed to assume the offensive.

Principle of surprise attack. Climate, terrain, and especially darkness must be used to the maximum advantage in springing attacks when and where the enemy least expects them. A major method of utilizing the surprise attack is to scatter the troops in the daytime, with only token opposition snipers for the enemy to operate against, and to group the forces during the night in order to mount a concentrated attack when the enemy cannot function well.

Principle of continuous attack. If an attack is once mounted, it must be continued. The troops cannot consider their fatigue or hunger, but must keep the enemy busy.

Principle of autonomy. There must be a high degree of autonomous operation. The chain of command is of almost no tactical significance. The commander's main function is to set an example of energetic courage for his own troops.

Principle of unity. War is like chess: one cannot play just his own men, he must stay several moves ahead of the enemy. Therefore, although each unit functions independently in tactical operations, there must be a high command to follow the action and formulate over-all plans for the campaign.

Principle of the military spirit. In war, the quality and quantity of arms are important; without them, one cannot win. Even with them, one can lose. The most important attribute of a victorious army is the military spirit. In every conceivable way, thought of possible defeat must be eliminated from the army and replaced with an iron will to win.

—From Kenmin Ho, "Mao's 10 Principles of War," *Military Review* 47 (July 1967):96-98. Reprinted by permission of *Military Review*.

# APPENDIX 62

## United States Army, "Principles of War," 1954

### 69. General

*The principles of war are fundamental truths governing the prosecution of war.* Their proper application is essential to the exercise of command and to successful conduct of military operations. The degree of application of any specific principle will vary with the situation and the application thereto of sound judgment and tactical sense.

### 70. Objective

*Every military operation must be directed toward a decisive, obtainable objective.* The destruction of the enemy's armed forces and his will to fight is the ultimate military objective of war. The objective of each operation must contribute to this ultimate objective. Each intermediate objective must be such that its attainment will most directly, quickly, and economically contribute to the purpose of the operation. It must permit the application of the maximum means available. Its selection must be based upon consideration of means available, the enemy, and the area of operations. Secondary objectives of any operation must contribute to the attainment of the principal objective.

### 71. Offensive

*Only offensive action achieves decisive results.* Offensive action permits the commander to exploit the initiative and impose his will on the enemy. The defensive may be forced on the commander, but it should be deliberately adopted only as a temporary expedient while awaiting an opportunity for offensive action or for the purpose of economizing forces on a front where a decision is not sought. Even on the defensive the commander seeks every opportunity to seize the initiative and achieve decisive results by offensive action.

### 72. Simplicity

*Simplicity must be the keynote of military operations.* Uncomplicated plans clearly expressed in orders promote common understanding and intelligent execution. Even the most simple plan is usually difficult to execute in combat. *Simplicity must be applied to organization, methods, and means in order to produce orderliness on the battlefield.*

## 73.  Unity of Command

*The decisive application of full combat power requires unity of command.*
Unity of command obtains unity of effort by the coordinated action of
all forces toward a common goal. Coordination may be achieved by
direction or by cooperation. It is best achieved by vesting a single commander with requisite authority. Unity of effort is furthered by willing
and intelligent cooperation among all elements of the forces involved.
Pearl Harbor is an example of failure in organization for command.

## 74.  Mass

*Maximum available combat power must be applied at the point of
decision.* Mass is the concentration of means at the critical time and place
to the maximum degree permitted by the situation. Proper application
of the principle of mass, in conjunction with the other principles of war,
may permit numerically inferior forces to achieve decisive combat superiority. Mass is essentially a combination of manpower and firepower and
is not dependent upon numbers alone; the effectiveness of mass may be
increased by superior weapons, tactics, and morale.

## 75.  Economy of Force

*Minimum essential means must be employed at points other than that
of decision.* To devote means to unnecessary secondary efforts or to
employ excessive means on required secondary efforts is to violate the
principle of both mass and the objective. Limited attacks, the defensive,
deception, or even retrograde action are used in noncritical areas to achieve
mass in the critical area.

## 76.  Maneuver

*Maneuver must be used to alter the relative combat power of military
forces.* Maneuver is the positioning of forces to place the enemy at a relative
disadvantage. Proper positioning of forces in relation to the enemy
frequently can achieve results which otherwise could be achieved only at
heavy cost in men and material. In many situations maneuver is made
possible only by the effective employment of firepower.

## 77.  Surprise

*Surprise may decisively shift the balance of combat power in favor of
the commander who achieves it.* It consists of striking the enemy when,
where, or in a manner for which he is unprepared. It is not essential that
the enemy be taken unaware but only that he becomes aware too late to

react effectively. Surprise can be achieved by speed, secrecy, deception, by variation in means and methods, and by using seemingly impossible terrain. Mass is essential to the optimum exploitation of the principle of surprise.

### 78. Security

*Security is essential to the application of the other principles of war.* It consists of those measures necessary to prevent surprise, avoid annoyance, preserve freedom of action, and deny to the enemy information of our forces. Security denies to the enemy and retains for the commander the ability to employ his forces most effectively.

—United States Army, FM 100-5, *Field Service Regulations—Operations*, 1954, pp. 25-27.

## APPENDIX 63

# UNITED STATES ARMY, "PRINCIPLES OF WAR," 1962

### 110.  General

The principles of war are fundamental truths governing the prosecution of war. Their proper application is essential to the exercise of command and to successful conduct of military operations. These principles are interrelated and, dependent on the circumstances, may tend to reinforce one another or to be in conflict. Consequently, the degree of application of any specific principle will vary with the situation.

### 111.  Principle of the Objective

Every military operation must be directed toward a clearly defined, decisive and attainable objective. The ultimate military objective of war is the destruction of the enemy's armed forces and his will to fight. The objective of each operation must contribute to this ultimate objective. Each intermediate objective must be such that its attainment will most directly, quickly, and economically contribute to the purpose of the operation. The selection of an objective is based upon consideration of the means available, the enemy, and the area of operations. Every commander must understand and clearly define his objective and consider each contemplated action in light thereof.

**112.  Principle of the Offensive**

Offensive action is necessary to achieve decisive results and to maintain freedom of action. It permits the commander to exercise initiative and impose his will upon the enemy; to set the pace and determine the course of battle; to exploit enemy weaknesses and rapidly changing situations, and to meet unexpected developments. The defensive may be forced on the commander, but it should be deliberately adopted only as a temporary expedient while awaiting an opportunity for offensive action or for the purpose of economizing forces on a front where a decision is not sought. Even on the defensive the commander seeks every opportunity to seize the initiative and achieve decisive results by offensive action.

**113.  Principle of Mass**

Superior combat power must be concentrated at the critical time and place for a decisive purpose. Superiority results from the proper combination of the elements of combat power. Proper application of the principle of mass, in conjunction with other principles of war, may permit numerically inferior forces to achieve decisive combat superiority.

**114.  Principle of Economy of Force**

Skillful and prudent use of combat power will enable the commander to accomplish the mission with minimum expenditure of resources. This principle is the corollary of the principle of mass. It does not imply husbanding but rather the measured allocation of available combat power to the primary task as well as secondary tasks such as limited attacks, the defense, deception or even retrograde action in order to insure sufficient combat power at the point of decision.

**115.  Principle of Maneuver**

Maneuver is an essential ingredient of combat power. It contributes materially in exploiting successes and in preserving freedom of action and reducing vulnerability. The object of maneuver is to dispose a force in such a manner as to place the enemy at a relative disadvantage and thus achieve results which would otherwise be more costly in men and materiel. Successful maneuver requires flexibility in organization, administrative support, and command and control. It is the antithesis of permanence of location and implies avoidance of stereotyped patterns of operation.

**116.  Principle of Unity of Command**

The decisive application of full combat power requires unity of command. Unity of command obtains unity of effort by the coordinated action of all forces toward a common goal. While coordination may be attained by cooperation, it is best achieved by vesting a single commander with the requisite authority.

**117. Principle of Security**

Security is essential to the preservation of combat power. Security is achieved by measures taken to prevent surprise, preserve freedom of action, and deny the enemy information of friendly forces. Since risk is inherent in war, application of the principle of security does not imply undue caution and the avoidance of calculated risk. Security frequently is enhanced by bold seizure and retention of the initiative, which denies the enemy the opportunity to interfere.

**118. Principle of Surprise**

Surprise can decisively shift the balance of combat power. By surprise, success out of proportion to the effort expended may be obtained. Surprise results from striking an enemy at a time, place, and in a manner for which he is not prepared. It is not essential that the enemy be taken unaware but only that he becomes aware too late to react effectively. Factors contributing to surprise include speed, deception, application of unexpected combat power, effective intelligence and counterintelligences, to include communication and electronic security, and variations in tactics and methods of operation.

**119. Principle of Simplicity**

Simplicity contributes to successful operations. Direct, simple plans and clear, concise orders minimize misunderstanding and confusion. If other factors are equal, the simplest plan is preferred.

—United States Army, FM 100-5, *Field Service Regulations—Operations,* 1962, pp. 46-48.

# APPENDIX 64

# VIRGIL NEY, "THE PRINCIPLES OF GUERRILLA WAR," 1962

1. The Environment.
2. Community Security.
3. Community Support.
4. Propaganda.

5. Proximity.
6. Deliberate Delay.
7. Personal Security.
8. Part-Time Function.
9. Modus Operandi.
10. Organization.

—Virgil Ney, *Notes on Guerrilla War: Principles and Practices,* p. 1.

## APPENDIX 65

# UNITED STATES ARMY, "PRINCIPLES OF WAR," 1968

**5-2.  General**
The principles of war are fundamental truths governing the prosecution of war. Their proper application is essential to the exercise of command and to the successful conduct of military operations. These principles are interrelated and, depending on the circumstances, may tend to reinforce one another, or to be in conflict. Consequently, the degree of application of any specific principle will vary with the situation.

**5-3.  Principle of the Objective**
Every military operation must be directed toward a clearly defined, decisive, and attainable objective. The ultimate military objective of war is the defeat of the enemy's armed forces. The objective of each operation must contribute to the ultimate objective. Each intermediate objective must be such that its attainment will most directly, quickly, and economically contribute to the purpose of the operation. The selection of an objective is based on consideration of the mission, the means available, the enemy, and the operational area. Every commander must understand and clearly define his objective and consider each contemplated action in light thereof.

**5-4.  Principle of the Offensive**
Offensive action is necessary to achieve decisive results and to maintain freedom of action. It permits the commander to exercise initiative and impose his will on the enemy, to set the pace and determine the course of

battle, to exploit enemy weaknesses and rapidly changing situations, and to meet unexpected developments. The defensive may be forced on the commander, but it should be deliberately adopted only as a temporary expedient while awaiting an opportunity for offensive action or for the purpose of economizing forces on a front where a decision is not sought. Even on the defensive, the commander seeks every opportunity to seize the initiative and achieve decisive results by offensive action.

### 5-5.  Principle of Mass

Superior combat power must be concentrated at the critical time and place for a decisive purpose. Superiority results from the proper combination of the elements of combat power. Proper application of the principle of mass, in conjunction with the other principles of war, may permit numerically inferior forces to achieve decisive combat superiority.

### 5-6.  Principle of Economy of Force

Minimum essential means must be employed at points other than that of the main effort. This principle is the reciprocal of the principle of mass. Economy of force does not imply husbanding, but the measured allocation of available combat power to the primary task as well as to supporting tasks, such as limited attacks, defense, cover and deception, or even retrograde action, to insure sufficient combat power at the point of decision.

### 5-7.  Principle of Maneuver

Maneuver is an essential ingredient of combat power. In contributes materially in exploiting successes and in preserving freedom of action and reducing vulnerability. The object of maneuver is to dispose a force in a manner that places the enemy at a relative disadvantage and thus achieves results that would otherwise be more costly in men and materiel. Successful maneuver requires flexibility in organization, combat service support, and command and control. It is the antithesis of permanence of location and implies avoidance of stereotyped patterns of operation.

### 5-8.  Principle of Unity of Command

The decisive application of full combat power requires unity of command. Unity of command obtains unity of effort by the coordinated action of all forces toward a common goal. While coordination may be attained by cooperation, it is best achieved by vesting a single commander with the requisite authority.

### 5-9.  Principle of Security

Security is essential to the preservation of combat power. Security results from the measures taken by a command to protect itself from espionage, observation, sabotage, annoyance, or surprise. It is a condition that results from the establishment and maintenance of protective measures that insure a state of inviolability from hostile acts or influences. Since risk is inherent in war, application of the principle of security does not imply undue caution and the avoidance of calculated risk. Security frequently is enhanced by bold seizure and retention of the initiative, which reduces the enemy's capability to interfere.

**5-10.  Principle of Surprise**

Surprise can decisively shift the balance of combat power. By surprise, success out of proportion to the effort expended may be obtained. Surprise results from striking an enemy at a time and place and in a manner for which he is unprepared. It is not essential that the enemy be taken unaware, but only that he becomes aware too late to react effectively. Factors contributing to surprise include speed, cover and deception, application of unexpected combat power, effective intelligence and counterintelligence (to include communications and electronic security), and variations in tactics and methods of operation.

**5-11.  Principle of Simplicity**

Simplicity contributes to successful operations. Direct, simple plans and clear, concise orders reduce misunderstanding and confusion. Other factors being equal, the simplest plan is preferred.

—United States Army, FM 100-5, *Operations of Army Forces in the Field,* 1968, pp. 5-1 to 5-2.

# APPENDIX 66

## COLONEL VASILI YE. SAVKIN, "THE LAWS OF WAR," 1972

The first law of war is that the course and outcome of war waged with unlimited employment of all means of conflict depends primarily on the correlation of available, strictly military forces of the combatants at the beginning of the war, especially in nuclear weapons and means of delivery.

The second law of war is that the course and outcome of war depends on the correlation of military potentials of the combatants.

The third law of war is that the course and outcome of war depends on its political content.

The fourth law of war is that the course and outcome of war depends on the correlation of moral-political and psychological capabilities of the people and armies of the combatants.

—Vasili Ye. Savkin, *The Basic Principles of Operational Art and Tactics (A Soviet View),* trans. and published under the auspices of the United States Air Force, pp. 89, 91, 92.

## APPENDIX 67

## COLONEL VASILI YE. SAVKIN, "THE LAWS OF ARMED CONFLICT," 1972

The first law of armed conflict is: methods and forms of armed conflict depend on the material basis of the battle and operation.

The second law of armed conflict is as follows: any battle or operation at any given moment of its development takes shape in favor of that opposing side whose troops possess the greater combat power in comparison with the enemy.

—Vasili Ye. Savkin, *The Basic Principles of Operational Art and Tactics (A Soviet View),* trans. and published under the auspices of the United States Air Force, pp. 99, 110.

## APPENDIX 68

## UNITED STATES ARMY, "THE PRINCIPLES OF WAR," 1978

**OBJECTIVE.**   Every military operation should be directed towards a clearly defined, decisive, and attainable objective. The ultimate military objective of war is the defeat of the enemy's armed forces. Correspondingly, each operation must contribute to the ultimate objective. Intermediate objectives must directly, quickly, and economically contribute to the purpose of the ultimate objective. The selection of objectives is based on consideration of the mission, the means and time available, the enemy, and the operational area. *Every commander must understand and clearly define his objective and consider each contemplated action in light thereof.*

**OFFENSIVE.**   Offensive action is necessary to achieve decisive results and to maintain freedom of action.   It permits the commander to exercise initiative and impose his will on the enemy, to set the terms and select the place of battle, to exploit enemy weaknesses and rapidly changing situations, and to react to unexpected developments.   The defensive may be forced on the commander as a temporary expedient while awaiting an opportunity for offensive action or may be adopted deliberately for the purpose of economizing forces on a front where a decision is not sought. Even on the defensive, the commander seeks opportunities to seize the initiative and achieve decisive results by offensive action.

**MASS.**   Superior combat power must be concentrated at the critical time and place for decisive results. Superiority results from the proper combination of the elements of combat power. Proper application of this principle, in conjunction with other principles of war, may permit numerically inferior forces to achieve decisive combat superiority at the point of decision.

**ECONOMY OF FORCE.**   This principle is the reciprocal of the principle of mass. Minimum essential means must be employed at points other than that of the main effort. Economy of force requires the acceptance of prudent risks in selected areas to achieve superiority at the point of decision. Economy of force missions may require limited attack, defense, cover and deception, or retrograde action.

**MANEUVER.**   Maneuver is an essential ingredient of combat power. It contributes materially in exploiting success and in preserving freedom of action and reducing vulnerability. The object of maneuver is to concentrate (or disperse) forces in a manner to place the enemy in a position of disadvantage and thus achieve results that would otherwise be more costly in men and materiel.

**UNITY OF COMMAND.**   The decisive application of full combat power requires unity of command. Unity of command results in unity of effort by coordinating the action of all forces towards a common goal. While coordination may be achieved by cooperation, it is best achieved by vesting a single commander with requisite authority.

**SECURITY.**   Security is essential to the preservation of combat power. Security results from the measures taken by a command to protect itself from espionage, observation, sabotage, annoyance, or surprise. It is a condition that results from the establishment and maintenance of protective measures against hostile acts or influences. Since risk is inherent in war, application of the principle of security does not imply undue caution and the avoidance of calculated risk.

**SURPRISE.** Surprise can decisively shift the balance of combat power. With surprise, success out of proportion to the effort expended may be obtained. Surprise results from striking the enemy at a time and/or place and in a manner for which he is unprepared. It is not essential that the enemy be taken unaware, but only that he become aware too late to react effectively. Factors contributing to surprise include speed, cover and deception, application of unexpected combat power, effective intelligence, variations of tactics and methods of operation, and operations security (OPSEC). OPSEC consists of signals and electronic security, physical security, and counterintelligence to deny enemy forces knowledge or forewarning of intent.

**SIMPLICITY.** Simplicity contributes to successful operations. Direct, simple plans and clear, concise orders reduce misunderstanding and confusion. Other factors being equal, the simplest plan is preferred.

—United States Army, FM 100-1, *The Army*, 29 September 1978, pp. 14-16.

# BIBLIOGRAPHY

*UNPUBLISHED SOURCES*

Ahern, George Patrick. "A Chronical of the Army War College, 1899-1919." Washington D.C., 1919.

Brodie, Bernard. "Principles of War and Their Application in Atomic Warfare." Lecture delivered at the U.S. Army Command and General Staff College, 7 March 1957.

Bundel, C. M. "Principles, Methods and Doctrines of War." Lecture delivered at the U.S. Army War College, 12 February 1927.

Crocker, David R. "Principles of Nuclear War." Student paper, U.S. Army War College, 19 March 1958.

Dickman, Joseph T. "Tactical Rides." Instructional material, U.S. Army, Infantry and Cavalry School, Ft. Leavenworth, Kansas, c. 1907.

Erickson, Hjalmar. "The Doctrine of War and of Training." Lecture delivered at the U.S. Army General Staff College, 17 April 1920.

————. "Remarks on Doctrines of War and of Training." Lecture delivered at the U.S. Army General Staff College, 20 April 1921.

————. "Some Remarks on War, Its Nature, Doctrines and Methods." Lecture delivered at the U.S. Army War College, 24 January 1922.

Français, G. F. "Cours d'art militaire, à l'usage des élèves de l'Ecole d'application de l'artillerie et du génie." Lithography of the School of Application, 1832.

Griess, Thomas E. "Dennis Hart Mahan: West Point Professor and

Advocate of Military Professionalism, 1830-1871." Ph.D. dissertation, Duke University, 1968.

Harris, Audley C. "Nationbuilding and the Principles of War." Student essay, Army War College, 1967.

Heraty, Captain. "The Principles of War." Typewritten copy bound in "Headquarters, USCC, Lectures," Office of the Commandant of Cadets, West Point, N.Y., c. 1925.

Montgomery, Bernard L. "High Command in War." Pamphlet for the Twenty-first Army Group, Germany, June 1945.

Pallister, Francis J. "Nuclear Weapons versus the Principles of War." Student thesis, Army War College, 25 June 1950.

"Science of War. Introductory." West Point, New York, c. 1875.

Shoemaker, John O. "The Principles of War: Sense or Nonsense in the Cold War?" Student essay, Army War College, 1966.

Starry, Donn A. "History, the Principles of War, and Military History." Keynote address to the Army Historians Conference, 2 May 1979.

Swift, Eben. "Remarks, Introductory to the Course in Military Art, at the Infantry and Cavalry School and Staff College, Fort Leavenworth, Kansas." Mimeographed copy bound in "Lectures Delivered at the Infantry and Cavalry School by Instructors and Student Officers of the Staff College during November and December 1904."

Thomas, C. B. "Principles of Revolutionary War." Student thesis, Army War College, March 1958.

Winecoff, Joseph L. "Influence of Nuclear Weapons on the Principles of War." Student individual study, Army War College, February 1957.

## GOVERNMENT DOCUMENTS AND OFFICIAL PUBLICATIONS

Cochenhausen, Friedrich von. *Die Truppenführung: Ein Handbuch für den Truppenführer und seine Gehilfen.* 11th ed. Berlin: E. S. Mittler, 1935.

_____. *Die Truppenführung: Ein Handbuch für den Truppenführer und seine Gehilfen.* Berlin, 1923.

Davis, Jefferson. *Report of the Commission to Examine into the Organization, System of Discipline, and Course of Instruction at the United States Military Academy.* 13 December 1860. In Serial Set 1089, Senate Miscellaneous Documents 3.

France. Army Ministry. Staff of the Land Forces. TTA 901, *Instruction générale sur les forces terrestres.* 27 September 1973.

———. Minister of War. *Décret du 26 octobre 1883 portant réglement sur le service des armées en campagne.* 7th ed. Paris: L. Baudoin, 1885.

———. Minister of War. *Décret du 18 mai 1895 portant réglement sur le service des armées en campagne.* Paris, 1895.

———. Minister of War. *Instruction sur le combat offensif des grandes unités.* Paris, 1916.

———. Minister of War. *Manual for Commanders of Infantry Platoons.* Trans. at the U.S. Army War College. Washington, D.C., 1917.

———. Minister of War. *Provisional Instructions for the Tactical Employment of Large Units.* Trans. Richard U. Nicholas. Fort Leavenworth, Kans., 1924.

———. Minister of War. Army Staff. *Instruction provisoire du octobre 1921 sur l'emploi tactique des grandes unités.* Paris, 1930.

———. Minister of War. Army Staff. *Instruction sur l'emploi tactique des grandes unités.* Paris, 1936.

———. War College. *Recueil de conférences. Problèmes opérationnels et logistiques.* May 1955.

———. War College and Staff School. *Notes relatives à la tactique.* June 1966.

Germany. Army. "The Attack in Position Warfare, 1 January 1918." In *Manual of Position Warfare for All Arms.* Trans. Great Britain, General Staff (Intelligence).

———. Army. "Essential Principles for the Defence of Positions as Laid Down in Instructions Issued by G.H.Q." Trans. Great Britain. General Staff. Intelligence. Army Headquarters, 2d Army, 1 August 1915.

———. Army. *The Field Service Regulations (Feld = Dienst Ordnung, 1900) of the German Army, 1900.* Trans. for the Intelligence Division, War Office, by Colonel H. S. Brownrigg. London: His Majesty's Stationery Office, n.d.

———. Army. *Manual of Position Warfare for All Arms.* Part 8. "The Principles of Command in the Defensive Battle in Position Warfare." Trans. Great Britain, General Staff, Intelligence. 1 March 1917.

———. Army. *Réglement du 22 mars 1908 sur le service en campagne dans l'armée allemande suivi des "Prescriptions pour les grandes manoeuvres."* Trans. General Peloux. Paris: Berger-Levrault, 1908.

_____. Federal Defense Minister. *Truppenführung.* Bonn, 25 October 1962.

_____. Federal Defense Minister. Army Service Regulation 100/100. *Command in Battle.* Trans. German Army Main Liaison Staff, U.S. Army Training and Doctrine Command. Bonn, 28 August 1973.

_____. Ministry of National Defense. *Command and Combat of the Combined Arms.* Fort Leavenworth, Kans., 1925.

Great Britain. *British Tactical Notes.* Ed. and prepared at the U.S. Army War College. Washington, D.C., 1918.

_____. *First Report of the Royal Commission Appointed to Inquire into the Present State of Military Education and into the Training of Candidates for Commissions in the Army.* London, 1869.

_____. *Report of the Commissioners Appointed to Consider the Best Mode of Re-organizing the System for Training Officers for the Scientific Corps Together with an Account of Foreign and Other Military Education.* London, 1857.

_____. *Report of the Committee Appointed to Consider the Education and Training of the Officers of the Army.* London, 1902.

_____. *Select Committee on the Royal Military College, Sandhurst* (Sandhurst Report). Parliamentary Paper 317. 1855.

_____. General Staff. *Instructions for Battle.* May 1917.

_____. Ministry of Defence. *Land Operations.* 15 July 1968.

_____. Royal Commission on Military Education. *Accounts of the Systems of Military Education in France, Prussia, Austria, Bavaria and the United States.* London, 1870.

_____. War Office. *Field Service Regulations, 1909* (amended 1914). London, 1916.

_____. War Office. *Field Service Regulations.* Volume II, *Operations* (Provisional). London, 1920.

_____. War Office. *Field Service Regulations.* Volume I, *Administration.* London, 1923.

_____. War Office. *Field Service Regulations.* Volume II, *Operations.* London, 1924.

_____. War Office. *Field Service Regulations.* Volume II, *Operations.* London, 1929.

_____. War Office. *Field Service Regulations.* Volume II, *Operations.* London, 1935.

Japan, Minister of War. *Réglement du 14 octobre 1907 sur le service en campagne dans l'armée japonaise suivi des prescriptions pour les manoeuvres.* Trans. Colonel Corvisart. Paris: Berger-Levrault, 1909.

McCleave, R. *General Principles of Infantry in Offense and Defense.* Fort Leavenworth, Kans., 1919.

Prussia. Minister of War. *Felddienst = Ordnung.* Berlin, 1908.

Union of the Soviet Socialist Republics. People's Commissariat of Defense. *Field Service Regulations, Soviet Army, 1936* (Tentative). Trans. Charles Berman. 1937.

United States. American Expeditionary Forces. *Infantry Drill Regulations* (Provisional). Part I. Paris, 1918.

United States Air Force. Air University. *Outlines of the Principles of Warfare from Clausewitz to the Present Time.* Maxwell Air Force Base, Ala., 1949.

United States Army. *Cavalry Service Regulations, 1914* (Experimental). Washington, D.C., 1914.

_____. *Field Service Regulations, 1905* (Amended 1908). Washington, D.C., 1908.

_____. *Field Service Regulations.* Washington, D.C., 1913.

_____. *Field Service Regulations.* Washington, D.C., 1914.

_____. *Field Service Regulations, 1923.* Washington, D.C., 1924.

_____. FM 100-1. *The Army.* 29 September 1978.

_____. FM 100-5. *Field Service Regulations—Operations* (Tentative). Washington, D.C., 1939.

_____. FM 100-5. *Field Service Regulations—Operations.* May 1941.

_____. FM 100-5. *Field Service Regulations—Operations.* June 1944.

_____. FM 100-5. *Field Service Regulations—Operations.* August 1949.

_____. FM 100-5. *Field Service Regulations—Operations.* 1954.

_____. FM 100-5. *Field Service Regulations—Operations.* February 1962.

_____. FM 100-5. *Operations of Army Forces in the Field.* September 1968.

_____. FM 100-5. *Operations.* July 1976.

_____. *Infantry Drill Regulations.* Washington, D.C., 1911.

_____. *Infantry Drill Regulations* (Provisional). Washington, D.C., 1919.

_____. *Infantry in Battle.* 2d ed. Washington, D.C.: Infantry Journal, 1939.

_____. SR No. 320-5-1. *Military Terms, Abbreviations and Symbols.* Washington, D.C., 1953.

United States Army Command and General Staff School. *Attack* (Tentative). Fort Leavenworth, Kans., 1937.

_____. *The Offensive* (Tentative). Fort Leavenworth, Kans., 1939.

_____. *The Principles of Strategy for an Independent Corps or Army in a Theater of Operations.* Fort Leavenworth, Kans., 1936.

United States Army Extension Courses. *Tactics and Technique of Infantry in Offensive Combat.* Washington, D.C., 1931.

United States Army Service Schools. *Lectures in Strategy.* Fort Leavenworth, Kans., 1905-1906.

United States Joint Chiefs of Staff. *A Dictionary of United States Military Terms.* Washington, D.C., 1963.

United States Marine Corps. FMFM 6-3. *Marine Infantry Battalion.* March 1978.

United States War Department. *Annual Report of the Commandant, U.S. Infantry and Cavalry School, U.S. Signal School and Staff College for the School Year ending August 31, 1906.* Washington, D.C., 1907.

_____. *Combat Instructions.* Washington, D.C., 5 September 1918.

_____. *Instructions for the Offensive Combat of Small Units.* Trans. from a French document at General Headquarters, Allied Expeditionary Force, France. Washington, D.C., 1918.

_____. TM 20-205. *Dictionary of U.S. Army Terms.* Washington, D.C., 1944.

_____. TR 10-5. *Doctrines, Principles, and Methods.* 23 December 1921.

_____. TR 10-5. *Doctrines, Principles, and Methods.* 15 August 1928.

_____. TR 10-5. *Doctrines, Principles, and Methods.* 10 August 1935.

_____. Military Intelligence Division. Tentative Lessons Bulletin No. 123. *British Survey on German Armored Formations.* Washington, D.C., 23 June 1941.

## BOOKS

Alger, John I. *Antoine-Henri Jomini: A Bibliographical Survey.* West Point, N. Y.: USMA Library, 1975.

_____. *Definitions and Doctrine of the Military Art, Past and Present.* West Point, N. Y.: Department of History, USMA, 1979.

Altham, Edward A. *The Principles of War Historically Illustrated.* Vol. 1. London: Macmillan, 1914.

Ambrose, Stephen. *Duty, Honor, Country: A History of West Point.* Baltimore: Johns Hopkins Press, 1966.

Andrews, Lincoln Clarke. *Fundamentals of Military Service.* Philadelphia: J. P. Lippincott Company [1916].

Aston, George Gray. *The Biography of the Late Marshal Foch.* New York: Macmillan, 1929.

_____. *Sea, Land and Air Strategy: A Comparison.* London: John Murray, 1914.

_____. *War Lessons, New and Old.* London: John Murray, 1919.

Barnard, Henry. *Military Schools and Courses of Instruction in the Science and Art of War.* Rev. ed. New York: Greenwood Press, 1969 [1872].

Beauregard, Pierre Gustave Toutant. *A Commentary on the Campaign and Battle of Manassas of July 1861 Together with a Summary of the Art of War.* New York: G. P. Putnam's Sons, 1891.

Berenhorst, Georg Heinrich von. *Aus den Nachlasse von Georg Heinrich von Berenhorst.* Ed. E. von Bülow. 2 vols. Dessau, 1845-47.

Bernhardi, Friedrich von. *On War of Today.* Trans. Karl von Donat. 2 vols. London: Hugh Rees, 1913.

_____. *The War of the Future in the Light of the Lessons of the World War.* Trans. F. A. Holt. 2d ed. London: Hutchison and Company, [1920].

Bigelow, John. *The Principles of Strategy Illustrated Mainly from American Campaigns.* 2d ed. Philadelphia: J. P. Lippincott, 1894.

Bird, Wilkinson Dent. *The Direction of War: A Study and Illustration of Strategy.* 2d ed. Cambridge, England: The University Press, 1920.

Bond, Brian. *Liddell Hart: A Study of His Military Thought.* New Brunswick, N. J.: Rutgers University Press, 1977.

_____. *The Victorian Army and the Staff College, 1854-1914.* London: Eyre Methuen, 1972.

Bond, Paul S., and Crouch, E. H. *Tactics, The Practical Art of Leading Troops in War.* New York: American Army and Navy Journal, 1922.

Bond, Paul S., and McDonough, M. J. *Technique of Modern Tactics: A Study of Troop Leading Methods in the Operations of Detachments of All Arms.* 3d ed. Menasha, Wis.: Collegiate Press, 1916.

Bonnal, Henri. *Les Conditions de la guerre moderne.* Paris: E. Boccard, 1916.

_____. *L'Esprit de la guerre moderne.* Paris: Chapelot, 1905.

Bonneau du Martray, Edmond. *Maximes, conseils et instructions sur l'art de la guerre ou aide-mémoire practique de la guerre à l'usage des militaires de toutes armes et de tous pays.* 36th ed. Paris, 1870.

_____. *Maxims, Advice and Instructions of the Art of War.* Trans. August Frederick Lendy. New York, 1862.

Boynton, Edward C. *History of West Point.* New York: Van Nostrand, 1863.

Brett, Maurice, ed. *Maxims of War.* London, 1905.

Brodie, Bernard. *Strategy in the Missile Age.* Princeton, N. J.: Princeton University Press, 1959.

_____. *War and Politics*. New York: Macmillan, 1973.

_____. *The Worth of the Principles of War*. Santa Monica, Calif.: Rand, 1957.

Bürde, J. *Tactical Principles*. London: Hugh Rees, 1908.

Burne, Alfred H. *The Art of War on Land Illustrated by Campaigns and Battles of All Ages*. London: Methuen and Company, 1944.

Buzelet, Charles Adrian de. *Cours de science militaire contenant les principes et les actions des grands généraux*. 2 vols. N.p., n.d. (c. 1808).

Caemmerer, Rudolf von. *Clausewitz*. In D. von Pelet-Narbonne, ed. *Erzieher des preussischen Heeres*. 2d ed. Oldenburg: G. Stalling, [1905].

_____. *The Development of Strategical Science during the Nineteenth Century*. Trans. Karl von Donat. London: Hugh Rees, 1905.

Caldwell, Vernon A. *Catechism of Uniform Tactical Training*. Menasha, Wis.: George Banta, 1918.

_____. *Five Tactical Principles and Uniform Tactical Training*. Menasha, Wis.: George Banta, 1916.

Califf, Joseph Mark. *Notes on Military Science and the Art of War*. Washington, D.C.: Chapman, 1891.

Callataÿ, Armand de. *Les principes de la tactique*. Brussels and Paris, 1912.

Callwell, C. E. *Small Wars: Their Principles and Practice*. 3d ed. London: Printed for H. M. Stationery Office by Harrison and Sons, 1906.

Carr, Edward H. *What Is History?* New York: Vintage Books, 1961.

Carrias, Eugène. *La Pensée militaire allemande*. Paris: Presses universitaires de France, 1948.

_____. *La Pensée militaire française*. [Paris]: Presses universitaires de France, [1960].

Cholet, Eugène. *A propos de doctrine: les leçons du passé confirmées par celles de la grande guerre*. Paris, 1919.

Churchill, Winston S. *My Early Life, A Roving Commission*. London: Thornton Butterworth, 1930.

Clausewitz, Carl von. *Hinterlassene Werke über Krieg und Kriegführung des Generals Carl von Clausewitz*. Vol. 3. 3d ed. Berlin: Ferdinand Dümmler, 1869.

_____. *On War*. Trans. Michael Howard and Peter Paret. Princeton, N.J.: Princeton University Press, 1976.

_____. *Principles of War*. Trans. Hans W. Gatzke. Harrisburg, Pa.: Stackpole, 1960.

Colin, Jean. *France and the Next War*. Trans. L. H. R. Hennesey. London: Hodder and Stoughton, 1914.

Collins, John M. *Grand Strategy, Principles and Practices.* Annapolis: Naval Institute Press, 1973.

Corbett, Julian S. *Some Principles of Maritime Strategy.* London: Longmans, Green and Company, 1911.

Cugnot, M. *Elémens de l'art militaire, ancien et modern.* Paris: Vincent, 1766.

Cullum, George W. *Biographical Register of Officers and Graduates of the United States Military Academy and Early History.* 2 vols. 3d ed. Cambridge, Mass.: Houghton Mifflin, 1891.

Culmann, F. *Stratégie, La Manoeuvre stratégique offensive dans la guerre de mouvements.* Paris: Lavauzelle, 1924.

Darrieus, Gabriel. *War on the Sea, Strategy and Tactics, Basic Principles.* Trans. Philip R. Alger. Annapolis: United States Naval Institute, 1908.

de Gaulle, Charles. *Le Fil de l'épée.* Paris: Berger-Levrault, 1944.

Delabarre-Duparcq, Nicolas Edouard. *Elements of Military Art and History: Comprising the History and Tactics of the Separate Arms and the Minor Operations of War.* Trans. George W. Cullum. New York: D. Van Nostrand, 1863.

de Pardieu, Marie Felix. *Critical Study of German Tactics and of the New German Regulations.* Trans. Charles F. Martin. Ft. Leavenworth, Kans., 1912.

Derrécagaix, Victor Bernard. *Modern War.* Trans. C. W. Foster. Washington, D.C.: J. J. Chapman, 1888.

Desmazes, René. *Saint-Cyr: son histoire, ses gloires, ses leçons.* Paris: Saint-Cyrienne, 1948.

Donaldson, John William Edward. *Military History Applied to Modern Warfare, A Guide to the Study of Military History Exemplified by Studies of the Campaigns of Austerlitz, Jena, Vimiero, Corunna, Salamanca, Waterloo, and the Shenandoah Valley.* 2d ed. London: H. Rees, 1907.

Douhet, Giulio. *The Command of the Air.* Trans. Dino Ferrari. London: Faber and Faber, 1943.

DuFour, Guillaume H. *Strategy and Tactics.* Trans. William P. Craighill. New York: Van Nostrand, 1864.

Dupuis, Victor César. *L'Age des casernes.* Paris: Fourner, 1923.

Eady, Harold Griffen. *Historical Illustrations to Field Service Regulations.* Vol. 2. London: Sifton, Praed and Company, 1927.

————. *Historical Illustrations to Field Service Regulations, "Operations," 1929.* London: Sifton, Praed and Company, 1930.

Earle, Edward Meade, ed. *Makers of Modern Strategy: Military Thought from Machiavelli to Hitler.* Princeton, N.J.: Princeton University Press, 1943.

Eccles, Henry E. *Military Concepts and Philosophy.* New Brunswick, N. J.: Rutgers University Press, 1965.

Edmunds, Frank Heartt. *Principles of the Art and Science of War and Their Application in Modern Warfare.* Fort Leavenworth, Kans.: Regimental Printing Office, Twentieth U.S. Infantry, 1883.

Ernst, Fritz. *Generäle: Portraits und Studien zur schweizerischen Biographie.* Zurich: Fretz und Wasmuth, 1942.

*Esprit des loix de la tactique et de différentes institutions militaires ou Notes de M. le maréchal de Saxe: contenant plusieurs nouveaux systèmes sur l'art de la guerre.* 2 vols. Haye: Pierre Grosse, 1762.

Falls, Cyril. *The Art of War from the Age of Napoleon to the Present Day.* London: Oxford, 1961.

———. *Ordeal by Battle.* New York: Oxford University Press, 1943.

Feuquières, Antoine Manassès de Pas, Marquis de. *Memoirs Historical and Military: Containing a Distinct View of All the Considerable States of Europe.* Trans. anonymous. 2 vols. New York: Greenwood Press, 1968 [1736].

Fiebeger, Gustave. *Elements of Strategy.* West Point, N. Y., [1906].

Field Officer, A. *Lectures on Land Warfare: A Tactical Manual for the Use of Infantry Officers: An Examination of the Principles Which Underlie the Art of Warfare, with Illustrations of the Principles Taken from Military History, from the Battle of Thermopylae, B.C. 480, to the Battle of the Sambre, November 1-11, 1918.* London, 1922.

Fix, Henri Constant. *La Stratégie appliqué.* Brussels: Merzbach, 1885.

Foch, Ferdinand. *Des Principes de la guerre; Conférences faite à l'Ecole supérieure de guerre.* 2d ed. Nancy and Paris: Berger-Levrault and Company, 1906.

———. *The Principles of War.* Trans. J. de Morinni. New York: H. K. Fly, 1918.

Foertsch Hermann, *The Art of Modern Warfare.* Trans. Theodore W. Knauth. New York: Veritas Press, 1940.

Folard, Jean Charles. *Abrégé des commentaires de M. de Folard sur l'histoire de Polybe.* 3 vols. Paris: La Veuve Gandouin, 1754.

Fortescue, John W. *Military History.* Cambridge, England: The University Press, 1914.

Frederick II. *Instruction pour les généraux qui auront à commander des detachments, des ailes, des secondes lignes et des armées prussiennes.* [Berlin, 1753].

Fuller, John Frederick Charles. *The Foundations of the Science of War.* London: Hutchison and Company, [1926].

_____. *Lectures on F.S.R. II.* London: Sifton, Praed, and Company, 1931.

_____. *Lectures on F.S.R. III (Operations between Mechanized Forces).* London: Sifton, Praed, and Company, 1932.

_____. *Memoirs of an Unconventional Soldier.* London: Nicholson and Watson, 1936.

_____. *Reformation of War.* London: Hutchison and Company, 1923.

_____. *The Second World War, 1939-45, A Strategical and Tactical History.* New York: Duell, Sloan and Pearce, 1949.

_____. *Training Soldiers for War.* London: H. Rees, 1914.

_____. *Watchwords.* London: Skeffington and Son, 1944.

Garthoff, Raymond L. *Soviet Military Doctrine.* Santa Monica, Calif.: Rand, 1953.

Gay de Vernon, Simon François. *Traité élémentaire d'art militaire et de fortification, à l'usage des élèves de l'Ecole polytechnique et des élèves des écoles militaires.* 2 vols. Paris: Allais, 1805.

_____. *A Treatise on the Science of War and Fortification Composed for the Use of the Imperial Polytechnik Schools, and Military Schools.* Trans. John Michael O'Connor. 2 vols. New York: J. Seymore, 1817-18.

Gilbert, Felix. *To the Farewell Address: Ideas of Early American Foreign Policy.* Princeton, N. J.: Princeton University Press, 1961.

Godwin-Austen, Alfred Reade. *The Staff and the Staff College.* London: Constable and Company, 1927.

Gourgaud, Gaspard. *Sainte-Hélène: Journal inédit de 1815 à 1818.* 2 vols. 3d ed. Paris: E. Flammarion, [1899].

Graham, James John. *Elementary History of the Progress of the Art of War.* London: R. Bentley, 1858.

Hahn, Roger. *The Anatomy of a Scientific Institution: The Paris Academy of Sciences, 1666-1803.* Berkeley: University of California Press, 1971.

Halleck, Henry W. *Elements of Military Art and Science.* New York: D. Appleton and Company, 1846.

Hamley, Edward Bruce. *The Operations of War Explained and Illustrated.* 5th ed. Edinburgh: William Blackwood and Sons, 1889.

Hanna, Matthew Elting. *Tactical Principles and Problems.* Menasha, Wis.: George Banta, 1910.

Henderson, George Francis Robert. *The Science of War, A Collection of Essays and Lectures, 1891-1903.* London: Longmans, Green and Company, 1905.

_____. *Stonewall Jackson and the American Civil War*. London: Longmans, Green and Company, 1949.

[Hess, Heinrich von]. *Allgemeine praktische Grundsätze der Strategie und höheren Taktik für Armee-, selbststandige Korps- und Divisions-Kommandanten*. Vienna: Hof- und Staatsdruckerei, 1867.

Higham, Robin, ed. *A Guide to the Sources of British Military History*. Berkeley: University of California Press, 1971.

_____. *The Military Intellectuals in Britain, 1918-1939*. New Brunswick, N. J.: Rutgers University Press, 1966.

Hittle, J. D., ed. *Jomini and His Summary of the Art of War*. Harrisburg, Pa.: Military Service, 1952.

Hohenlohe-Ingelfingen, Kraft Karl August zu. *Letters on Strategy*. Trans. Walter Haweis James. 2 vols. London: K. Paul, Trench, Trübner and Company, 1918.

Howard, Michael. *Studies in War and Peace*. New York: Viking Press, 1972.

_____. ed., *The Theory and Practice of War: Essays Presented to Captain B. H. Liddell Hart on His Seventieth Birthday*. Bloomington: Indiana University Press, 1965.

Howland, Charles R. *A Military History of the World War*. Fort Leavenworth, Kans.: General Service Schools Press, 1923.

Immanuel, Friedrich, ed. *Lehnerts Handbuch für den Truppenführer*. 21st ed. Berlin: E. S. Mittler and Son, 1903.

James, Walter H. *Modern Strategy: An Outline of the Principles Which Guide the Conduct of Campaigns*. 2d ed. Edinburgh: W. Blackwood, 1904.

Jomini, Antoine-Henri. *The Art of War*. Trans. G. H. Mendell and W. P. Craighill. Philadelphia: J. B. Lippincott and Company, 1862.

_____. *Histoire critique et militaire des campagnes de la révolution*. Third and last parts. 2d ed. Paris: Magimel, Anselin and Pochard, 1816.

_____. *Histoire critique et militaire des guerres de Frédéric II*. 3 vols. 3d ed. Paris: Magimel, Anselin and Pochard, 1818.

_____. *Précis de l'art de la guerre*. 2 vols. New ed. Paris: Tanera, 1855.

_____. *Summary of the Art of War*. Trans. O. F. Winship and E. E. McLean. New York: G. Putnam and Company, 1854.

_____. *Tableau analytique des principales combinaisons de la guerre*. 3d ed. Paris: Anselin, 1830.

_____. *Traité de grande tactique*. First and second parts. Paris: Giguet and Michaud, Magimel, 1805.

_____. *Traité de grande tactique*. Fifth part. Paris: Giguet and Michaud, Magimel, 1806.

———. *Traité de grandes opérations militaires.* Third and fourth parts. Paris: Giguet and Michaud, Magimel, 1807 and 1809.

———. *Traité des grandes opérations militaires.* 4 vols. 2d ed. Paris: Magimel, 1811.

———. *Treatise on Grand Military Operations.* . . . Trans. Samuel B. Holabird. 2 vols. New York and London: D. Van Nostrand, 1865.

[Karl, Archduke of Austria]. *Grundsätze der höherer Kriegskunst für die Generäle der österreichischer Armee.* Vienna: Hof- und Staats-Druckerei, 1806.

———. *Grundsätze der Strategie erlautert durch die Darstellung des Feldzugs von 1796.* Vienna: Anton Strauss, 1813.

Karl, Archduke of Austria. *Ausgewählte Schriften weiland seiner kaiserlichen Hoheit des Erzherzogs Karl von Oesterreich.* Vienna, 1893.

———. *Principes de la stratégie developpés par la relation de la campagne de 1796 en Allemagne.* Trans. and ed. Antoine-Henri Jomini. 3 vols. Paris: Magimel, Anselin and Pochard, 1818.

Kearsey, Alexander H. C. *The Events, Strategy and Tactics of the Palestine Campaigns, with Illustrations of the Principles of War.* London: H. Rees, 1928.

———. *Notes on Training for War: Staff College, with Schemes and Solutions and Historical Illustrations of the Principles of War.* London: H. Rees, 1926.

———. *A Study of the Strategy and Tactics of the East Prussian Campaign 1914; Illustrating the Principles of War.* 2d rev. ed. London: Sifton Praed, 1932.

Kingston-McCloughry, Edgar J. *War in Three Dimensions: The Impact of Air-Power upon the Classical Principles of War.* London: Cape, 1949.

Kuznetsaw, F. *Principles of Modern Offensive Combat.* Trans. Charles Berman. (Originally published in Moscow, 5 June 1938.)

Lecomte, Ferdinand. *Le Général Jomini, sa vie et ses écrits.* 3d ed. Lausanne: B. Benda, 1888.

Lendy, Auguste F. *The Principles of War: or Elementary Treatise on Higher Tactics and Strategy.* 2d ed. London: Mitchell and Son, 1862.

Liddell Hart, Basil H. *The British Way in Warfare: Adaptability and Mobility.* Rev. ed. New York: Penguin Books, 1942.

Lippett, Francis J. *A Treatise on the Tactical Use of the Three Arms: Infantry, Artillery and Cavalry.* New York: D. Van Nostrand, 1865.

Lloyd, Henry. *Introduction à l'histoire de la guerre en Allemagne.* Trans. Germain de Mesmon. London: n.p., 1784.

———. *Mémoires militaires et politiques du général Lloyd.* Paris: Magimel, 1801.

Lloyd George, David. *The War Memoirs of David Lloyd George.* Vol. 6. Boston: Little, Brown and Company, 1937.

Lucas, Pascal Marie. *L'Evolution des idées tactiques en France et en Allemagne pendant la guerre de 1914-1918.* Paris: Berger-Levrault, 1932.

Luvaas, Jay. *The Education of an Army: British Military Thought, 1815-1940.* Chicago: University of Chicago Press, 1964.

Lyautey, Louis Hubert Gonzalve. *Lyautey l'africain: Textes et lettres du Maréchal Lyautey.* Ed. Pierre Lyautey. Vol. 3. Paris: Plon, 1956.

McCleary, Oliver S. *The Principles of War.* [Salt Lake City: Private printing, c. 1930].

MacDougall, Patrick L. *The Theory of War Illustrated by Numerous Examples from Military History.* 2d ed. London: Longman, Green, Longman and Roberts, 1858.

Machiavel, Nicholas [Niccolò Machiavelli]. *The Art of War.* [Trans. Ellis Farneworth]. Albany, N. Y.: Henry C. Southwick, 1815.

Mahan, Alfred Thayer. *The Influence of Sea Power upon History, 1660-1783.* 7th ed. Boston: Little, Brown, 1894.

_____. *Lessons of the War with Spain and Other Articles.* Boston: Little, Brown, [1889].

_____. *Naval Strategy Compared and Contrasted with the Principles and Practice of Military Operations on Land.* Boston: Little, Brown, 1911.

Mahan, Dennis Hart. *Advanced-Guard, Outpost, and Detachment Service of Troops, with the Essential Principles of Strategy and Grand Tactics, for the Use of Officers of the Militia and Volunteers.* New ed. New York: John Wiley, 1864.

_____. *A Complete Treatise on Field Fortifications with the General Outlines of the Principles Regulating the Arrangement, the Attack and Defense of Permanent Works.* New York: Greenwood Press, 1968 [1836].

Maillard, Louis. *Les Eléments de la guerre.* Paris: L. Baudoin, 1891.

Mao Tse-tung. *Selected Military Writings of Mao Tse-tung.* Trans. Foreign Languages Press. Peking: Foreign Languages Press, 1968.

Marmont, Auguste. *The Spirit of Military Institutions; or Essential Principles of the Art of War.* Trans. Henry Coppée. Philadelphia: J. B. Lippincott, 1862.

Matloff, Maurice, ed. *American Military History.* Washington, D.C.: Office of the Chief of Military History, United States Army, 1969.

Maurice, Frederick. *British Strategy: A Study of the Application of the Principles of War.* London: Constable and Company, 1929.

Meinecke, Friedrich. *Machiavellism, The Doctrine of Raison d'état and Its Place in Modern History.* Trans. Douglas Scott. New Haven, Conn.: Yale University Press, 1957.

Mercur, James. *Elements of the Art of War.* 2d ed. New York: J. Wiley, 1889.

Michie, Peter S., ed. *The Life and Letters of Emory Upton.* New York: D. Appleton, 1885.

Moltke, Helmuth von. *Moltkes militarische Werke.* Ed. the Great General Staff. Vol. 4, *Kriegslehren.* Part 3, Die Schlacht. Berlin: E. S. Mittler und Sohn, 1912.

Montecuccoli, Raimund. *Ausgewaehlte Schriften des Raimund Fürsten Montecuccoli General-Lieutenant und Feld-Marschall.* Ed. Alois Veltzé. Vol. 1, *Militaerischen Schriften.* Vienna and Leipzig: W. Brumüller, 1899.

Montgomery, Bernard L. *The Memoirs of Field-Marshal the Viscount Montgomery of Alamein, K.G.* Cleveland: World Publishing Company, 1958.

Mordacq, Jean Jules Henri. *La Stratégie, Historique évolution.* Paris: L. Fournier, 1912.

Moss, James A. *Applied Minor Tactics.* Menasha, Wis.: George Banta, 1917.

Musée de Payerne. *Général Antoine-Henri Jomini, 1779-1869.* Payerne, 1969.

Napoleon I. *Maximes de guerre et pensées de Napoléon.* Paris: J. Dumaine, 1874.

_____. *War Maxims, with his Social and Political Thought.* Trans. and ed. Lucien Edward Henry. London: Gale and Polden, [1899].

Naylor, William K. *The Marne Miracle Illustrating the Principles of War.* Washington, D.C.: United States Infantry Association, 1923.

_____. *Principles of Strategy with Historical Illustrations.* Fort Leavenworth, Kans.: Army Service Schools Press, 1921.

Ney, Virgil. *Evolution of the United States Army Field Manual Valley Forge to Vietnam.* Combat Operations Research Group Memorandum 244. Fort Belvoir, Va.: U.S. Army Combat Developments Command, January 1966.

_____. *Notes on Guerrilla War: Principles and Practices.* Washington, D.C.: Command Publications, 1962.

Okunev, Nikolai A. *Considérations sur les grandes opérations de la campagne de 1812 en Russie; des mémoires sur les principes de la stratégie; de l'examen raisonné des propriétés des trois armes; et d'un mémoire sur l'artillerie.* New ed. Brussels: J.-B. Petit, 1841.

Palit, Dhariti K. *The Essentials of Military Knowledge*. London: C. Hurst, 1967.

Pappas, George S. *Prudens Futuri: The US Army War College, 1901-1967*. Carlisle Barracks, Pa.: Alumni Association, U.S. Army War College, 1967.

Paret, Peter. *Clausewitz and the State*. New York: Oxford University Press, 1976.

_____. *Innovation and Reform in Warfare*. Harmon Memorial Lecture, United States Air Force Academy, 1966.

Pettit, James S. *Elements of Military Science for the Use of Students in Colleges and Universities*. New Haven, Conn.: Tuttle, Morehouse and Taylor, 1895.

Phillips, Thomas R., ed. *Roots of Strategy: A Collection of Military Classics*. Harrisburg, Pa.: Military Service Publishing, 1955.

Picard, Ernest. *Précepts et jugements de Napoléon*. Paris: Berger-Levrault, 1913.

Prussian General Officer, A [Bülow-Dietrich]. *The Spirit of the Modern System of War*. London: T. Egerton, 1806.

Puleston, W. D. *The Life and Work of Captain Alfred Thayer Mahan*. New Haven, Conn.: Yale, 1939.

Reed, Hugh T. *Elements of Military Science and Tactics*. 7th ed. Chicago: The author, 1889.

Ritter, Gerhard. *Frederick the Great, A Historical Profile*. Trans. and ed. Peter Paret. Berkeley: University of California Press, 1968.

Robinson, Oliver P. *The Fundamentals of Military Strategy*. Washington, D.C.: United States Infantry Association, 1928.

Rocheaymon, C. de la. *Introduction a l'étude de l'art de la guerre*. 4 vols. Weimar: Bureau d'industrie, 1802-1804.

Rocquancourt, Jean T. *Cours élémentaire d'art et d'histoire militaires à l'usage des élèves de l'Ecole royale spéciale militaire*. 4 vols. 2d ed. Paris: Anselin, 1831-1838.

Rogniat, Joseph. *Considérations sur l'art de la guerre*. 3d ed. Paris: Anselin and Pochard, 1820.

Rüstow, Wilhelm von. *Die Feldherrnkunst des neunzehnten Jahrhunderts*. 2 vols. 3d ed. Zurich: F. Schulthess, 1878-1879.

Saint Cyr, Gouvion. *Mémoires pour servir l'histoire militaire sous le directoire, le consulat, et l'empire*. Paris: Anselin, 1831.

Savkin, Vasili Ye. *The Basic Principles of Operational Art and Tactics (A Soviet View)*. Trans. and published under the auspices of the United States Air Force. (Originally published in Moscow 1972.)

Savoye, Charles de. *Réglement sur le service en campagne*. 2d ed. Paris: J. Dumaine, 1866.

Schalk, Emil. *Campaigns of 1862 and 1863 Illustrating the Principles of Strategy.* Philadelphia: J. B. Lippincott and Company, 1863.

_____. *Summary of the Art of War.* Philadelphia: J. B. Lippincott and Company, 1862.

Serrigny, Bernard. *Réflexions sur l'art de la guerre.* 2d ed. Paris: Charles-Lavauzelle, 1921.

Silva, Marquis de. *Considérations sur la guerre présente entre les russes et les turcs.* Turin: Reyceud, 1773.

_____. *Pensées sur la tactique et la stratégique ou, Vrais principes de la science militaire.* Turin, 1778.

Simon, Walter M. *European Positivism in the Nineteenth Century: An Essay in Intellectual History.* Ithaca, N. Y.: Cornell University Press, 1963.

Smith, Dale O. *U.S. Military Doctrine: A Study and Appraisal.* New York: Duell, Sloan and Pearce, 1955.

Smyth, John. *Sandhurst, the History of the Royal Military Academy, Woolwich, the Royal Military College, Sandhurst, and the Royal Military Academy, Sandhurst, 1741-1961.* London: Weidenfeld and Nicholson, 1961.

Soady, France James. *Lessons of War as Taught by the Great Masters and Others; Selected and Arranged from the Various Operations of War.* London: W. H. Allen, 1870.

Steele, Matthew F. *American Campaigns.* 2 vols. Washington, D.C.: Combat Forces Press, 1951.

Sun Tzu. *The Art of War.* Trans. Samuel B. Griffith. Oxford: Clarendon Press, 1963.

Szabad, Emeric. *Modern War: Its Theory and Practice.* New York: Harper, 1863.

Thomas, Hugh. *The Story of Sandhurst.* London: Hutchison, 1961.

Trythall, Anthony J. *"Boney" Fuller: The Intellectual General, 1878-1966.* London: Cassell, 1977.

United States Military Academy. *Jomini, Clausewitz, and Schlieffen.* West Point, N.Y.: Department of Military Art and Engineering, 1964.

_____. *Notes for the Course in the History of the Military Art.* West Point, N. Y.: Department of Military Art and Engineering, 1954.

_____. *Notes on Combat Maneuvers.* West Point, N.Y.: Department of Military Art and Engineering, 1943.

_____. *Operations in Belgium and France, 1940.* West Point, N. Y.: Department of Military Art and Engineering, c. 1941.

Verdy du Vernois, Julius von. *Studies in the Leading of Troops.* Trans. William Gerlach. Kansas City: Hudson Press, 1906.

_____. *A Tactical Study Based on the Battle of Custozza.* Trans. G. F. R. Henderson. New York: Greenwood Press, 1968 [1894].

Vial, Jules. *Cours d'art et d'histoire militaires.* 2 vols. Paris, 1861.

Vizetelly, Henry. *Berlin under the New Empire.* 2 vols. London, 1879.

von der Goltz, Colmar. *Kriegführung: Kurze Lehre ihrer wichtigsten Grundsätz und Formen.* Berlin: R. v. Decker, 1895.

_____. *Das Volk in Waffen. Ein Buch über Heerwesen und Kriegführung unserer Zeit.* 4th ed. Berlin: R. v. Decker, 1890.

Voysey, R. A. E. *An Outline of the Principles of War.* Diss, England, 1934.

Wagner, Arthur L. *Organization and Tactics.* Kansas City, Missouri: Hudson-Kimberly, 1894.

_____. *Strategy.* Kansas City, Mo.: Hudson-Kimberly, 1904.

Wavell, Earl. *Soldiers and Soldiering: or Epithets of War.* London: Cape, 1953.

Wellington, Arthur Wellesley, Duke of. *The Principles of War, Exhibited in the Practice of the Camp; and as Developed in a Series of General Orders of Field-Marshal the Duke of Wellington, K.G. etc., etc., etc. in the Late Campaign on the Peninsula.* London: W. Clowes, 1815.

Wheeler, Junius B. *A Course of Instruction in the Elements of the Art and Science of War.* New York: D. Van Nostrand, 1879.

Wilkinson, Spenser. *The French Army before Napoleon.* Oxford: Clarendon Press, 1915.

Willisen, Wilhelm von. *Theorie des grossen Krieges angewendet auf den russisch-polnischen Feldzug von 1831.* Vol. 1. Berlin, 1840.

Willoughby, Charles A. *Maneuver in War.* Harrisburg, Pa.: Military Service, 1939.

Wisser, John P. *Practical Instruction in Minor Tactics and Strategy.* New York: D. Appleton, 1888.

Wylie, J. C. *Military Strategy: A General Theory of Power Control.* New Brunswick, N. J.: Rutgers University Press, 1967.

Young, Frederick W. *The Story of the Staff College, 1858-1958.* Aldershot: Gale and Polden, 1958.

## ARTICLES

Ali, F. B. "The Principles of War." *Journal of the Royal United Service Institution* 108 (May 1963): 159-65.

Allen, George. "The Life of Jomini." *United States Service Magazine* 2 (October 1864):351-64.

Armstrong, Donald. "The New Power and the Old-age Principles." *Infantry Journal* 57 (October 1945):46-48.

Atlas, Edward. "The Shape of War as It Is." *Infantry Journal* 50 (February 1942):66-71.

Baker, R. H. "The Origins of Soviet Military Doctrine." *Journal of the Royal United Service Institution for Defence Studies* 121 (March 1976):38-43.

Betts, Benjamin D. "Principles of War Applied to Cavalry." *Cavalry Journal* 52 (September-October 1943):27-28.

Bonnal, Henri. "De la méthode dans les hautes études militaires en Allemagne et en France." *Minerva: Revue des lettres et des arts* 1 (October 1902):15-29.

Booth, K. "History or Logic as Approaches to Strategy." *Journal of the Royal United Service Institution for Defence Studies* 117 (September 1972):34-41.

"Brief Discussion of the Principles of War, A." *Military Digest* 1 (December 1936):16-20.

Britt, A. S. "The Battle of Cowpens: An Application of Certain Principles of War." *Military Review* 30 (December 1950):47-50.

Brown, C. R. "The Principles of War." *United States Naval Institute Proceedings* 75 (June 1949):621-33.

Bundel, Charles M. "What Is Wrong with Our Principles of War?" *Infantry Journal* 33 (October 1928): 329-47.

Burne, Alfred H. "The Battle of Kadesh and the Principles of War." *Army Quarterly* 4 (April 1922):115-23.

Campbell, John W. "Evolution of a Doctrine: The Principles of War." *Marine Corps Gazette* 54 (December 1970):39-42.

Carmichael, George K. "Principles of War and Their Application to Strategy and Tactics." *Naval War College Review* 3 (October 1950):23-42.

Clarke, F. A. S. "The First Principle of War." *Army Quarterly and Defence Journal* 77 (January 1959): 242-49.

Coakley, P. "Economy of Principles." *Australian Army Journal* 84 (May 1956):37-44.

Coe, Edward H. "The Campaigns of Joshua." *Military Engineer* 27 (March-April 1935):90-95.

Connolly, R. D. "The Principles of War and Psywar." *Military Review* 36 (March 1957):37-46.

Conolly, Richard L. "The Principles of War." *United States Naval Institute Proceedings* 79 (January 1953):1-9.

Crawford, Charles. "Our Backward Military Science." *Literary Digest* 55 (July 1917):29-30.

Cullum, George. "Jomini's Life of Napoleon." *United States Service Magazine* 2 (August 1864):128.

Dany, Jean. "La Littérature militaire d'aujourd'hui." *Revue de Paris* 2 (April 1912):611-24.

de Gaulle, Charles. "Doctrine a priori ou doctrine des circonstances?" *Revue militaire française* 15 (1925):306-28.

Disbrey, W. D. "The Application of the Principles of War to Air Power." *Military Review* 31 (October 1951):89-95.

Doty, Ralph E. "Joshua and the Principles of War." *Infantry Journal* 44 (August 1930):178-79.

Edmond, Emil. "The First Principle of War." *Military Review* 41 (February 1961):12-15.

"Eight Principles of War as Applicable to the Platoon Commander's Job, The." *Military Review* 23 (September 1943):35.

Elting, John R. "Jomini: Disciple of Napoleon?" *Military Affairs* 27 (Spring 1964):17-26.

Erickson, Hjalmar. "Doctrines and Principles of War." *Infantry Journal* 20 (January 1922):47-55.

_____. "War, Its Nature, Doctrines and Methods." *Coast Artillery Journal* 57 (October 1922):306-14.

Ernle-Erle-Drux, Reginald A.K.P. "Principles of War." *Journal of the Royal United Service Institution* 107 (February 1962): 65-66.

Fallwell, Marshall L. "The Principles of War and the Solution of Military Problems." *Military Review* 35 (May 1955):48-62.

Fletcher, J. "Intelligence: A Principle of War." *Military Review* 50 (August 1970):52-57.

François, H. "Des Principes de guerre." *Revue militaire française* 3 (April 1922):103-10.

Fuller, J. F. C. "The Foundations of the Science of War." *Army Quarterly* 1 (October 1920):90-111.

_____. "Major-General Henry Lloyd, Adventurer and Military Philosopher." *Army Quarterly* 12 (July 1926):300-14.

[Fuller, J. F. C.] "The Principles of War with Reference to the Campaigns of 1914-15." *Journal of the Royal United Service Institution* 61 (February 1916):1-40.

Garthoff, Raymond L. "Soviet Doctrine on the Decisive Factors in Modern War." *Military Review* 39 (July 1959):3-22.

Greenwood, John E. "New Principle." *Marine Corps Gazette* 38 (July 1954):12-15.

Gruzman, D. B. "Some Thoughts on the Principles of War." *Australian Army Journal* 148 (September 1961):41-47.

H. H. "Naval History: Mahan and His Successors." *The Military Historian and Economist* 3 (January 1918):7-19.

Henderson, G.F.R. "Strategy and its Teachings." *Journal of the Royal United Service Institution* 42 (July 1898): 761-86.

Ho, Kenmin. "Mao's 10 Principles of War." *Military Review* 47 (July 1967):96-98.

Howard-Williams, E. L. "The Principles of War and the R.A.F.: Concentration." *Royal Air Force Quarterly* 4 (October 1933):353-60.

Hughes, E. S. "The Fundamentals of War." *Army Information Digest* 9 (March 1954):353-58.

Huston, James A. "Re-examine the Principles of War." *Military Review* 35 (February 1956):30-36.

Irvine, Dallas D. "The French Discovery of Clausewitz and Napoleon." *Military Affairs* 4 (1940):143-61.

Johnston, Edward S. "A Science of War." *Review of Military Literature: The Command and General Staff School Quarterly* 14 (June 1934): 89-123.

Johnston, Frank L. "The Principles of War." *Naval War College Review* 4 (October 1951):1-26.

Jomini, Antoine-Henri. "L'Art de la guerre." *Pallas: Eine Zeitschrift für Staats = und Kriegs = Kunst* 1 (1808):31-40.

Jones, Archer. "The New FM 100-5: A View from the Ivory Tower." *Military Review* 58 (February 1978):27-36.

Kalakuka, Theodore. "Streamlined Principles of War, and the Greatest of These Is Preparation." *Military Digest* 4 (March 1939):53-55.

Keegan, John D. "On the Principles of War." *Military Review* 41 (December 1961):61-72.

Keener, Bruce. "The Principles of War: A Thesis for Change." *Naval War College Review* 17 (September 1964):51-61.

Kelley, Richard L. "Applying Logistics Principles." *Military Review* 57 (September 1977):57-63.

Kennedy, K. C. "The Principles of War." *Canadian Army Journal* 5 (November 1951):69-74.

Kinter, William C. "Stalin on War." *Marine Corps Gazette* (August 1948): 54-59.

Krulak, V. H. "A Principle in Jeopardy." *Marine Corps Gazette* 40 (November 1956):26-27.

Lathrop, A. B. "Principles of War in a Nuclear Age." *Military Review* 39 (June 1959):21-27.

Laughton, John K. "The Scientific Study of Naval History." *Journal of the Royal United Service Institution* 18 (1874):508-27.

Lecomte, H. "Hérésies stratégiques." *Revue militaire suisse* 9 (September 1923):385-94.

Liddell Hart, Basil H. "The 'Ten Commandments' of the Combat Unit. Suggestions on Its Theory and Training." *Journal of the Royal United Service Institution* 64 (May 1919):288-93.

Lippman, Gordon J. "Jomini and the Principles of War." *Military Review* 38 (February 1959):45-51.

Loomis, D. G. "Communist Concepts of the Principles of War." *Canadian Army Journal* 12 (October 1958):4-22.

_____. "Principles of War and the Canadian Army." *Canadian Army Journal* 15 (Winter 1961):33-37.

Luvaas, Jay. "G. F. R. Henderson and the American Civil War." *Military Affairs* 20 (Fall 1956):139-53.

MacBride, D. J. "Fundamental Principles of War." *Army Journal* (Australia) 272 (January 1972):33-61.

McCracken, Alan R. "Quotable Principles of War." *United States Naval Institute Proceedings* 61 (December 1935):1826-28.

McGranahan, William J. "The Fall and Rise of Marshal Tukhachevsky," *Parameters* 8 (December 1978):62-72.

Macklin, W. H. S. "The Principles of War." *Canadian Army Journal* (April 1948):1-13.

Mahan, Alfred Thayer. "The Panama Canal and the Distribution of the Fleet." *North American Review* 200 (September 1914):406-17.

_____. "The Practical Character of the Naval War College." *United States Naval Institute Proceedings* 19 (1893):162-63.

_____. "Subordination in Historical Treatment." *American Historical Association Annual Report,* 1902.

Mahan, F. A. "Professor D. H. Mahan." *Professional Memoirs, Corps of Engineers, U.S. Army and Engineering Department at Large* 9 (1917):72-76.

Merat, L. "Un Principe—un procédé: Economie des forces, concentration sur le théâtre principal." *Revue militaire générale* 11 (15 March 1922):187-98.

Michel, Henri, "Pour l'enseignement de l'organization à l'Ecole supérieure de guerre." *Revue militaire française* 3 (1922):196-220.

"Military History and the Principles of War." *Canadian Army Journal* 4 (December 1950):1-2.

Milotta, David E. "One Eye on the Last War." *Infantry Journal* 61 (August 1947):12-13.

Moreno, Aristides. "Command and General Staff School." *Infantry Journal* 22 (January 1923):22-30.

Morrison, James L. "Educating the Civil War Generals: West Point, 1833-1861." *Military Affairs* 38 (October 1974):108-11.

[Napier, William]. "Traité des grandes opérations militaires, contenant l'histoire critique des campagnes de Frédéric II, comparées à cellas l'Empereur Napoléon; avec un recueil des principes généraux de l'art de la guerre." *Edinburgh Review* 35 (July 1821):377-409.

Naylor, William K. "The Principles of War." *Infantry Journal* 22 (February-April 1923):144-62, 297-306, 416-25.

Nazareth, J., and Wright, M. J. W. "Two Views on the Principles of War." *Military Review* 41 (February 1961):26-36.

Neumann, William L. "Franklin Delano Roosevelt: A Disciple of Admiral Mahan." *United States Naval Institute Proceedings* 78 (July 1952): 713-19.

"Obituary, Brig. Gen. Hjalmar M. Erickson." *Nevada State Journal,* 3 March 1949.

"Operations of Modern Warfare." *Quarterly Review* 120 (October 1866): 513.

Parker, Frank. "The Ever-changing Application of the Unchanging Principles of War." *Military Review* 19 (December 1939):5-9.

Phillips, Thomas R. "Word Magic of the Military Mystics." *Infantry Journal* 46 (September-October 1939):402-14.

"Phormio." "Economy of Forces: A Plea for the Older Meaning." *Journal of the Royal United Service Institution* 75 (August 1930): 492-96.

――――. "The Value of Time: A Principle of War?" *Journal of the Royal United Service Institution* 75 (November 1930):701-7.

Preston, A. W. "British Military Thought, 1856-1890." *Army Quarterly* 89 (October 1964):57-74.

Pride, W. F. "The Principles of War and Their Application to Small Cavalry Units." *Cavalry Journal* 35 (1926):54-59, 192-98.

"Principles of Modern Warfare." *Military Review* 28 (November 1948):101.

"Principles of War, The," *Marine Corps Gazette* 28 (March 1944):74-75.

"Principles of War, The." *Military Review* 28 (October 1948):88-89.

Reinhardt, George C. "The Tenth Principle of War." *Military Review* 33 (July 1953):22-26.

Rhodes, Charles D. "How Best to Instruct Our Officers in Tactics." *Journal of the Military Service Institute* 43 (September-October 1908):202-21.

Richards, J. C. C. "The Principles of War." *Canadian Army Journal* 15 (Spring 1961):2-7.

Richmond, Herbert W. "The Principles of War, a Criticism." *Journal of the Royal United Service Institution* 74 (November 1929):714-20.

Salisbury-Jones, A. G. "The Sandhurst of France: Some Impressions of the Ecole spéciale militaire de Saint-Cyr." *Army Quarterly* 6 (April 1923):77-89.

Scammel, J. M. "Military Education and Indoctrination." *Infantry Journal* 18 (March 1921):256-59.

Serong, F. P. "A Matter of Principle." *Military Review* 32 (December 1952):83-85.

"Signifer" [Edward S. Johnson]. "Reunion on the Styx." *Infantry Journal* 42 (January-February, March-April, May-June 1935):3-7, 127-33, 237-46.

Skelly, Frank H. "The Principles of War." *Military Review* 29 (August 1949):15-19. Reprinted in *Canadian Army Journal* 3 (September 1949):13-15.

Solomon, M. A. "Concentration of Force." *Military Review* 28 (August 1948):36-41.

"Soviet Doctrine of War, The." *Military Review* 28 (December 1948):79-82.

Stearley, Ralph F. "The Principles of War." *Air Force* 27 (January 1944):30-31.

Steele, Matthew F. "Conduct of War." *Journal of the Military Service Institution* 42 (January-February 1908):22-31.

Stevenson, R. M. "Principles of War and the Canadian Army." *Canadian Army Journal* 15 (Spring 1961):7-12.

Swain, Richard M. "On Bringing Back the Principles of War." *Military Review* 60 (November 1980):40-46.

Swift, Eben. "An American Pioneer in the Cause of Military Education." *Journal of the Military Service Institution of the United States* 44 (January-February 1909):67-72.

Unwin, J. H. "Principles of War—The Acid Test." *Journal of the Royal United Service Institution* 92 (May 1947):216-20.

Usborne, C. V. "The Principles of War—A Dialogue." *Journal of the Royal United Service Institution* 74 (August 1929):465-77.

_____. "The Principles of War—Another Dialogue." *Journal of the Royal United Service Institution* 75 (February 1930):60-69.

"Value and Originality of 'The Foundations of the Science of War,' The." *Army Quarterly* 12 (July 1926):354-61.

Wallace, Josiah A. "The Principles of War in Counterinsurgency." *Military Review* 46 (December 1966):72-81.

Watson, S. J. "The Principles of War as Applied by England, the United States and Russia." *Military Review* 31 (April 1951):86.

Watteville, H. G. de. "The Principles of War." *Journal of the Royal United Service Institution* 75 (May 1930):267-75.

Weller, Richard. "In My Opinion . . . The Principles of War Will Get You if You Don't Watch Out." *Air University Quarterly Review* (Spring 1954):63.

Wharry, D. F. "Nuclear Fission and the Principles of War." *Journal of the Royal Artillery* 83 (January 1956):45-64.

Whitehead, J. G. O. "The Word 'Strategy.' " *Army Quarterly* 34 (April 1937):113-17.

Whitton, F. E. "Economy of Forces." Letter to the Editor. *Journal of the Royal United Service Institution* 75 (November 1930):834-35.

————. "The Mystery of Strategy." *Quarterly Review* 249 (October 1927):273-90.

Wise, Jennings C. "The Battle of Elah." *Infantry Journal* 16 (March 1920):744-48.

Wolff, Herbert E. "9 + 1 = 10." *Infantry* 55 (March-April 1965):30-33.

Wright, M. J. W. "The Principles of War—An Analysis." *Army Quarterly* 80 (July 1960):200-5.

Zook, David H. "John Frederick Charles Fuller: Military Historian." *Military Affairs* 23 (1959):185-93.

# INDEX

Moss, James A., 235-36
Mountain warfare, principles for,
57, 102
Movement, principle of, 114, 115;
in Fuller's *F.S.R. III*, 134; must
be combined with fire, 135; included in early lists, 140; replaced
by "Fire and Movement" in
U.S. doctrine, 141; as French
law of war and strategy, 152
Mutual confidence, principle
of, 71
Mutual support, 135

Napier, William, 37-38, 39, 40
Napoleon: influence of, on
military thought, 16-18; impression of Jomini on, 21; influence
of, on MacDougall, 39;
memoires of, referred to by
Halleck, 46; admiration of, by
Civil War leaders, 54; maxims
of, learned by Foch, 68; endorsement of principles suggested by Foch, 69; maxims of,
mentioned by Steele, 86, 87;
credit to, from Colin, 98-99;
ideas of, in Fiebeger, 99-100;
Jomini's examples taken from,
129; strategy of, discussed by
Ritter, 132; maxims of, discussed
by Naylor, 136; influence of, on
1920s lists, 140-41; relationship
of campaigns of, to Jomini's
theory, 177; and study of principles by application, 181
Napoleon Club (West Point), 54
Naval War College (Newport,
R.I.), 87, 90, 91
Naval warfare, principles of,
70-71, 88-93

Navy, U.S., adopted principles,
165
Naylor, William K., 136, 138,
139-41, 148 n.56
Newport, R.I., 83
New Zealand, 149, 152
Ney, Virgil, 165, 264-65
*Notes on Guerrilla War* (Ney),
165, 264-65
*Notes relative à la tactique*,
152-53
Nuclear war, principles in, 154,
162, 163

Object: principle of the, 117; as
"true" principle of war, 163
Objective: antecedents in de Silva,
12; prevision of modern principle in 1815 list, 28; principle of,
attributed to Clausewitz, 28,
186; mentioned by Rüstow, 59;
hostile army as the, 61-62, 136,
177-78; principle of the, 71, 114,
115; discussed by Henderson,
80; as expressed by Wagner, 85;
as expressed by Dickman, 88; as
expressed in 1936 Soviet *FSR*,
134; in *Infantry Drill Regulations*, 135; discussed by
Erickson, 138; included in early
lists, 140; evolution of concept
in U.S. regulations, 144; in
post-WWII Soviet doctrine, 158;
in U.S. *FSRs*, 161, 166; in a
class above other principles,
190. *See also* Maintenance of
the objective
O'Connor, John Michael, 41-42
Offensive: importance of, 58; as
expressed by Maillard, 66; as expressed in 1913 French regula-

Staff School; Staff school
(Paris)
Staff rides, 56, 68
Staff school (Paris), 35
Stalin, Joseph, 155-56, 159
Starry, Donn A., 168,
172 n.42
Steele, Matthew F., 85-87, 178,
224
"Strategical Principles" (Fuller),
115-16
Strategic offensive, principle
of, 76
*Stratégie appliqué, La* (Fix),
64
*Strategische Briefe* (Hohenlohe-
Ingelfingen), 59
Strategy: principles of, xxii,
xxiii, 53, 86; Clausewitz's
discussion of, 28, 30; discussed
by Marmont, 37; not studied in
Britain, 37; at USMA under
Mahan, 42, 43-44; defined by
Moltke, 57; teaching of, at Fort
Leavenworth, 85; naval, 92; as
expressed by Naylor, 139; for an
independent corps, 142; problems of, discussed by Mao, 158;
defined, 176, 177
*Strategy* (Wagner), 84-85
Strength at the decisive point:
as expressed by Jomini, 20-23,
25-26, 46; as expressed by
Lloyd, 20, 46; as expressed by
Archduke Charles, 24; as expressed by Willisen, 33; as expressed by Français, 35; as expressed by Marmont, 36-37; as
expressed by MacDougall, 39; as
expressed by Graham, 41; as expressed by Forrest, 54; as ex-

pressed by Maillard, 66; as expressed by Darrieus, 70; as expressed by Mercur, 82; as
discussed by Wagner, 84; as expressed by Steele, 86; as expressed
by Colin, 99; as expressed in
*Décret du 26 octobre 1883*, 101;
as expressed in British *FSR*,
103; as expressed in 1930s and
1940s German writings, 133; as
expressed in post-WWII French
doctrine, 153; associated with
mass and concentration, 189.
*See also* Concentration; Jomini,
fundamental principle of; Mass
Successive decentralization of
means, as principle of war, 128
*Summary of the Art of War*
(Schalk), 52-53
Sun Tzu, 4-5, 160, 197
Superiority of means, 129
Superiority of the offensive, as
principle of war, 128
Surprise: as principle of war, xviii,
122, 124, 129, 160, 163; importance of, 4; principle of, attributed to Clausewitz, 28, 186;
principle of, 63, 76, 107, 114,
115, 130; as expressed by
Henderson, 79; as expressed by
Steele, 86; as expressed in 1917
French sources, 108; as expressed
in 1935 British *FSR*, 125; as expressed by François, 128; as expressed in *L'évolution des idées
tactiques*, 129; as expressed in
1936 French instructions, 131;
as expressed by Foertsch, 133;
as German leadership principle,
133; in Fuller's *F.S.R. III*, 134;
as expressed by Trotsky, 133; in

**About the Author**

LIEUTENANT COLONEL JOHN I. ALGER, currently assigned
to the Congressional Activities Team in the office of the U.S. Army
Chief of Staff, received his Ph.D. from Stanford University. He is
the author of *Antoine-Henri Jomini: A Bibliographical Survey* and
*Definitions and Doctrine of the Military Art—Past and Present*,
both published at the United States Military Academy.